# Children's Rights

## Legal and Educational Issues

Heather Berkeley, Chad Gaffield, and
W. Gordon West, Editors

The Ontario Institute for Studies in Education / Symposium Series 9

THE ONTARIO INSTITUTE FOR STUDIES IN EDUCATION has three prime functions: to conduct programs of graduate study in education, to undertake research in education, and to assist in the implementation of the findings of educational studies. The Institute is a college chartered by an Act of the Ontario Legislature in 1965. It is affiliated with the University of Toronto for graduate studies purposes.

The publications program of the Institute has been established to make available information and materials arising from studies in education, to foster the spirit of critical inquiry, and to provide a forum for the exchange of ideas about education. The opinions expressed should be viewed as those of the contributors.

The original versions of the papers in this book appeared in *Interchange*, 1977-78, Vol. 8, Nos. 1-2.

ISBN 0-7744-0169-9     Printed in Canada

1 2 3 4 5 6   MD   28 18 08 97 87

# Contents

# General Overviews

# Children's Rights in the Canadian Context

Chad Gaffield/OISE and W. Gordon West/Queen's University

In recent years, the issue of children's rights has become a focal point of concern and controversy. Contesting the selective imagery of the North American child as indulged and protected by a liberal and affluent society, many have uncovered the darker side of childhood dependency as a vulnerable and manipulable status. The crux of the children's rights issue has been one of explicating the destructive dimensions of age-ascribed dependency, while attempting to formulate the bases for the child's rights to self-determination. Concern has thus not been restricted to the child's need for recourse to civil rights, in cases where dependency has not been reciprocated with attention and care, but has extended as well to the exploration of the life-stage of childhood as potentially rich in unseen talents and misunderstood competencies (e.g., Friedenberg, 1959; Goodman, 1960).

Television documentaries, journal articles, and a variety of monographs have all concluded that children are socially oppressed, economically exploited, and legally deprived. Why, then, should another paper focus on the subject of children's rights in Canada?

The rationale is primarily the need for systematic examination and analysis of the precise nature of childhood in Canada. Although there has been general recognition of the unequal status of Canadian children, the exact dimensions of this inequality have not been defined and specific ways of more justly integrating children into our society have not been effectively suggested.

Important theoretical and practical aspects need to be delineated if the abstract call to rights is to gain real and realizable content. Two of these are examined in this paper:

1. Though we do not ignore the economic, familial, and ideological position of children and youth, we focus on educational and legal positions. The subordinate status of the Canadian child has not yet been sufficiently explored in the institutional settings of the school and the court. It is clearly in these institutions that the protective needs of childhood are formally espoused, and yet in actuality are violated. These spheres consist of institutional networks consciously created within living memory to provide links between the family and state and corporate command posts. They make explicit claims to embody rational policy, formulated in the best interests of youth, and hence are most open to challenge on those grounds. They are not as sacred and beyond re-evaluation as economic, ideological, and familial matters. Yet, as this paper makes evident, our legal and educational treatment of children is peculiar to a certain economic order.

3

2. In the context of locating concretely the legitimate bases for children's rights is our concern that study and reform be responsive to the particular features of Canadian society. Too frequently, American legal decisions, policy changes, and research findings have been non-reflectively assumed to bear direct relevance to the Canadian experience. In this regard, we draw attention to the fact that, unlike the United States, Canada does not have a deeply entrenched civil liberties tradition. Canada's founding legislation is not based on the individualistic premises of "life, liberty, and the pursuit of happiness," but rather on the conservative principles of "peace, order, and good government." Moreover, Canada has not experienced government by diverse political parties whose alternating leadership provides a force of dynamic change within which wrongs can be righted (Porter, 1965). Our federal government has always been dominated by brokerage parties of the centre that characteristically do not aid oppressed minority groups unable to mobilize support on their own behalf.

With respect to children's rights, development is partly hindered by the fact that, without a legal basis for demanding civil liberties, Canadian advocates cannot rely on general human rights arguments. Rather, it is necessary to document the Canadian need for change in the way in which we treat children before legislative and attitudinal changes can be realistically anticipated. Although some of our arguments draw upon evidence from the United States, their inclusion is intended to stimulate similar reflection in Canada rather than to imply immediate analogy. Thus, our aim is to provide a foundation upon which responses to the need for Canadian children's rights can be successfully constructed.

**The Historical and Contemporary Status of Children**
Children, particularly since the 19th century, have been seen as a likely source of social disorder, and much judicial and educational legislation has been enacted in the hope of limiting the potential chaos youth can cause. The fear that children will disrupt important societal activity is largely a product of a changed economic world in which children's traditional contribution is no longer needed or is relegated to less vital areas. In medieval society, for example, children were generally included in the adult world when they reached age seven (Ariès, 1962). They performed important productive activities such as spinning cloth, doing farm chores, and working as servants. They were valued and respected for the part they played in the overall financial well-being of the household, which included servants, apprentices, and distant cousins as well as immediate relatives. After age seven, the Church recognized children as responsible adults, the law held them potentially accountable for their actions, and they were treated with the characteristic severity of traditional peasant society. In a political world where few had many rights, they were not noticeably inferior. The upper-class few who went to schools were seen as apprentice clergy, clerks, or rulers, and experienced a suprisingly unstructured, non-age-graded, often student-governed education that would be the envy of many present day reformers.

The commercial and industrial revolutions of the 1700s and 1800s brought widespread changes. Working-class children joined their parents in the great immigrations from country farms to city factories, sharing in their new monetary independence and industrial drudgery. The expanding middle class continued to use the apprenticeship system, but increasingly sought professional positions for its sons, which could be secured only through "higher" education. The English "public" school created the status of adolescence by acting as an *in loco parentis* holding ground of character development and discipline.

In the middle 1800s, this new status was diffused to and imposed upon all youth. Increased mechanization and fear on the part of adult unions of losing jobs coincided with humanitarian motives in the 1833 and 1847 British Factory Acts restricting child labor. By 1860, there was a declining percentage of children in schools or factories, and these "street arabs" threatened the burghers into imposing compulsory education in the Acts of 1870, 1876, and 1880 (Musgrove, 1964, pp.76-77). Schooling became the prerequisite to all economic positions in a dynamic that continues to unfold today.

These economic factors were linked with more humanitarian ones originating in the enlightenment and the spread of political liberalism and democracy. The former presaged modern social science, with its emphasis on the importance of environment in shaping children. The latter required the development of minimal skills of reading and writing to produce a citizenry deserving of the extended franchise. Such movements toward liberation, however, were always carefully tempered in actual practice: school curricula were carefully engineered to reproduce the existing class order (Johnson, 1976). The potential of the enlightment may thus be seen as thwarted by the political and economic powers, although natural rights arguments still rely on intellectual justifications developed at that time.

This pattern of imperial Britain was imposed on the colonies in North America. Compulsory education was instituted in Ontario, for instance, in 1880, and enforcing legislation passed in 1891. The utility of youth on the rural farming frontier gave way to factory labor. Urbanization and population concentration, the necessity of assimilating immigrants, and the push for moral anti-child labor reform combined to support the advent of schooling. Social workers in settlement houses, YMCAs, and the Boy Scouts joined in the campaign to uplift and control youth in city streets, and continue to do so now. Thus, the tension and mutual distrust between children and educational systems that are now accepted as characteristic of our society developed from the attempt to re-assign children to a status of secondary importance in schools after the basis of their equal status had been undercut by a changed economic structure. The rights of children were traditionally founded on their valued labor contribution and, as this was undermined by the onset of industrial capitalism and the separation of place of work from the home, these rights were consequently dissipated. While older workers gained new political rights, children were left behind.

Contemporary law still requires children and adolescents to attend school until they are 16 years of age. Within educational institutions, they are defined as students, and are subjugated to the administrative authority of teachers and principals (Levin & Sylvester, 1972). Although their civil rights in these settings have been somewhat expanded recently (e.g., in dress code decisions – Goldstein, 1970), they are still subject to relatively arbitrary rules and hindered by the expense and time-consuming nature of any attempted rectification through the courts. Nonetheless, Gallup reports public sentiment as feeling that school discipline is too lax (Gallup Poll, 1974). Since job opportunities are increasingly tied to years and stream of educational experience, subjection to mystifying invalid testing (see Mackay, in this volume) is an assault on liberty, and social pressures to remain in school persist far beyond the legal minimum age of leaving.

Contemporary inequities in the treatment of young people (especially

5

students) have been identified by critics of the school system and highlighted by the establishment of educational alternatives (e.g., free schools) and proposals to revamp entire government systems (e.g., the Hall-Dennis report – Ontario Department of Education, 1968). As the enthusiasm for these efforts has worn thin with their co-option by conservatives, however, critics have come to see the educational system as only one part of the institutional network oppressing children.

The origins of the juvenile justice system lie in the same movement as the educational changes (Houston, 1972; Platt, 1969). For those children who did not conform in the regular schools, additional measures were developed that extended the scope of prohibitions specified in adult criminal legislation and school acts. The poor were identified as being particularly crime-prone by professional social pathologists, who attempted to emulate the success of positivistic natural science in predicting social disease. "Predelinquent" children of unfit parents thus became eligible for state intervention as much as did those who had already committed a crime.

The passing in 1908 of the Canadian Juvenile Delinquents Act legally entrenched the inferior status of the young. Leon (in this volume) demonstrates how the child-savers won the day in the battle with police over the spoils. A new social problem was firmly identified, and new institutions were established in dealing with youth.

Juveniles are still denied the franchise (political power) and are subjected to special closed courts and provisions in different laws, and their everyday behavior is significantly constrained. For example, it is prohibited for anyone under 18 to drink alcoholic beverages, and for anyone under 16 to smoke tobacco, drive a car, or engage in sexual intercourse. Compulsory education and curfew laws (though the latter are rarely enforced, they are publicly supported – see Gallup Poll, 1975) can determine a juvenile's physical location for about 12 to 14 hours of each weekday. Youths are prohibited access to certain books and movies. Vague "incorrigibility" clauses and prosecution of solvent-sniffing by some judges are other offences specially limited to juveniles.

"The present Juvenile Delinquents Act of Canada defines as a delinquent any child who violates any provision of the Criminal Code, or any federal or provincial statute, or any by-law or ordinance of any municipality; a child 'who is guilty of sexual immorality or any similar vice' (a condition that, according to Freud, would include all normal children); and a child 'liable by reason of any other act to be committed to an industrial school or juvenile reformatory under the provisions of any dominion or provincial statute' (and that includes a great many children, even those accused of petty crimes)." (Grygier, 1965, p.31)

Juveniles clearly retain a second-class status under our laws.

Juvenile courts lack elementary safeguards of due process. Judges have access to confidential information on defendents before they are convicted, hardly a situation guaranteed to uphold the "innocent until proven guilty" principle. Information that may be relevant to the defence is held by the crown prosecutors and denied to the child's lawyer (when the child has one) (Bad day, 1975). The courts are not public and hence not under the safeguard of public scrutiny (Juvenile court, 1975). In becoming an administrative welfare problem, children lost their civil rights to self-defence.

Given that they thus have far more laws to break and are more easily convicted in such courts, it is not surprising that young people are predominant in criminal statistics. At least 15% of the juvenile offences are for status crimes, actions for which only juveniles are liable. In addition, in the last decade in Ontario 40% to 50% of incarcerated juveniles were placed in training schools under "needy children" clauses and not for any criminal offence (see Weiler, in this volume, on effects of the recent revocation of such clauses in Ontario). Similar treatment of both neglected and delinquent youth in the same institution has been justified by the argument that delinquency-prone conditions can be identified and treated. While it is unclear whether such children get positive help, they certainly get confined in inadequately funded programs.

The most successfully replicated explanation of delinquency – control theory – predicts that individuals who lack conventional commitments (e.g., jobs), constraining attachments (e.g., families), and socially approved beliefs are most likely to commit crimes. Ironically, adolescent status inherently places its incumbents in such a position and hence seems to encourage delinquency. Even if juveniles were subject only to adult law in adult courts, their dependent social situation would be more likely to encourage criminal activities. While self-report studies verify that almost all adolescents commit some offences, working-class adolescents are much more likely than middle-class ones to appear in court (by a ratio of roughly 5:1 rather than the 1:1-1/2 ratio for self-report offences). Theft is a prototypical crime: some 80% of the specifically identified violations of the criminal code are property offences, with the rate being three times higher for juveniles than for adults (Statistics Canada, 1969). Of all thieves successfully prosecuted, about 40% are juvenile, and the modal age is 15 to 17 years. A growing body of research argues that a significant proportion of such adolescent crime is committed by young persons "precociously" claiming adult status (Buff, 1971; Centre for New Schools, 1974; West, 1975). The connection to propertylessness is obvious.

Although this discussion has focussed on schools and legal systems, the repercussions of deprived status plague children and youth in other sectors of our society, particularly the economy. In 1971, children and youth comprised almost half of the Canadian population: some 10.4 million of 21.5 million Canadians were under 24 years of age (Committee on Youth, 1971). The postwar baby boom somewhat exaggerated the predominance of youth in the population. This boom was responsible for much of our economic growth, as it constituted a market opportunity for the provision of new physical facilities (homes, schools, recreation centres), jobs for caretakers (teachers, youth workers, and professors), and general consumer demand, especially in the new teenage market. It also created pressure on schools and courts, and particularly on the job market.

Private industry has simply been unable to absorb this increase in the labor supply. Of the increase in the American laboring population from 1951 to 1966, teachers and students (above age 18, considered as job holders) account for 45% of the new jobs, defence for a further 21%, and private industry for only the remaining 33% (Rowntree & Rowntree, 1968). Although the Canadian defence industry is negligible, the relation between education and the labor force is doubtlessly similar here. Whereas the overall 1970 Canadian unemployment rates for males and females were 6.6% and 4.5% respectively, for 14- to 19-year-olds they were 15% and 11.4%, and for 20- to 24-year-olds they were 10.55% and 5.1%. Youth has continued to be unemployed at two to three times the national average, and constitutes about 45% of the total

7

unemployed (Committee on Youth, 1971; Employment, 1975). In light of these figures, the much criticized Local Initiatives Program and Opportunities for Youth program can be seen as attempts to meet a potentially disastrous national emergency rather than as precursors of a new era of civil participation and social service. Education was forced to "take up the slack" and become the country's largest industry by 1970, consuming 8% of the GNP, occupying 6.5 million students and teachers, and consuming 20% of the total government spending, over $6 billion.

Young persons remain severely handicapped economically. Labor laws effectively prohibit employment of juveniles; in terms of training, experience, and seniority, the young stand at a disadvantage to other workers. As a result, when they are employed their pay is differentially lower. They consequently must rely to an unusual extent upon alternative sources of income (e.g., parents, welfare, or crime). To the extent that work roles are the primary source of personal identity in our society, juveniles who are denied jobs can be expected to experience identity crises and adolescent "angst," and to look elsewhere (e.g., in various "youth cultures") to create worth-while selves (Hughes, 1958, pp.42-43).

"Adolescent behavior that adults call irresponsible simply reflects the failure of society to provide any responsible position for them." (Friedenberg, 1966, p.46)

The free market economy justifies itself by arguing that the market responds to consumer demand and hence satisfies the wants of the general population (Meyer, 1973, pp.38-39). Only the consumers can know what they most want in "maximizing [their] utilities." They vote with their dollars to encourage efficiency and production in those sectors of the economy which provide for their needs, thus attracting capital to those areas. This argument assumes that each person has the money to articulate individual needs and wants into consumer demands. For the vast majority of the population such money comes only from employment. Any group, therefore, restricted in employment or institutionally held to a low income is handicapped in articulating its consumer demand on the market. Children and youth (as well as the old, unemployed, single mothers, etc.) are systematically unsatisfied and oppressed by the market system in conjunction with the law. (This is to ignore the gross facts of capital accumulation, and the gross distortion of free market demand by tariffs, corporate wealth, and advertising, which affect the entire population.) Labor market problems of our economy are thus fought on the backs of the young (and the very old).

**Proposed Changes**
There have been many attempts to implement children's rights within the schools over the last decade. Such innovations as open primary schools, child-centred education, open-choice high school credit systems, alternative high schools within the system, and parent–student–teacher councils have been implemented. Yet the grading system remains as firmly entrenched as ever; every child is expected to develop the same skills in the same areas examined on standardized tests that are developed expressly to discriminate among children (MacKay, in this volume). The ranking system is fully blown into streaming or tracking, and specifically job-oriented community colleges, whereby working-class and immigrant children (D'Oyley, in this volume) are

channelled into curriculum divisions preparatory to working-class jobs, and middle-class ones are slotted to become managers and technicians. This is all justified by the "IQ ideology": in such a meritocracy as ours, social position and the goods that go with it are merited by the amount of testable intelligence one has.

The teacher/pupil ratio has remained constant. Funds that could have been used to fundamentally alter this condition of education have instead been used to buy expensive hardware from the education techology industries (Martell, 1974). Thus, any chance of altering the teacher-pupil distance from one demanding authority–submission to one of honest encounter is precluded (Ryan & Greenfield, 1975). School–community councils remain firmly subordinated to central educational bureaucracies and ministries, as much by their own role-definition as by overt coercion (Eastabrook, in this volume).

Administrative discretion still remains unclarified and unsystematized within schools (Manley-Casimir, in this volume). Magsino (in this volume) demonstrates in great detail how the legislative support for students' rights is weak. And compulsory attendance remains.

Both the Ontario and federal governments have recently taken steps to modify legislation governing delinquency and training schools. Legal aid has brought duty counsel lawyers to juvenile courts, so that due process is informally more encouraged. However, such progress remains based on casual agreements between individual judges and lawyers, rather than being grounded in statutes. Duty counsel lawyers often see themselves as representing the community, the parents, or the court, at least as much as the child. They tend to interact regularly with other court officials, and hence are subject to informal pressures to be more cooperative with them than they are informally beholden to their "clients." It remains unclear, of course, whether the lawyer's client is the paying state, the legally responsible parents, or the child (Platt, 1969).

Ontario has revoked Section 8 of the Training Schools Act, which allowed dependent children to be incarcerated "if no suitable community facility were available" (Weiler, in this volume). Child welfare organizations, which would be held responsible for providing alternative services to such children, succeeded in delaying the implementation of this legislation for over a year, seeking adequate government financing for the new programs. Children continued to suffer while these two squabbling "parents" bartered as to whom would be stuck with "support payments." The very organizations which claim to have the best interests of the child at heart were ironically revealed to be much more concerned with their own budgets, aggrandizements, boundaries, and relationships. Weiler makes clear that the revocation of Section 8 still allows dependency cases to be incarcerated under a formerly seldom-used clause in the federal Juvenile Delinquents Act.

The federal government has announced its intention to replace the Juvenile Delinquents Act with the Young Offenders Act. Insofar as all status offences (e.g., truancy and sexual immorality) would be eliminated, the law is progressive; maximum three-year sentences would replace the present indefinite terms. The raising of the age of juveniles from 16 to 18 would protect this group from any harshness to which adults are subjected, but the group would also lose any rights that it had as adults. The oppressed age group would thus be expanded. Children below 14 would lose all vestiges of responsible personhood in being deprived of the opportunity for a court trial. They would be relegated to the administration of the same types of welfare bureaucracies that have so obviously failed to uplift the old, the native peoples, and the poor. It is hard to avoid considering the pressing organizational advantages of the new legislation: with the baby boom generation now almost grown up, the revocation of Section 8, and the increased use of group homes, the training schools will become even emptier and hence available for new older customers, since the adult reformatories are jammed. Under the guise of state humanitarianism, the administered population will be redistributed so that staff and facilities will be least disrupted.

The continued lack of evidence of successful reformation gives firm support to Conly's (in this volume) call for abolition.

Youth is faring no better in the economy. When they appeared most rebellious and most likely to become politically organized, they were co-opted into the Company of Young Canadians, Opportunities for Youth, and Local Initiatives Programs. All of these were thinly disguised welfare measures, subject to administrative control and approval, and of short-term duration. None were allowed to become serious economic enterprises by using funds for capital expenses – it is hardly surprising that a government supported by business would brand such activities as unfair competition. When the government needed obvious spending cuts to propagandize its war on inflation, youth was among the victims as these programs were cut.

The scandalous rates of continuing youth unemployment have forced revision of the Job Corps: "Canada Works" and "Young Canada Works" have stricter discipline and control.

Simultaneous changes in welfare distribution have tightened the noose to prevent young unemployed persons from being supported if living at home. The often heard charge that the battle against inflation is being fought on the backs of the workers is, given the predominance of youth among the unemployed, more accurately depicted as a strangulation of our young.

The Ontario government has increased postsecondary tuition fees as well, without any promise of proportionate increases in grants, cutting back in the one alternative to jobs it previously supported.

## The Special Character of Children's Rights Advocacy

How is it that children's rights remain in dispute, with only pyrrhic victories? Children, it seems, are among the less promising groups to organize. One of the most obvious and most important characteristics of children is the temporary nature of their status. With respect to rights, this characteristic partly explains the failure of children to organize themselves. Members of youth leadership groups change constantly and, by definition, become part of the exploitive adult world. Similarly, children, conscious of their ephemeral situation, tend to identify less with their peers than with older age groups. Their ambition is to escape from childhood rather than to deal with it.

Of course, even if children did develop a critical consciousness, they are further disadvantaged by their physical size. Children are early confronted with defeat through the threat or use of force, regardless of the logic or reasonableness of their desires. For example, the accepted practice of spanking children establishes parent–child, adult–youth relationships that are based on the underpinnings of "might is right." Children cannot control their own activity except when this activity meets with parental acceptance. If children deserve certain rights that infringe on adult hegemony, only special provision will prevent the classic strong–weak tyranny.

Definition of children's rights is by itself inadequate to guarantee protection since children are severely disadvantaged by inadequate knowledge of the ways in which society functions. Information about recourse to judicial authority, for example, is largely inaccessible to children and it is unlikely that an abused child would know where to find protection. How children can be better prepared to stand for themselves is perhaps the central question that emerges from discussion of the need for children's rights.

Unlike other members of oppressed groups, children cannot easily find solace away from control by the adult world. Members of minority groups can seek refuge in community groups and often can share burdens and find comfort in family settings. Children, however, are supervised in all aspects of their lives and they are not assured of support and encouragement even in their own dwellings. In fact, their legal and educational oppression may be only extensions of mistreatment at home.

The issue is further complicated by the generally good intentions of children's caretakers (parents, teachers, training school attendants, etc.) who are given nigh impossible tasks and then blamed for any failures. The law requires juveniles, their families, and teachers to maintain ongoing association in frequently pressure-cooker intimacy. In addition to economic dependence on parents, minors require parental permission for contracts (e.g., marriage, purchases, club memberships). The family and teachers are thus delegated the responsibility of controlling juvenile behavior in ways that they may find personally disagreeable or abhorrent. Standing guard over the oppressed is a nasty and thankless task in the best of circumstances. For many parents (especially working-class ones) and many teachers and staff (isolated in under-staffed, inadequately equipped schools), it is an impossible one. With custody functions delegated to parents and teachers, the responsibility for creating the conditions that may engender ensuing rebellions is avoided by the schools, the state, and the corporations, who maintain their hegemony by such bureaucratically fostered division of people amongst themselves. The mystification becomes complete when the truants, the delinquents, and the unemployed assume blame for their situation and actions, believing their troubles result from their own stupidity, emotional disturbance, and shiftlessness.

Youth are further pressed to serve our society in peculiar ways. They are used as an ideological vanguard to test ideas and add some dynamism to the existing order. Although most youth are as conservative as their parents, the few rebels serve as scapegoats upon which sexual fantasies and dreams that the "golden age has passed" (Jahoda & Warren, 1965) and decadent fears can be projected. The girls are seen as precocious and the boys as shiftless and undisciplined (Musgrove, 1964, pp.102ff).

To summarize, one of the most salient characteristics of juvenile status in education, law, and the economy is "denied adulthood." As with blacks, this institutionalized, often legalized, oppression is mystifyingly justified by claims to be in the interests of the oppressed. Children are deemed to be of a fundamentally different nature than citizens (e.g., immature, dependent, ignorant, frivolous). Social and educational science has developed professorships, research programs, bodies of literature, and graduate programs around the unquestioned assumption of such social beliefs. Developmental psychology, learning theory, delinquency research, adolescent counselling, etc., all function "scientifically" to legitimize the status of children by presupposing them to be fundamentally different, incomplete, irrational, etc., and then documenting their peculiarities. And, in our society, they often *are* such; but we fail to recognize the self-fulfilling vicious-circle nature of this oppression until we learn that children of other societies and times act much as adults do when they are allowed and expected to. In our society, it is illegal for a person under 16 to act maturely, i.e., as an adult. An elementary glance at the status of children is thus enough to identify them as a legally and socially oppressed group (see Kelly, 1969).

Our legal structure creates a special group of second-class persons, called children, who are denied citizenship rights and responsibilities (Ariès, 1962). Unlike some oppressed adult groups, their structural position within society is so weak as to require advocacy mainly by allies.

## Why Children's Rights?

This discussion has asked that youth and children be given citizenship rights within society. It consists fundamentally of requests for liberal reforms to release the young from oppression. It relies on humanitarian appeals for the establishment of civil liberties that would apply to all, regardless of age. Given their inherent weaknesses discussed above, it is especially imperative that children have rights institutionalized in the law. They should not simply be delegated to various social agencies who claim to act "in the best interests of the child."

But there are further reasons that push beyond liberal reforms for extending such rights to children. Endowing children with rights would require that we develop their and our ability to become self-aware, to analyze, and to choose. Mel Hurtig's surveys and the Symons report on Canadian studies in our universities indicate the horrendous depths of our ignorance of ourselves. As a result, for example, we have slavishly copied French, English, and American educational ideas in adopting classical colleges, private schools, and mass education, without questioning the relevance of these educational forms to our culture and economy (Lockheart, 1975). We are only now seriously engaging in debate on how to organize a multicultural society of two historically predominant "founding peoples" that must incorporate the cultural richness of other groups (which now compose roughly a third of us, and as much as half of some school jurisdictions – see D'Oyley, in this volume). The ecological crisis and our unique position on the northern half of a continent rich in finite resources that are required for our continued survival must surely impress upon us the need for our children to learn rapidly how to become respectful stewards of our inheritance.

This expansion of the discussion of children's rights from the demands for liberal democratically inspired citizenship claims has incorporated the issue within the wider structural dilemmas of our time. This implies that children's rights cannot be dealt with as a separate entity, divorced from the endemic problems of Canadian society. Thoroughgoing changes in schools, juvenile justice systems, and economic opportunities cannot be effected without changes in our political and economic leadership and institutions. The refusal to ground the discussion of children's rights within such a context can result only in the piecemeal reforms of the past decade, which have been subject to widespread co-option within the present system.

Children's rights will not be achieved in isolation from the liberation of other sectors of society. The analysis implies the fundamental need for unity among all movements, in particular with the most successful and powerful movement of this century, that of working people, especially since training school inmates and school failures are largely working class. Only in such alliance can just socialization of the young be achieved. Reciprocally, without children's liberation, the young of all oppressed groups will continue to be

12

dominated by the existing hegemony. Alternatively, re-education of our children holds the promise of re-establishing human life as not absolutely reducible to economic exchange value.

To do these things, of course, requires renewal of our best and most progressive political traditions. We have inherited from Britain not only the liberal democratic traditions present in the United States, but also a collectivist tradition of Tory rule, corporate exploitation, and our own socialist movements. Our more recent and incomplete industrialization has left us with recently fresh memories of rural community. Our children need to learn skills required for participation in a thoroughgoing democratic community, where the public control all aspects of their lives, not merely the formally democratic ones (Heap, 1974; Porter, 1965). The rightful recognition of people's knowledge should lead not only to a demystification of our educationally supported intellectual hierarchies, but also to a just society. Our children deserve no less.

## Note
Prepared for the annual meeting of the Canadian Sociology and Anthropology Association, Fredericton, N.B., June 1977.

## References

Ariès, P. *Centuries of childhood*. New York: Vintage, 1962.

Bad day in court for young offenders. *Toronto Star*, Oct. 20, 1975, p.6.

Buff, S. Greasers, dupers, and hippies. In L. Kapp (Ed.), *The white majority between poverty and affluence*. New York: Doubleday Anchor, 1971.

Center for New Schools. A quantitative-qualitative study of student subcultures in an alternative high school. Paper presented at the Annual Convention of the American Educational Research Association, Chicago, 1974.

Committee on Youth. *It's your turn*. . . . Ottawa: Information Canada, 1971.

Employment singles out a victim: youth. *Toronto Star*, July 19, 1975, p.B1.

Friedenberg, E. Z. *The vanishing adolescent*. New York: Dell, 1959.

Friedenberg, E. Z. Adolescence as a social problem. In H. S. Becker (Ed.), *Social problems*. New York: Wiley, 1966.

Gallup Poll. Need more discipline in schools 56% say. *Toronto Star*, Apr. 27, 1974, p.7.

Gallup Poll. 60 per cent believe curfew a good idea for children. *Toronto Star*, July 25, 1975, p.7.

Goldstein, S. R. Reflections on developing trends in the law of student rights. *University of Pennsylvania Law Review*, 1970, **118**.

Goodman, P. *Growing up absurd*. New York: Vintage, 1960.

Grygier, T. Crime and society. In W. T. McGrath (Ed.), *Crime and its treatment in Canada*. Toronto: Macmillan, 1965.

Heap, J. *Everybody's Canada*. Toronto: Burns and MacEachern, 1974.

Houston, S. The Victorian origins of juvenile delinquency. *History of Education Quarterly*, Fall 1972.

Hughes, E. C. *Men and their work*. Glencoe, Ill.: Free Press, 1958.

Jahoda, M., & Warren, N. The myths of youth. *Sociology of Education*, 1965, **38**(2).

Johnson, R. Notes on the schooling of the English working class. In I. R. Dale, G.

Esland, & M. Macdonald (Eds.), *Schooling and capitalism*. London: Routledge and Kegan Paul, 1976.

Juvenile court judge rules out publicity. *Toronto Star*, Sept. 30, 1975, p.4.

Kelly, H. Adolescents: A suppressed minority group. *Personnel and Guidance Journal*, 1969, **47.**

Levin, M., & Sylvester, C. *Rights of youth*. Toronto: Ontario Institute for Studies in Education/General Publishing, 1972.

Lockheart, A. Future failure: The unanticipated consequences of educational planning. In E. Zureik & R. Pike (Eds.), *Socialization and values in Canadian society*. Toronto: McClelland & Stewart, 1975.

Martell, G. The politics of reading and writing. *This Magazine*, 1974, **8**(2), 12-15.

Meyer, P. The exploitation of the American growing class. In D. Gottlieb (Ed.), *Children's liberation*. Englewood Cliffs, N.J.: Prentice-Hall, 1973.

Musgrove, F. *Youth and society*. London: Routledge and Kegan Paul, 1964.

Ontario Department of Education. *Living and learning*. Report of the Provincial Committee on the Aims and Objectives of Education in the Schools of Ontario. Toronto: The Department, 1968.

Platt, A. *The child savers*. Chicago: University of Chicago Press, 1969.

Porter, J. *The vertical mosaic*. Toronto: University of Toronto Press, 1965.

Rowntree, J., & Rowntree, M. The political economy of youth. *Our Generation*, 1968, **6**(1-2), 155-186.

Ryan, D., & Greenfield, T. B. *The class size question*. Toronto: Ministry of Education, Ontario, 1975.

Statistics Canada. *Crime statistics*. Ottawa: Information Canada, 1969.

West, W. G. Adolescent deviance and the school. *Interchange*, 1975, **6**(2), 49-55.

# A Status Report on Child Advocacy in the United States

Patrick C. Lee/Teachers College, Columbia University

Child advocacy is an emerging specialty in the area of child care that cuts across professional and national boundaries and focuses on the rights and prerogatives of children. It deals with issues such as these: What are the rights of children in legal proceedings that intimately affect their lives, such as divorce and custody cases and juvenile court actions? What are children's rights to physical and psychological well-being and to protection from abuse, neglect, and hunger? What are children's rights in the educational arena: expulsion and suspension from school, mandatory use of drugs for "hyperactive" children, freedom of expression of ideas, protection from corporal punishment, and access to school records? What are the rights of children to a stable and caring environment in the family, in institutions, and in foster care? What protections do children have from commercial exploitation by television advertising, the toy industry, and manufacturers of children's foods, candies, and clothing? Or to put it more simply, do children have rights and, if not, what rights should they have and how can they be realized?

These questions are being raised as concerned Americans become aware that 515 000 children are treated in hospital emergency rooms each year because of injuries from toys, that approximately 500 000 are abused and battered by adults, that almost one million suffer from serious physical neglect or sexual abuse, and that over one million accidentally swallow poisons each year. Moreover, there are about 400 000 children with high lead levels in their blood from chewing on lead-based paint, hundreds of thousands of youngsters are in jails and lockups, over 500 000 school children are on amphetamines and Ritalin for presumed hyperactivity, over one million children have been "pushed out" of school, and, while almost one million are erroneously placed in special education classes, there are about four million who should receive such services and do not. This gruesome catalog of facts and figures indicates that there are serious breakdowns in what might be called the "child support system" of American society.

## The Child Support System

Children live in the context of a support system that is made up of an intricate network of goods and services provided by society. Some of these services are formally organized parts of the public sector, e.g., day care, schooling, and special education programs. Some derive from the private sector, e.g., children's toys, foods, and television programming. A third kind of "service," perhaps less tangible and less explicitly developed than the others, includes factors like a secure cultural identification, family integrity, and a sense of community. The key

15

component of this loosely jointed support system is the family, for it mediates in primary and enduring ways between the child and the other components of the system. When the family mediates effectively and when the various elements of the system are available and of high quality, the child's well-being is markedly enhanced. However, the breakdown of the system in terms of quality or availability of services can seriously interfere with the child's healthy development.

The abuses just listed are examples of breakdown in the child support system and they constitute the grist of the child advocacy movement. It should be mentioned that child advocacy is not centrally or hierarchically organized, and thus is not a "movement" in the strict sense of the term. Rather, it is a loose network of separate groups that have been independently formed, usually for the purpose of pursuing specific issues or representing specific causes. There are, however, important commonalities shared by most advocacy efforts. Taken collectively, the movement's focus is on the relationship between children and their support system, and its objective is that the system be made more responsive to the needs of children. It accomplishes this objective in several ways. It draws attention to breakdowns and irregularities in the child support system. It attempts to pull the disparate elements of the system into a coherent, integrated whole. It translates child care customs into children's rights. This means that services for children come not out of an adult sense of responsibility, or even out of love, but because children have a *right* to services. And, finally, child advocates lobby that children's rights be recognized, codified, and affirmatively developed.

This paper attempts to make a status report on the child advocacy movement in the United States. In doing so it raises and provides tentative answers to these questions: Is there a need for child advocacy? Which issues are currently at the cutting edge of the movement? Where has the movement failed and where has it succeeded? Finally, which bodies of opinion in American society are opposed to child advocacy? While it is clear that the American experience does not bear a point-for-point correspondence with that of Canada, or any other nation, it may provide a basis for analysis of issues that are extra-national in scope. Canada, in particular, has a child support system that shares many elements in common with the American system, e.g., universal compulsory education, the juvenile justice system, and special regulatory codes for children's television. Given these commonalities, there is good reason to expect that Canadian and American advocates could learn much from each other.

## Is There a Need for Child Advocacy?

This question may seem superfluous after having listed some of the abuses, accidents, and misfortunes that befall children in contemporary America. It would appear that there is a need for child advocacy, and that it is needed not only by children with special disadvantages or disabilities, but by ordinary children as well. It may be more to the point to consider *why* there is a need for child advocacy. Several reasons are apparent.

First, children are politically disenfranchised. They cannot vote and, during most of their childhood years, they are psychologically incapable of sustained political organization; they therefore do not enjoy the concessions ordinarily made to viable political constituencies.

Second, they are economically disadvantaged. It is illegal for them to work, although a small minority of children provide cheap labor in family-owned businesses and during harvest time in rural, agricultural areas. Moreover, they have no *de facto* control over substantial funds, they have no access to money

16

that is legally theirs without permission of trustees, and they are not significant producers of capital. Economically they are restricted to the role of consumer and must rely upon "grants" from adults even to play this role. Thus they experience all the vulnerabilities of economic creatures with none of the prerogatives or advantages.

Third, their legal status is essentially passive. They have no legal initiatives, cannot bring suit on their own behalf, can be incarcerated for non-criminal behavior, and have a severely constricted and qualified range of rights. With the exception of limited *parens patriae* protections, they are essentially the chattels of their biological families.

Finally, because of their relative gullibility, inexperience, and lack of caution, they are subject to multiple and arbitrary victimizations on a daily and casual basis. They are destructively and, occasionally, fatally exploited by the economics and customs of an adult-oriented and -governed culture. Even in those instances where they question and resist adult influence, they are handicapped by their small physical size and are almost certain to succumb to actual or threatened physical coercion. One might want to view children as "developmentally disadvantaged" – they simply haven't learned the rules of the adult cultural game well enough to win, except on a chance basis.

Given the four ways in which they are handicapped, the list of childhood misfortunes begins to make sense. In some important respects children are a colonized nation. They are undereducated, patronized, essentially unable to protect themselves, completely dependent upon the benevolence of adults for their welfare, governed by laws and customs imposed upon them by adult society, and physically occupied. Their one resource is that they grow physically, a factor that allows them to hope for self-determination in the future. The child advocacy movement, in a sense, is attempting to lift the colonial yoke by securing extensive legal prerogatives for children, and by ensuring that children not be victimized and exploited because of their youthful vulnerabilities.

**Brief Historical Overview**

Before we consider specific issues, it might be useful to review briefly the origins and history of the Child Advocacy Movement (cf., Kahn, Kamerman, & Mc-Gowan, 1972). The movement can be understood as having gone through two periods of development, which, for the sake of better terms, may be called the "old advocacy" and the "new advocacy." The old advocacy began in 19th century America primarily out of citizen concern for orphaned and abandoned children, i.e., for those who were failed by the family and community support system. Out of this precedent of society as a *backup* parent there evolved a more vigorous and intrusive brand of advocacy that defined society (or the state) as an *alternate* parent. Thus, the legal principle of *parens patriae* was affirmatively developed, creating a basis for intervening in the lives of children who were abused or received inadequate care in the family context. Concomitant with this development, child advocacy steadily expanded its purview and initiated a large number of programs, legal reforms, and institutions, which, taken collectively, resulted in children being given a special status in law and society. This new status was developed to protect them not only from failings in the nurturant and educative functions of the family, but also from the failure of the broader economic and judicial systems of American society to meet their special needs. A testimony to the effectiveness of the old advocacy is that its effects are everywhere present in contemporary society in the form of compulsory universal schooling, child labor laws, the juvenile court system, the foster care apparatus, and institutions for the severely handicapped, to mention only its most important contributions. Taken as a whole, these contributions have evolved into a major part of the contemporary child support system.

With the passage of time, however, many of the reforms won by the old advocates came under the control of a new class of bureaucrats, the "child service establishment," and degenerated into arbitrary and unilateral encroachments upon the lives of children and their families. The solutions of the past often become the problems of the present, and the new advocacy emerged in response to this historical paradox as well as to the social and political turmoil of the 1960s. At that time Americans were shocked to discover that unacceptably large numbers of children suffered from the effects of racism, classism, poverty, inadequate educational opportunity, and poor dietary and health care (cf., Harrington, 1962). This discovery led to a broader examination of the ways in which children, both privileged and poor, were victimized by a social and economic structure that increasingly viewed them as objects to be processed and markets to be cultivated. For example, universal compulsory education appeared to be more compulsory than educative; the juvenile justice system, while protecting children from the harshness of the regular courts, also denied them the fundamental right of equal protection under the law; and institutions for the handicapped were utterly non-rehabilitative, serving only as places for detaining children unwanted by "normal" society.

Moreover, the new advocates were faced with a second set of problems that grew out of industrial and technological developments of the post-war era. An enormous child-oriented industry had emerged almost unnoticed since the Second World War. Drugs, toys, cereals, children's clothing, and, perhaps most perniciously, children's television had become major enterprises with one common objective – the maximization of profits through the creation and cultivation of the "child market" (cf., Helitzer & Heyel, 1970). The proliferation of various child industries that were accountable more to stockholders than to the developmental needs of children required new methods and priorities within the revived child advocacy movement. The new technology of information gathering and processing also began to create problems for children. Foremost among these is the "computerization" of children through the compilation and centralization of records, particularly in schools. These records often constitute an inordinate violation of due process and privacy and, again, have presented new challenges to child advocates.

In summary, there are several respects in which the old and the new advocacy differ. The old advocates built an extensive system of child-serving institutions to supplement and improve upon the family; their objective was to provide actual instrumental protection to children; and their ideology was grounded in a commitment to social service. Although the new advocates are spiritual brethren to those who came before them, they have priorities and a style of their own. Their primary focus is not on improving the family, but on improving the child-care apparatus created by the old advocates. They are less concerned with mounting child-protection programs and more with the affirmation of children's rights. And, finally, their ideology seems to grow more out of the American civil libertarian tradition than out of a child-service consciousness. These distinctions, of course, are not absolute, as there is much of the old sensibility among the new advocates, but they do capture the essential ways in which the new advocates differ from their predecessors.

## The Leading Edge of Child Advocacy

The child advocacy movement is active on several fronts and will probably be a significant part of the North American scene at least through the 1970s. The issues currently attracting most attention in the United States are children's rights, the juvenile court system, deinstitutionalization, child abuse and neglect, special education, and commercial exploitation of children.

### Children's Rights

This is probably the single most overarching issue in child advocacy today. It pervades all other aspects of action for children, either implicitly or explicitly, and may ultimately constitute the most far-reaching legacy the movement will leave to children. Why there is such interest in children's rights becomes immediately apparent when one reviews the legal status of children.

First, children have no legal initiative. They cannot sue an offending party, but must have someone sue for them. Rather than exercising generic rights and prerogatives, they are the recipients of specific legal protections. For example, although they are protected against abuse by parents or guardians in New York State, they have no generic right not to be abused – thus, older siblings could abuse them with legal impunity.

Second, the substantive definitions in law assign different values to the same act, depending on whether the actor is an adult or a minor. For example, the right to travel for a 21-year-old would be called "running away" for a 15-year-old. The latter, as a "juvenile status offense," is punishable under law. Parenthetically, there are about 500 000 runaways each year in the United States, indicating a manifest desire to "travel" on the part of many minors.

Third, the state has assumed enhanced legal control over children. For example, they must attend school and they cannot work. This is not to say that formal education or child labor laws are injurious; and it is not to claim that in every instance these laws are enforced against "offending" children; it is only to point out that children's behavior is subject to more control by law than is adults' behavior.

Fourth, there is insufficient gradation of rights according to age. After 16 and 18 years of age some additional rights and privileges accrue to young people (e.g., the right to vote for 18-year-olds), but 15-year-old adolescents are legally categorized with 15-week-old infants, completely ignoring the vast developmental differences between children of these ages.

It is difficult to anticipate precisely where the concern with children's rights will lead, since it is an extremely complex area and there are differing opinions on both fine and gross points of law among legal experts. In general, however, it seems safe to expect that the law will eventually allow less discretion to those who control the lives of children, that children will have greater legal control over their own destiny, and that some of the specific protections children now enjoy will be lost. These latter will be replaced by new rights that will, in turn, become the basis for new legal and extra-legal actions on behalf of children.

### The Juvenile Court System

This issue is, of course, basically indistinguishable from children's rights. It is described separately because the legal vulnerability of children seems to be most manifest in the context of the judicial system, which was designed specifically to protect them from the rough and tumble advocacy of the regular courts. Ever since the famous *Gault* case of 1967, in which a youthful offender was put away

19

for six years for a crime that had a maximum sentence of two months for an adult, there has been a strong reform movement directed at the juvenile courts (cf., Stansby, 1973).

Three specific foci are receiving most attention. First, judges have traditionally decided cases on the basis of the "best interests of the child" doctrine. Critics now argue that this places too much unregulated discretion in the hands of judges, and they are proposing that it be replaced by the "least detrimental alternative" doctrine (Goldstein, Freud, & Solnit, 1973). This latter simply means that a judge should realistically survey the options open to a child in any given case before making a decision. Application of the "best interests" principle has allowed too many judges to hand down idealistic decisions with complete disregard for the realities of children's lives. Second, critics are trying to reduce the number of so-called "juvenile status offenses," which are often arbitrary and occasionally represent perversions of the rights enjoyed by adults. The example of runaway children is a neat perversion of the adult's right to travel. In 1969, 80% of the children institutionalized as delinquents were not guilty of criminal acts, but were put away for status offenses like pregnancy, truancy, disobeying their parents, and, in the words of one critic, for "having trouble growing up" (Rodham, 1973, p.491). Finally, the Children's Defense Fund's (1976) Juvenile Justice Division has recently completed a study indicating that as many as half a million children and adolescents are held in adult jails each year. Of these, 43% are 15 years of age or younger and 88% are charged only with property or minor offenses. These statistics, however, fail to capture the revolting human and physical conditions of the jails in which youngsters are confined. They are often placed in cells with hardened adult prisoners, a situation that can lead to multiple rapes and other atrocities perpetrated by the adults on the youngsters.

*Deinstitutionalization*
The movement toward deinstitutionalization of children is a collaborative effort of lawyers, physicians, and journalists. Essentially its purpose is to re-examine the reasons why various classes of children have been consigned to institutions, and to "normalize" the lives of those children for whom institutions are either unnecessary or destructive (Wolfensberger, 1972). For example, the One to One project in New York City is an attempt to get mentally retarded youngsters (many of whom apparently are *not* retarded) out of huge, dehumanizing settings (often called "warehouses") and into small community-based homes headed by parent surrogates where their lives can approximate normality. In addition to the ethical and moral incentives for the movement, there are also economic incentives. A basic economic rule in the provision of human services is that services become more expensive to the degree that they depart from the normal state of affairs. Thus, it is less expensive to keep children in neighborhood homes than it is to support huge residential institutions.

The same economic formula holds for foster care arrangements. While not as costly as large institutions, they do cost more than having children cared for in their family of origin, even when the natural family is subsidized. Many advocates, therefore, are arguing that there are two reasons for reducing the number of children assigned to foster care agencies. Foster care usually costs the state more than providing natural families with whatever special services are required to retain their integrity, whether these services involve food supplements, housekeeping help, temporary counseling, or the availability of day care arrangements.

And, although foster care is intended to be a temporary arrangement for children before adoption or return to their natural family, it often turns out to be a prolonged limbo in which children are shunted from one foster home to another without any permanent resolution of their case (Mnookin, 1973).

Thus the deinstitutionalization movement is directed against those institutions, such as foster care and residential facilities, that were originally established to serve the "best interests" of the child, but have turned out to be counterproductive and costly, both in human and monetary terms.

### Child Abuse and Neglect

This is probably the most sensational of the problems that concern child advocates today. In the last five years it has received more public and media attention than any of the other issues discussed in this paper. An indication of the great interest and concern it has generated is the U.S. Congress' creation in 1974 of the National Center on Child Abuse and Neglect, an agency budgeted for $50 million over the next two years. Actually abuse and neglect are two separate syndromes, referring, respectively, to beating, battering, and torturing children and to ignoring the physical and psychological needs of children to the point where they fail to thrive. As might be expected, these syndromes are most evident with children below five years of age, during the time of life when they are most helpless and dependent upon others. They are also found in all socioeconomic classes, although poor people are more likely to bring their sick and battered children to public facilities for aid, thus making abuse and neglect appear to be lower-class phenomena. People who can afford the cost probably bring their children to privately practicing pediatricians, who, in addition to treating the children, also treat the matter as privileged.

For this reason, there is little agreement about the incidence of child abuse and neglect even among those who agree that these are serious problems. Estimates of child abuse in the United States vary from 60 000 to over two million cases a year. In an attempt to reconcile these discrepant figures, Light (1973) has reanalyzed data from a number of sources and arrived at estimates of 665 000 to 1 675 000 cases of abuse and neglect each year, including approximately 50 000 fatalities. At this time, these would appear to be the best estimates available.

The most sensible means for dealing with these syndromes are threefold. First, as a preventive measure, family planning and parent training should become more public, accepted, and integral aspects of the lives of young people of child-bearing age. Unwanted children should not be conceived and it should not be assumed that all people have the "instincts" or competence to be good parents. Second, parents who are discovered to be abusing or neglectful should be provided with group psychiatric care, family aid, and parent training. These methods have been shown to be quite effective in reducing repetition of neglect and abuse. Third, a much more efficient detection and referral system than currently exists is needed. The vast majority of cases go unreported while hundreds of thousands of small children are trapped in horrible circumstances from which there is no escape. How to devise and implement such a system is an extremely difficult question, but it seems that without the answer to it, treatment will reach only a few of those, both parents and children, who need it (cf. Alvy, 1975).

### Special Education

The two basic child advocacy issues in the area of special education are whether

21

all children who need special education are getting it, and whether all who are getting it need it. With regard to the first point, there have been some significant breakthroughs in the last four years as a result of parents taking school districts to the federal courts. These cases have focused on mentally retarded children, an area that has two advantages from a child advocacy point of view. Since genetically determined mental retardation cuts across socioeconomic class lines, it is one of the few areas of advocacy in which middle-class and impoverished parents have worked together. Also, what is in the best interests of the parents of mentally retarded children is in the best interests of the children themselves, i.e., that the children receive high quality, on-going, and low-cost treatment. (It should be mentioned that the interests of parents and their children do not always overlap. For example, in child abuse cases parents are often defendants.) Two recent federal court decisions, the *Pennsylvania* case and the *Reid* case in New York, have mandated that public schools provide education appropriate to all children, regardless of the educational deficits they may have. Thus, the legal foundation has been laid for publicly supported special education for those who need it (cf. Lippman & Goldberg, 1973).

However, there are still staggering problems in the realm of special education that require money, improvement of diagnostic procedures, and extraordinary dedication to solve. For example, only about 35% of the children who need special education are receiving it, leaving about four million children without essential services. Moreover, there are approximately one million youngsters stuck in special classes who should be in regular classes. Several studies have indicated that 25% to 60% of children diagnosed as mentally retarded are, upon retesting, not retarded at all; but they may very well become retarded, both functionally and in terms of self-perception, if allowed to spend their school years in segregated special classes. Most schools and school districts do not periodically re-evaluate special children – this means that a child placed in a special class is usually tracked there permanently. It should be added that the children who suffer most from misdiagnosis and erroneous placement are from cultural and ethnic minority groups, e.g., blacks and Chicanos (Kirp, 1974).

A closely related issue is the designation of special and regular children as "hyperkinetic," "behaviorally disordered," or suffering from "minimal brain dysfunction," to mention only a few of the labels presently enjoying widespread use in schools (Schrag & Divoky, 1975). There are several problems in the assignment of children to such categories. One is that the diagnostic procedures on which labels are based are themselves often faulty and of uncertain validity. For example, minimal brain dysfunction clearly suggests organic damage, but no "hard signs" of such damage are required in order to assign the label to a child. Furthermore, the fact that follow-up diagnostic procedures often fail to confirm earlier diagnoses suggests that many diagnoses are false positives. Another problem, and directly related to the first one, is that once children are labeled, there is a tendency for the label to follow them throughout their school years. The label thus becomes a self-fulfilling prophecy, which encourages the children's successive teachers to relate to them as though they continued to be, for example, "hyperkinetic." The burden of proof seems to be on the children to demonstrate that the label no longer applies, rather than on the school for showing that it does apply. A third problem is that there is a stigma associated with most of these labels that is unmistakable to the school staff, to the children's peers, and to the labeled children themselves. There is a body of sociological opinion that holds that the "secondary deviance" deriving from the perception of this stigma often has more serious consequences than the "primary deviance" that prompted the use of the label in the first place. Because of these several problems, many advocates are working on alternative ways of identifying children who need special help, without burdening them with offensive labels. Unfortunately, this is no easy task, and no satisfactory and workable alternative has yet been found (cf. Gove, 1975; Hobbs, 1975).

*The Commercial Exploitation of Children*

The two areas in which children are most vulnerable to commercial exploitation are children's television and children's products. The astounding figures on the number of hours logged by children in front of the television set and the number of commercials to which they are exposed have become oft-told tales. Up to puberty, youngsters spend more time watching television than they do at any other waking activity, including schooling, playing games, and all the other activities traditionally associated with childhood. The American consumer organization that has most vigorously advocated on behalf of children in this area has been Action for Children's Television (ACT). In recent years some of ACT's work appears to be getting results, as both the U.S. Federal Communications Commission (FCC) and the Federal Trade Commission have forced the television industry to reduce the number of commercials on some children's programming and to reserve the first two hours of "prime time" for family-oriented programs. It is also noteworthy that in Canada the Canadian Radio-Television Commission (CRTC) (1974) mandated that, as of 1975, all commercials be removed from Canadian Broadcasting Corporation programming directed at children below 13 years of age. Although the CBC has never become as totally dependent on commercial revenue as have American broadcasters and networks, approximately one third of its income is from advertisers. It will be interesting to see what effect the CRTC prohibition will ultimately have upon the financial status of the CBC. The American industry and regulatory agencies will probably watch these developments quite closely, because they may augur directions for future regulation of American children's programming.

A second issue in the area of children's programming is violence. Again the raw numbers of violent episodes on children's TV are startling on the face of it. But the real issue here is whether this deluge of violence has any long- or short-term effects on either the behavior or psychological development of youngsters. The U.S. Surgeon General's (1972) report on *Television and Social Behavior* does not conclude that violent programming has any long-term effects on "normal" children, although the report does find that television influences children who may be inclined toward violence in the first instance. Many researchers, however, including some who worked on the Surgeon General's project, feel that there is sufficient evidence to conclude that televised violence does have detrimental effects and that the industry is, in effect, hoist on its own petard because, in approaching advertisers, its argument is precisely that television does influence children (e.g., Liebert, Neale, & Davidson, 1973).

As mentioned earlier, 515 000 American children were given emergency treatment in hospitals as a result of toy-related injuries in 1973. Approximately 76 000 children under five years of age were hurt in automobile accidents in 1973, primarily because of faulty car seats for babies and preschoolers. The U.S. Federal Consumer Product Safety Commission now has 1 500 toys on its banned list, considerably more than the U.S. Food and Drug Administration's (FDA) list of 800 toys. About 6 000 children below age five are injured each year because their sleepwear catches fire. Finally, the Poison Control Center of the FDA estimates that over one million preschool children a year swallow potentially or actually toxic substances, and in 1970 226 deaths resulted. These figures indicate that many of the things young children find most fascinating, e.g., their toys and the contents of containers, are too hot, too sharp, too flammable, too shoddy, or too poisonous for their health, and, in some instances, for their lives. At the moment most regulatory agencies and advocacy groups in the United States appear to be stymied about how to deal with such problems, which, while large in total scope, actually consist of many isolated incidents. Banned lists and court cases are helpful, but potentially dangerous materials for children are being produced at an accelerating rate. An example of this acceleration is found in Poison Control Center figures: 17 years ago the center estimated that 600 000 children below 15 years of age swallowed toxic substances, as compared now with the over one million poisoned children under *five* years of age. Thus the danger of commercial products to children is increasing and it would not seem that enhanced parental vigilance is the only answer. Something must be done to stop the flow at its source. (Facts and figures cited here are taken from recent official reports of the agencies mentioned.)

*Other Issues*
The foregoing, of course is not an exhaustive survey of child advocacy issues. Some others include the provision of day care services to young children of working mothers; breakdown in the delivery of essential immunizations to children, e.g., polio vaccine; school record-keeping practices; and the use of psychopharmacological drugs in school settings. The first two issues are addressed in the $2 billion Child and Family Services Act of 1975, which (contrary to its misleading date) is currently being considered for passage by the U.S. Congress. The third issue, school records, has been addressed by the Family Rights and Privacy Act of 1974. This act, more popularly known as the "Buckley Amendment," regulates the kinds of information that can be kept in children's school records and opens records to the inspection of students and their parents. The fourth issue, the use of psychoactive drugs on children, is not the subject of any current federal legislation, but is certainly a major concern of many advocates (e.g., Grinspoon & Singer, 1973; Schrag & Divoky, 1975). It should be mentioned that none of these matters would ever have been considered by the U.S. Congress without a great deal of preliminary lobbying and grassroots action by child advocates.

*The Next Several Years*
It is difficult to predict which issues will become most important over the next several years. It depends on which issues become authentic scandals. For example, child abuse has probably already assumed the dimensions and sensationalism associated with scandal. In early 1977, the Children's Defense Fund released the results of a four-year study on children in jails which may also be viewed as scandalous. Since encarcerated children are subject to the same physical assault and psychological terror as abused children, one might expect them to evoke the same kind of public sympathy as abused children. However, the public may reserve its sympathy for abused innocent children and withhold it from children in jails, who, while abused, are presumed to be "guilty" of punishable offenses.

This lack of sympathy for socially deviant children may have undermined public response to an earlier report by the Children's Defense Fund, issued in 1974, on school "pushouts." This study found that almost two million American children between seven and 17 years of age were not enrolled in school at all and that hundreds of thousands more attended school only on a sporadic basis. In some areas of the United States, e.g., selected census tracts in Maine, Colorado, Kentucky, and Massachusetts, approximately 10% of school-age children do not attend school. As might be expected the number of pushouts is greatest among the non-white, the poor, and those from single-parent families, i.e., precisely those most in need of high quality schooling to compensate for other disadvantages in their lives. In a nation that prides itself on universal education for promoting equality of opportunity, these findings could have been viewed as scandalous. But apparently they were not so viewed, and have been swept aside by other issues related to children who are *in* school, such as busing, the return to curricular fundamentals, and access to student records.

A second factor that will determine the direction of the next several years has to do with the ability of child advocacy groups to make continued progress in achieving their objectives. Unless ACT and the Children's Defense Fund, for example, have a measurable impact on the societal status of children, they and their causes will falter significantly. However, if they make gains, their causes will be the salient issues in child advocacy over the next decade.

Finally, much depends on how sustained the commitment of advocates remains. The probability is not high that the U.S. government will provide strong, affirmative funding of advocacy projects during this era of enormous budget deficits. Under these conditions, private commitment and financial backing may be stretched to the breaking point. So the questions remain: Can the commitment to child advocacy grow? And, if not, can it at least sustain itself against temporary but discouraging odds?

**Where Has Child Advocacy Succeeded?**
There are four respects in which child advocacy has had at least initial success. Its most conspicuous success has been in the area of child abuse and neglect, although there is some possibility that the success may be more apparent than real. Child abuse and neglect have become fashionable issues, thus creating the danger that they may fall out of fashion as readily as they fell in. Nevertheless, despite the misgivings of some observers, in 1974 the U.S. Congress appropriated almost $100 million over a period of five years specifically to combat these two syndromes. Moreover, a variety of treatment, public education, and research programs have been established through the use of these funds and the initiative of many state legislatures. Although these projects differ in excellence and promise, their number and regional spread indicate that a national commitment to solve the problem of child maltreatment may be emerging.

It should not be assumed, however, that the problem is under control. On the contrary, the vast majority of abused and neglected children go undetected and neither they nor their families are receiving treatment. Much more must be learned about the epidemiology of child maltreatment, and public consciousness must be raised to new levels of vigilance and concern before the fundamental problem of detection is resolved.

Another success has been in the area of special education. As mentioned earlier, a number of major federal court cases have been won over the last four years by parents of mentally retarded children. More recently, the U.S. Congress has taken positive legislative action in the form of two assistance bills for the handicapped. One bill, passed in late 1975, established a matching funds program that assures states of federal financial assistance for meeting the special education needs of handicapped children and adolescents (The Education for All Handicapped Children Act of 1975). The second bill also established a grants program for the states, but made the conferral of grants contingent upon each state's development of a "complete system" of advocacy for disabled children by October 1977 (The Developmentally Disabled Assistance and Bill of Rights Act of 1975). This combination of court mandates and federal incentive funds has simultaneously pushed and pulled the states to provide a more complete range of services for handicapped youngsters.

The third success is that child advocacy has generally done well in the courts – the special education cases, as well as a number of "right to treatment" cases for delinquent, emotionally disturbed, and retarded children in residential facilities in Pennsylvania and Alabama. Many of these were class-action suits, a legal device borrowed from consumer advocates. Basically, the class-action strategy requires only a sample of children to take legal action on behalf of an entire category of children. In this sense, it is analogous to a class action taken against the manufacturer of a defective product – it is not necessary that all purchasers of the defective product be actual plaintiffs, although all owners of the product stand to benefit if the case is won.

Thus, in its first gambits child advocacy has often enjoyed the benefits of judicial activism, i.e., the aggressive *interpretation* of existing law by the courts. However, there are limits to the new interpretations judges can place on old law. The next step must involve legislative action, i.e., the *creation* of new law. This two-step sequence was taken in the case of special education. In most other areas of child advocacy, however, the movement has not got beyond the courts and into legislative bodies.

Finally, child advocacy has been reasonably successful in raising the general level of public consciousness regarding the needs of children. Public interest seems to be particularly active in the areas of child maltreatment, school records, and children's television. The first area tends to bring out strong, perhaps instinctive, feelings of adult protectiveness toward children. This, coupled with the fact that child maltreatment is a totally non-partisan issue, may account for the nearly universal outrage and sympathy it has evoked. The other two issues, school records and children's television, cross socioeconomic class lines and touch on the lives of almost all children and families. They are also congruent with the larger "consumerism" movement in which the public is requiring greater accountability of tax-supported institutions, e.g., the schools, and of those institutions licensed and regulated by government agencies, e.g., television broadcasters. Illustrative of the degree of public sensitivity to the children's television issue is that the FCC received over 100 000 letters in support of an ACT petition a few years ago. Reportedly this was the strongest expression of public response to *any* matter the FCC has handled in its history.

**Child Advocacy's Failures**
Just as it is difficult to pinpoint clear and unambiguous successes, it is also somewhat misleading to label certain issues as failures. It probably makes better sense to view lost or underdeveloped causes as temporary setbacks. By the same token, successes should also be reckoned as tentative rather than fully won.

One major problem in the movement is that it has not yet developed the notion of children as a *class*, i.e., as a special interest group in its own right. All children, regardless of their individual differences, have a broad range of common experiences that are specifically a function of their socially ascribed status as children. Despite this cultural reality, advocates tend to specialize in one kind of child or another, e.g., the mentally retarded or the juvenile offender; this specialization has had the unfortunate effect of pitting one group against another in a competition for limited resources. For example, increased aid to special education limits aid to the education of poor children. The current U.S. federal mandate that 10% of each state's Head Start enrollment consist of handicapped children is a clear example of this kind of trade-off. Money originally targeted for poverty-level children now has to justify itself again by serving the needs of poor handicapped children as well. The result is diluted services for all Head Start children and frustrated efforts for many Head Start workers, who are expected to accomplish yet another major task with only minor additional resources.

A second tentative failure is that child advocacy has not yet developed a coherent and consensual reference system. At the present time its major frame of reference seems to be the self-interest of adult groups. The special education effort described, although clearly a success, provides a lesson about the realities of advocacy that is not altogether edifying. Child advocacy succeeds best when it is wedded to vested adult interests – in the case of special education, teachers' unions, teacher training colleges, special educators, and parents of handicapped children had overlapping interests that enabled them to coalesce into a solid and powerful lobby. Some observers detect an underlying weakness in child advocacy when its successes rely upon measures, i.e., old-fashioned power politics, that are not available to most of its causes. What is needed is a fully developed system of advocacy that is grounded in consensual morality and children's rights rather than the self-interest of adult groups; that reviews programs against projected plans for every major human service in order to separate functional from dysfunctional programs; and that coordinates and integrates children's services, rather than leaving them in their present state of segmentation and disarray.

Another problem is that, despite its claim to advocate on behalf of children, the movement has made no systematic effort to find out what children themselves want. There are many experts who draft hypothetical "bills of rights" for children or who purport to know what children's best interests are, but none of these pronouncements, however well intentioned they may be, are grounded in research on children's perceptions of their own rights and prerogatives; and there is no existing body of research to which advocates could turn if they were so inclined. Such research could conceivably set well informed directions and priorities for the movement as well as yield much information about gaps between the way adults and children define children's best interests. For example, a pilot study done at Columbia University found that there was considerable agreement between children and their parents on the child's right to personal territory and privacy in the home, indicating that children and adults have similar perceptions in this respect. However, children and their parents appear to be polarized on the child's role in decision-making in the family context. This is the area in which children were found to have strongest convictions regarding their rights, while simultaneously being the area in which parents were least willing to share power. Clearly children perceive themselves as being more competent in decision-making than parents are prepared to accept. In a sense, this finding epitomizes the status of children in American society: they are usually loved and protected, but *always* infantilized and patronized (Corso & Lee, 1975). This status may in part explain why advocates and social scientists have done so little to discover how children perceive their own rights.

A fourth area of concern is that advocacy on behalf of *young* children is underdeveloped. The movement has focused largely on the needs of 10- to 16-year-old youngsters because of their potential for delinquency. They can actually do harm to society, whereas smaller children are harmless, helpless, and rightless. The irony of this particular failure, even by self-interest standards, is that intervention earlier in life is almost always less expensive and more effective than is later intervention. Again, this is an indication of the shortsightedness of American society and of many child advocates.

Finally, just as young children have received relatively little sustained focus, multiply victimized children have, if anything, received even less attention. For example, there are almost 400 000 children of migrant laborers who are seriously deprived of almost every service of modern society, including medical care, schooling, and child labor laws, to mention only a few. Their parents are mostly leaderless, unorganized, and terribly poor, with a mean annual family income of $3 600, an average that falls about $1 000 below the official U.S. Department of Labor poverty line. Child advocacy has barely touched the lives of these children (Spingarn, 1973).

## Who Is Opposed to Child Advocacy?

It is difficult, at first thought, to imagine that anyone would be opposed to child advocacy, but the movement confronts two significant kinds of opposition. One comes from vested economic, institutional, and community interests and the other lies in conservative sentiment and ideology.

Economic interests opposed to child advocacy are found in the children's television industry, manufacturers of children's products, producers of children's foods and drugs, and important parts of the advertising industry. Television broadcasters have ready access to large audiences of children; manufacturers of children's commodities want access to the children's market; and advertisers get the first two groups together for the mutual economic benefit of all three (Melody, 1973). For this reason they are extremely wary of any government agency or social–political movement that would interfere with the orderly and unobtruded pursuit of profits. The recent regulatory gambits by the U.S. Federal Communication and Trade Commissions have left the "children's industry" in a state of disappointment and anger for two reasons: First, and most important, new regulations pose the necessity of either accepting reduced profits or devising new means of maintaining current levels of profitability; and second, external regulations deprive the industry of the prerogative of self-regulation. Economic systems, particularly capitalistic systems, abhor the introduction of any important factors that are not governed by economic laws. The dynamics of government regulation and child advocacy are political or social in nature, and thus represent palpable threats to the integrity of a system that has learned to prefer business as usual.

The child service establishment represents a second vested interest in the status quo. Schools, teachers' unions, and foster care agencies, to name a few, are often opposed to child advocacy programs for reasons similar to those of the children's industry. Child advocacy calls upon the child service establishment to be accountable, reminds them that they are not doing their best, and threatens to deprive them of hard-earned economic gains. For example, there are currently about 250 000 children in publicly supported foster care in the United States. Although foster care is supposed to be a temporary remedy for children caught in unstable living conditions, it is not unusual for youngsters to remain in foster care for five years or more (cf. Mnookin, 1973). Foster families are paid by the state for holding children and foster placement agencies derive their budgetary appropriations from the number of children they place and the number of families they supervise. Thus, there are economic *dis*incentives for seeking permanent resolution of cases either by returning children to their original families or by placing them for adoption. Often foster care agencies claim they cannot find adopting parents for children, but in many cases this is patently untrue. For example, in New York City the Council on Adoptable Children has over 1 000 parents wanting to adopt precisely those children who are most difficult to place for adoption. But agencies have no incentive for allowing such children to be adopted – in fact they have an economic incentive not to allow it. The net effect is to leave many of the 250 000 children in sustained states of limbo, shuttling among foster homes at great cost to them personally and to society financially.

Finally, communities are often opposed to child advocacy programs that, for real or imagined reasons, are presumed to be detrimental to the community's best interests. Many communities are opposed to the deinstitutionalization movement because it means that retarded or unusual children are to be taken from remotely located institutions and placed in small homes in the communities themselves. Such opposition appears to be grounded in two fears, economic and psychological. The economic fears are of decrease in property value, loss of or destruction to property itself, and increased school taxes because of the special classes such children would require. The psychological reaction comes from fear of the different. There is an emotional value placed on being with one's own kind, on being with "normal" people. Communities often fail to recognize that retarded youngsters make for reliable, neat, and conscientious neighbors, and often pose fewer problems than "normal" children.

In addition to vested interests that see themselves as having something to lose by child advocacy, there is also a body of conservative sentiment in America that is simply opposed to any movement construed as interfering with family integrity or parental authority over children. Citizens of a more conservative persuasion often blame social programs and movements for causing the very disruptions that caused the programs to be created in the first place. For example, "day care" is a fighting word among many conservatives, who see it as a threat to the integrity of the family. It was on the strength of this fear that then President Richard Nixon successfully blocked the Comprehensive Child Development Act of 1971 and it continues to be the basis of a widespread smear campaign against the Child and Family Services Act of 1975 (cf. Francke & Camper, 1976). The fact of the matter is that there are strong economic and social forces in contemporary American society that are creating alternative models of family life. Approximately 40% of American mothers are currently in the labor force, up from 10% in 1940. Almost four and a half million of these working mothers have a combined total of six million children under the age of six, indicating an obvious need for day care services on a massive scale. It should be noted that almost two thirds of American working women are single, divorced, widowed, separated, or have husbands who earn less than $7 000 a year. Clearly these people work, not out of boredom or disrespect for traditional familial values, but because they and their families need the income.

Aside from the economic incentives that are increasingly drawing mothers to work, the incidence of divorce alone has had a tremendous impact on the American family. In the United States in 1975 there was one divorce for every 2.1 marriages, a dramatic gain of 85% over 1960 when the ratio of divorce to marriage was 1 to 3.9. There are now approximately one million divorces and over half a million legal separations annually in the United States, and these involve well over one million dependent children each year.[1] It is manifestly absurd to blame day care or any other child care program, legislation, or movement for bringing such powerful economic and social realities into existence. On the contrary, it would seem that an expanded day care apparatus would provide millions of working or divorced mothers with safe, humane, and educationally beneficial places to leave their children while they spend their working hours contributing to an economy that seems glad to have them.

**Implications for Canada**

In attempting to generalize from the American to the Canadian experience, one must remain mindful of basic differences in the traditions and structure of the two societies. At the risk of oversimplification, American society is more centralized than Canadian society and has a stronger overt civil libertarian tradition. This encourages American society to define itself as a collection of individuals. Canada, however, tends to be more regionalized and more frankly defines itself as a collection of human groups or subcultures. There is, of course, a dynamic tension in both nations between *officially* held norms and the *informal* ways in which people identify themselves both as individuals and as members of communities. Thus, while American citizens are legally protected by explicit constitutional guarantees that apply equally to all individuals, they may in fact derive a major part of their security and individual identity from affiliation with regional or subcultural groupings. Conversely, Canadian citizens enjoy overt protections specifically through membership in certain human categories, whether they be defined in cultural, regional, or language terms. But they also share with Americans the British tradition of common law, with its cumulative specification of rights accruing to individuals as individuals.

One way in which regionalism vs. centralism affects the status of children is found in the degree of federal control over education. In Canada education is entirely under the control of the provinces and Ottawa has little if anything to do with public school programs. Any advocacy initiative on behalf of school children, therefore, would have to be provincially based. In the United States, however, the federal government has assumed an increasing hegemony over public education, despite the fact that education is *officially* under the control of the separate states. Washington has encroached upon state control through the creation of matching funds and affirmative action programs. Thus, the states have gradually accepted financial aid formulas that also involve acceptance of federal specification of educational standards. A recent example of this *de facto* usurpation of state functions by the federal government is found in the special education legislation described earlier. The upshot of all this is that American advocates have more options open to them than do their Canadian counterparts, since they can operate at both the state and federal levels.

The frank recognition of multiculturalism and bilingualism in Canada, however, readily opens to Canadian advocates options that American advocates do not enjoy. For example, in Canada it would be unusual for French-speaking children to have their IQ underestimated by having to take an English test, and be erroneously assigned to a special education class. If this were to happen, the burden of proof would be on the school, not on the advocate or the child. There are, then, certain protections for children who are officially recognized as members of language or cultural categories. In the United States, however, it is not at all unusual for Spanish-speaking children, for example, to take English IQ tests and be tracked accordingly. In this case the burden of proof is on the child and the advocate, not the school. Thus the American civil libertarian tradition grants all individuals the same rights, but also implies that they meet the same cultural norms.

Despite these *caveats*, there is much that Canadian and American advocates can share with each other. There are strong similarities in the child support systems of the two societies – and so one should not be surprised if the two systems are subject to similar breakdowns and in need of similar advocacies. These latter may differ in detail, but not in their essential thrust.

## Notes

The author would like to express his appreciation to Gita Kedar Voivodas and Patricia Vardin for their colleagueship in the areas treated by this paper. He would also like to extend special thanks to Professor Voivodas and Chad Gaffield for critical reading of the manuscript.

[1] Figures cited in this section are taken from recent official reports of the Women's Bureau of the U.S. Dept. of Labor and Census Bureau of the U.S. Dept. of Commerce.

## References

Alvy, K. T. Preventing child abuse. *American Psychologist*, 1975, **30**, 921-928.

Canadian Radio-Television Commission. *Radio frequencies are public property*, Mar. 31, 1974.

Children's Defense Fund. *Children out of school in America*. Washington, D.C.: Children's Defense Fund of the Washington Research Project, 1974.

Children's Defense Fund. *Children in adult jails*. Washington, D.C.: Children's Defense Fund of the Washington Research Project, 1976.

Corso, V., & Lee, P. C. An interview study of children's rights. Unpublished manuscript, Teachers College, Columbia University, 1975.

Francke, L. B., & Camper, D. Child-care scare. *Newsweek*, Apr. 5, 1976, p.77.

Goldstein, J., Freud, A., & Solnit, A. J. *Beyond the best interests of the child*. New York: Free Press, 1973.

Gove, W. R. (Ed.) *The labeling of deviance: Evaluating a perspective*. New York: Halsted Press, 1975.

Grinspoon, L., & Singer, S. B. Amphetamines in the treatment of hyperactive children. *Harvard Educational Review*, 1973, **43**, 515-555.

Harrington, M. *The other America: Poverty in the United States*. New York: Macmillan, 1962.

Helitzer, M., & Heyel, C. *The youth market*. New York: Media Books, 1970.

Hobbs, N. *The futures of children: Categories, labels, and their consequences*. San Francisco: Jossey-Bass, 1975.

Kahn, A. J., Kamerman, S. B., & McGowan, B. G. *Child advocacy: Report of a national baseline study*. New York: Columbia University School of Social Work, 1972.

Kirp, D. Student classification, public policy, and the courts. *Harvard Educational Review*, 1974, **44**, 7-52.

Liebert, R. M., Neale, J. M., & Davidson, E. S. *The early window: Effects of television on children and youth.* New York: Pergamon Press, 1973.

Light, R. J. Abused and neglected children in America: A study of alternative policies. *Harvard Educational Review*, 1973, **43**, 556-598.

Lippman, L., & Goldberg, I. I. *Right to education: Anatomy of the Pennsylvania Case and its implications for exceptional children.* New York: Teachers College Press, 1973.

Melody, W. *Children's television: The economics of exploitation.* New Haven: Yale University Press, 1973.

Mnookin, R. H. Foster care – in whose best interest. *Harvard Educational Review*, 1973, **43**, 599-638.

Rodham, H. Children under the law. *Harvard Educational Review*, 1973, **43**, 487-514.

Schrag, P., & Divoky, D. *The myth of the hyperactive child.* New York: Pantheon Books (Random House), 1975.

Spingarn, N. D. Children on the road. *New Republic*, Apr. 7, 1973, 13-14.

Stansby, J. F. In Re Gault: Children are people. In A. E. Wilkerson (Ed.), *The rights of children: Emergent concepts in law and society.* Philadelphia: Temple University Press, 1973.

U.S. Surgeon General. *Television and social behavior.* (4 vols.) Washington, D.C.: U.S. Dept. of Health, Education, and Welfare, 1972.

Wolfensberger, W. *The principle of normalization in human services.* Toronto: National Institute on Mental Retardation, 1972.

# Legal
# Issues

# New and Old Themes in Canadian Juvenile Justice: The Origins of Delinquency Legislation and the Prospects for Recognition of Children's Rights

Jeffrey S. Leon/University of Toronto

Recent proposals purporting to give increased recognition to the rights of children in the Canadian juvenile justice system will most likely generate extensive debate on the preferred methods for dealing with "young persons in conflict with the law" (Solicitor-General's Committee, 1975) or "young offenders" (Solicitor-General Canada, 1977) in Canada. This was the case in 1971 when the Young Offenders Bill was introduced to the House of Commons (see Cousineau & Veevers, 1972; Fox & Spencer, 1972), and has also been characteristic of related American experiences in the field (Noyes, 1970; Stapleton & Teitelbaum, 1972). This paper provides a social-historical context for the debate by outlining the origins of existing juvenile delinquency legislation in Canada, the Juvenile Delinquents Act (see also Fiser, 1966; McGrath, 1965; Parker, 1967a, 1967b; Scott, 1952; Scott, n.d.; Stewart, 1970). Further, in tracing the development of traditional juvenile court procedures, the philosophies and assumptions about children that were favored by the early 20th-century Canadian reformers who introduced the present system are exposed (cf. Fox, 1970; Hart, 1910; Lou, 1927; Mennel, 1973; Parker, 1968; Platt, 1969, 1974; Schultz, 1973).

The "liberation" of children through the creation of new statutory rights will lead not only to the imposition of duties on others but also to an alteration in the rights previously exercised by others (primarily by parents). As one commentator has recently noted, "any broad assertion that age is . . . irrelevant to legal autonomy inescapably collides with certain biological and economic realities" (Mnookin, 1975, p.3). It is then necessary to consider the *degree* to which children of various ages are to remain dependent on the decision-making powers of others. In a sense, such a determination is crucial in order to distinguish dependency from domination. The functional needs of children for "protection" may, at some point, translate into intergenerational conflict. And, in this regard, an assessment of the extent to which the dependent status of children is reflected in the new as well as the old themes in Canadian juvenile justice suggests that, with a few important exceptions, there may be more to the promise of, than to the proposals for, securing legal rights for children.

For the historical aspects of this paper, reliance was placed on several primary sources of data, including the writings of, and the correspondence among, key proponents of special delinquency legislation; the proceedings of selected child welfare conferences; government reports; and legislative debates. Secondary accounts of related concerns with juvenile behavior during various periods of Canadian history have also been utilized. For the more contemporary matters, both published and unpublished documents were consulted. It might be noted that the theoretical implications of the Canadian history of delinquency legislation for the sociology of law, as well as the extensive legal considerations involved therein, have been dealt with elsewhere (Hagan & Leon, 1977; Leon, 1977).

## From a Status of Dependency to a State of Delinquency

Underlying the notion of a separate system for juvenile offenders is the assumption that young people should be spared the full impact of the criminal law. Traditionally, the philosophy of the modern juvenile court has been traced to the *parens patriae* jurisdiction of the English Chancery Court. It was there that the law placed "the care of individuals who cannot take care of themselves."[1] Whether this power is viewed as the original *legal* basis for the development of delinquency legislation (Langley, 1975; Wang, 1972) or as a rationalization for such development (Fox, 1970, p.1192; Lemert, 1970, p.25) is less significant than the subsequent implications. The imposition of a dependent status on children has meant that children have been denied, or have relinquished, certain substantive rights and procedural safeguards in order to expedite their special treatment (cf. Catton, 1976; Ketcham, 1961). A dependent status confers privileged treatments, allows certain indulgences, and imposes certain liabilities (cf. Stapleton & Teitelbaum, 1972, p.11), effectively resulting in both the "legal classification of society" and the "legal protection of certain social relations and individual connections" (Graveson, 1953, p.142). As one writer has noted: "It is a deficiency of citizenship. Dependents are only limited citizens" (Matza, 1964, p.193).

The dependent status of children has two main implications, one historical and the other contemporary. The social and legal status of infancy has, for the most part, rendered it unnecessary to ask *whether* children *should be* protected. That is not to say that all children have always been subject to the same types of protections (cf. Musgrove, 1964; Sanders, 1970). Rather, it is the specific incidents of this status, as justifying a variety of social and legal responses, that are subject to variation over time. Hence, the question is *which children* should be subject to *what* protective social and legal mechanisms, to *what* extent, and as applied *by whom*. At common law, the criminal law was concerned that a child be of sufficient age to have the *capacity* to form a criminal intent.[2] The common law, as well as various statutory enactments, extended the protected status of childhood in giving effect to perceived needs for the protection of children from their own actions, and for the protection of children from the acts of, or the failure to act by, others.

With the application of this status in the context of a third interrelated notion, the perceived need to protect others from children, special measures for the control and prevention of delinquency were formulated. The interspersion of the rationale for protection *from* children with justifications for the protection *of* children was central to the social and legal concerns debated at the turn of the century. Different responses were made to these concerns by various individuals and groups competing for predominant roles in an expanding child-saving movement. Analysis of the institutional development that resulted from certain of these efforts indicates that the protection associated with the dependent status of children was successfully refined from its initially vague expressions to a specific delinquency program of protection through prevention by probation. The emergence of the juvenile court, with its special procedures and dispositions (the most significant of which was organized probation), may thus be viewed as the culmination of several interrelated child-saving ventures.

Because "in theory, the juvenile justice system is [and was] totally committed to rehabilitation and to 'the best interests of the child',"[3] yet at the same time
is concerned with the *prevention* of delinquent/criminal behavior, there was
considerably less concern with the rights of children at the adjudication stage of
the trial than with the "treatment" of children at the disposition stage. In effect
the trial process was to be part of the treatment process. Since "strict adherence
to the procedures of the ordinary courts might well work to the detriment of the
child," stated Mr. Justice McRuer, a judge must assume the role of "a social
physician charged with diagnosing the case and issuing the prescription"
(1968, p.554; cf. Steinberg, 1972, 1974; Thomson, 1973). Yet as indicated by
current juvenile justice reformers, "elements such as deterrence, punishment,
detention and the resulting stigma have surfaced in the juvenile justice process
despite initial intentions to the contrary" (Solicitor-General's Committee,
1975, p.4; cf. Ketcham, 1961). In response to such a realization, the legal
profession has taken a renewed interest in the juvenile court (Isaacs, 1968;
Johnson, 1970; also Catton & Erickson, 1974; Djootes, Erickson, & Fox,
1972; Erickson, 1974, 1975).

Since it is likely that children will retain, to some extent, their dependent
status, a contemporary examination of the incidents of that status is in order.
Recently, pointed attacks have been made by social scientists on certain
assumptions that underlie the social and legal policies that treat children as
"less responsible" persons (Skolnick, 1975). Reevaluations of the roles of the
child, the family, and the state in the protection process have been suggested
(Goldstein, Freud & Solnit, 1973; Wald, 1975, 1976). In the Canadian context, such inquiries are crucial to reform of the juvenile justice system. Given
that their dependent status has made children particularly vulnerable to the
intrusion of those who profess to know what is in the child's "best interests,"
the proposed Canadian reforms require critical examination. To give children
"rights" without providing the necessary mechanisms to make these rights
effective would result in confusion for all concerned. The draft Young Offenders Act appears to tread a fine and perhaps necessary line between the
"protection of dependents" and the "provision of legal rights." Which children are given what rights and with what effect? is a crucial question to be
addressed. The historical origins of delinquency legislation are not without
relevance for the prospects of reform.

## Early Concerns with the Welfare of Children[4]
Concern with child welfare in Canada did not originate with the late 19th-
century reformers' "discovery" of urban social problems (Houston, 1974,
p.2; cf. Splane, 1965). The family, as a unit for the socialization of children,
had long been supplemented by state efforts. Being late in the 18th century, for
example, legislative measures made provision for the care, support, and
protection of children who were orphans or who had been deserted by their
parents. This concern, originally directed towards children without parents
(and more specifically, without a father), was later extended to children with
inadequate parents.

With the focus on control, or the lack thereof, in the family context,
distinctions between behavior that might be attributed to parental absence or
neglect and behavior that might be characterized as criminal or delinquent were
not relevant. The rationale for the control of juvenile misbehavior, and hence
for the *prevention* of *future* criminal behavior, mixed the perceived need for the
protection of others from children with the perceived need for the protection of

children from themselves and others. The question was not as much one of whether children would be held *accountable* for their behavior (criminal or otherwise), but rather one of how best to *treat* children in order to effect adequate socialization before they became "convicted criminals." If the family was not capable, then the state would intervene to reform the child. For example, in a series of letters published in the *Montreal Gazette* (and also in pamphlet form) in 1857 under the pseudonym "Philanthropy," it was suggested that the "evil must be reached at its source; the noxious weed must be nipped in the bud; the child must be separated from parents who would only train it up to vice." And while acknowledging the apparent harshness of such measures, the author queried whether it was "not much harder to allow such children to become actual criminals, and then be obliged to do the same thing with much less chance of success."

In sum, "the distinction in states between *neglected* and *criminal* in effect translated as *potentially* vs. *actually* criminal" (Houston, 1972, p.263). This attitude towards the prevention of criminality was reasserted by those who later drafted Canada's delinquency legislation in terms of the idea "that there should be no hard and fast distinction between neglected and delinquent children, but that all should be recognized as of the same class, and should be dealt with with a view to serving the best interests of the child" (Scott, 1906, 27/10, see also Parker, 1968). Given such goals, the recognition of "rights" for the child in the court process was simply not considered necessary.

Concern with controlling the delinquent behavior of children was, moreover, part of an extensive concern with child-saving in general (cf. Marks, 1975; Morrison, 1971; Parker, 1967a, p.746). The notion, as expressed by a later Canadian legislator, that "idleness begets delinquency" (Senate Debates, 1907, 24/04, p.901) was reflected in the early emphasis placed on apprentice-ship and the promotion of education. Private individuals and volunteer organizations were involved during the mid-19th century in organizing institutions, with the directors having the power to bind out as apprentices children who were under their charge (Splane, 1965, p.223). The promotion of schooling under the impetus of Egerton Ryerson and others was, like apprenticeship, associated with crime prevention and the effective preparation of children for productive roles in later life (see Prentice, 1974). The attitudes expressed by this movement continued to be voiced by later reformers. Deviation from an idealized model of family life, and the failure of children to attend school, would result in children "rapidly acquiring an education of the wrong kind" (*Proceedings*, 1909, p.99).

Though these and later "child welfare" efforts were tenuously linked by their "concern with the predicament of disadvantaged and delinquent children" (Morrison, 1971, p.4), the development of special procedures for processing *delinquent* children resulted from unique organizational forces. Yet the distinctions between neglect and delinquency were never well-defined; the modified treatment of children convicted of crimes had long reflected doubt as to the true "criminality" of their behavior (Houston, 1972).

Two statutes enacted in Canada in 1857 were relevant to the treatment of children convicted of criminal offences. An Act for Establishing Prisons for Young Offenders provided for the construction of "reformatory prisons" in Upper and Lower Canada to which certain young offenders could be sent in order to "be detained and corrected, and receive such instruction and be subject to such discipline, as shall appear most conducive to their reformation and the repression of crime." During this period, then, lengthy sentences to special institutions were justified by the belief that reformation could be effected for the benefit of the child and society.[5] The second statute, An Act for the More Speedy Trial and Punishment of Young Offenders, provided for special summary trial procedures, and increased powers to discharge certain juvenile offenders in order "to avoid the evils of their long imprisonment previously to trial."

While enthusiasm for the reformatory varied even in this early period (Houston, 1972, 1974), the later advocates of delinquency legislation expressed the definite desire to keep all but the most "serious cases" out of institutions such as juvenile reformatories and industrial schools, which were regarded as "no more than a necessary evil" (Scott, 1908, p.897). "What wise parent," argued Scott, "would place a naughty child with other naughty children in order to make him better?" (p.897). The fulfilment of this desire was not, however, immediately forthcoming.

The failure to distinguish children implicated by their parents' absence or inadequacy from children who had committed an offence, all of whom were regarded as potential criminals and hence as subjects for preventive treatment, was also reflected in the provisions of An Act respecting Industrial Schools, passed in Ontario in 1874. This Act allowed for the establishment of residential schools[6] to which police magistrates could commit certain children for purposes of "teaching and training." In offering an alternative that was more severe than public school, but less severe than the reformatory, the industrial school was to accept a variety of candidates, including any child found begging, wandering, destitute, out of control, or "who, by reason of the neglect, drunkenness or other vices of parents, is suffered to be growing up without salutary parental control and education, or in circumstances exposing him to lead an idle and dissolute life." In 1884, those eligible for committal were expanded to include, at the discretion of the judge, any child "who has been found guilty of petty crime."[7] Thus, as more benign treatment-oriented responses to the behavior of children were developed, the perceived needs to protect children and to protect others from children dictated similar preventive measures. In the final decades of the 19th century, a period of rapid urbanization in Ontario, reform efforts directed towards children were gradually professionalized and bureaucratized (Morrison, 1971, 1976). These developments provided the background for the eventual enactment of juvenile delinquency legislation in Canada.

The reformers of this period idealized the family, emphasizing the natural home as the preferred child-rearing milieu (Kelso, n.d.a., pp.4-5; Morrison, 1971, pp.92-112). The industrial school was considered as complementary to the family in which adequate control was lacking (Morrison, 1974). Nevertheless, as previously noted, the view that "if a child can be saved from the industrial school it should be done" (Scott, 1907, 08/07) was destined to be popular among the principal advocates of delinquency legislation. Further, in addition to their concern with children who might be institutionalized, these reformers noted the potentially undesirable results that might follow from the court's direct release of children to home environments where control was presumably deficient. "Release on suspended sentence without more," wrote Scott (1908), "is in the majority of cases, equally or even more objectionable . . . [the child] goes back to what caused his downfall without anything extraneous to aid him in avoiding further lapses" (p.897). As such, this disposition was "as a rule of little use in preventing juvenile crime" (p.898). At the crux of the eventual delinquency legislation, then, was the extension of probation, a measure for the protection of children through the prevention of "crime," that would both keep children out of institutions and provide them with supervision in their home environment. The conflict generated among the groups that supported and resisted this change is documented below. It would appear that the intent of the legislation, as suggested by its proponents, was to expand probation work as a significant alternative to the established dispositions of institutionalization (in reformatories and industrial schools) and discharge. In the words of Scott (1907): "We wish to see the work spread" (11/06).

## The Development of Child-Saving: Legislation and Organization

It was during the latter two decades of the 19th century that certain persons, who were eventually to take up the cause for the enactment of legislation for a specialized juvenile court with probation services, achieved prominence in the Canadian child-saving movement. In 1887, J. J. Kelso, a crusading newspaper reporter and "moral entrepreneur" (Becker, 1963, ch.8), who went on to a long and influential career as Ontario's first Superintendent of Neglected and Dependent Children, brought together several prominent men and women[8] in the Toronto community to organize the Toronto Humane Society,[9] an organization that set for itself a "broadly educational" mission: "better laws, better methods, [and] the development of the humane spirit in all the affairs of life" (Kelso, 1911, p.17; see also Bain, 1955; Morrison, 1971).

Generally consistent with such objectives, An Act for the Protection and Reformation of Neglected Children, prepared under Beverley Jones, was passed in Ontario in the following year (Kelso, 1911, p.20). This Act allowed for the committal of neglected children[10] to certain institutions (including industrial schools and refuges), or to authorized charitable societies, to be "kept, cared for and educated." Further, with regard to provincial offences, the Act provided for the appointment of "commissioners, each with the powers of a police magistrate, to hear and determine complaints against juvenile offenders." Also, persons under 21 years of age were "as far as practicable, [to] be tried, and their cases [to] be disposed of, separately and apart from other offenders, and at suitable times to be designated and appointed for this purpose." At this stage, though special court procedures were being introduced for some offenders (at least in legislation), institutional commitment rather than probation was considered a necessary mode of care when the family home proved unable to meet this task (Morrison, 1971, p.292, 1974; Splane, 1965, pp.266-267). Yet as Kelso consistently emphasized, "The aim . . . is not to steal children from their parents and place heavy burdens upon the charitable, but by every available means to make the home and family all it ought to be" (*Annual Report*, 1895). And, as indicated, the close connections between neglect and delinquency remained.

Trends in Ontario child-saving were furthered by the enactment of An Act respecting the Custody of Juvenile Offenders and An Act respecting the Commitment of Persons of Tender Years in 1890. These statutes favored the committal of boys to industrial school rather than the reformatory. In subsequent reflections on this change in attitude towards the use of reformatories (which he helped to foster), Kelso noted the principle, as set out by his department, "that the family home is the best place in which to develop sturdy self-reliant character in children, whether good or bad" (*Annual Report*, 1906, p.101). The industrial schools had a "good showing," he claimed, "considering the wretched home life from which many of the children were taken." However, "in studying the histories of lads in the Penetang Reformatory, many youths were found there for so-called crimes that almost every man in the country of any spirit has committed at some time or other in his boyhood!" pp.101-102). "These are cruelties and hardships," Kelso prophesied, "that will not occur so frequently when we have a properly equipped Children's Court and probation system" (p.102). Kelso ultimately played a major role in clearing the reformatory of its juvenile population and placing the former inmates in foster homes.

Most significant to the trends in institutional treatment at the turn of the century were the findings of the Commission of Inquiry into the Prison and Reformatory System of Ontario. The Commissioners handed down a report in 1891 that was critical of the methods previously used to control and reform children. The Ontario Reformatory for Boys was characterized as a "great mistake": "The new structure was but a more commodious prison" (*Report of the Commissioners*, 1891, pp.87-88).[11] This document in many respects appears to have provided a general "blueprint" for future responses to juvenile behavior in Ontario. The Commissioners' recommendations covered a variety of matters, including enforcement of compulsory school attendance laws;[12] establishment of industrial schools; control of child immigration; relocation of the reformatory, together with the incorporation of a cottage system and earned remission; alteration in the institutional facilities for girls; and introduction of various after-care programs and facilities (pp.214-218). Furthermore, several of the recommendations focussed specifically on differential processing of juvenile offenders, before, during, and after trial. The Commissioners' recommendations touched on arrest; the use of summons for trivial offences; separate detention; special trials without publicity; committal to the refuge or reformatory only after all other corrective measures had been tried; discharge under parental supervision; suspended sentences under police supervision; and expansion of the powers and duties assigned to probation officers.

Shortly after the Commissioners submitted their report in 1891, Kelso organized a public meeting, and with the support of the Commission's chairman (Mr. Langmuir) and one of its most influential members (Dr. Rosebrugh) (see also Morrison, 1971, p.297), the Toronto Children's Aid Society and Fresh Air Fund was founded (with Kelso as president). In the letter announcing the meeting, several possible objects of the proposed society, including "the separate trial of juvenile offenders and young girls," were mentioned. Among the matters demanding attention was "the appointment of a probation officer to ascertain and submit to the court full particulars of each child brought up for trial and to act in the capacity of the child's next friend" (Kelso, 1911, p.69). Kelso's (1891) primary concerns were outlined in a letter to a local newspaper:

"I happened to be at the Police Court the other day and the first thing that caught my attention was the presence before the bar of no less than seven boys, not one of whom was eighteen years of age. They were charged with larceny in various degrees, and one had gone so far as to have served a term at Kingston Penitentiary. The number of boys who come up in the Police Court from day to day is a problem that calls for the most careful enquiry. . . . Should we not organize at once a society that will remove children from such unfortunate conditions and afford them an opportunity to grow up good men and women."

It was, as noted, Kelso's philosophy that a "family" home was the best location for prevention of juvenile misbehavior. However, some families required assistance to effect this task. "Children should never be treated or spoken of as criminals. . . . Wherever there is an offence there is a cause behind it and our children's court and probation system," Kelso later emphasized, "should be able to reach that cause and by some means or other remove it for the safety and protection of the children in the home" (*Annual Report*, 1906, p.15).

As the organization of reform efforts developed into an expansive bureaucracy, there was a concomitant trend towards a rationalization of child-saving efforts by supplementing (and to a degree replacing) the work done by volunteers and philanthropic citizens with that of paid professionals. "What is needed," wrote Kelso [n.d.a], "is personal service, the complete organization of charitable forces, harmony of action, and the appointment of trained and experienced workers, instead of isolated action, rivalry and jealousy and spasmodic and amateur administration" (p.20). With this shift, a number of child-savers began to develop vested interests in the perpetuation of their own positions in the growing scheme of child welfare.

Increased activity also led to the formation of an effective lobby that sought and secured legislation at both provincial and federal levels to legitimize and ensure the legality of their programs for reform. Reflecting back on these efforts, Kelso indicated that "any defect in the work is not due to any defect in the law, for we have as much if not more law than we can assimilate, and the Governments are ready to give new measures whenever they are asked to do so" (*Proceedings*, 1903, p.21).

For example, when Alderman John Baxter was appointed a Commissioner in 1890 by the provincial Attorney-General, his authority over children charged with criminal offences was challenged. Senator G. W. Allen, who was president of the Toronto Working Boys' Home, joined Kelso in exerting pressure for the enactment of federal legislation (Bain, 1955, pp.72-76). The first Criminal Code of Canada, enacted in 1892, included a section providing for the in-camera and separate trial of persons under the age of 16 years if it was "expedient and practicable" to do so.

In 1893 the Ontario Legislature enacted a comprehensive Child Protection Act that gave explicit recognition and authority to children's aid societies and their agents or officers to apprehend and detain children in need of protection because of ill-treatment or neglect. Further, the Act allowed for the investigation of charges against a child (for provincial offences), inquiry into the child's family environment, examination of all the facts and circumstances of the case, and the submission of a report to the court.[13] Provision was also made for the separate detention and trial of children in certain locations.[14]

It was assumed, however, that these procedures could not encompass children charged with federal criminal offences. To this end, Senator Allen introduced An Act respecting Juvenile Offenders to the Senate in 1893 "at the insistence of the Prison Reform Conference and Prisoner's Aid Societies of Ontario" (Senate Debates, 1893, 07/03, p.298). This bill was eventually withdrawn, but in the following year, at the request of "persons interested in the care of children" (House of Commons Debates, 1894, 15/05, p.4941), An Act respecting Arrest, Trial and Imprisonment of Youthful Offenders was enacted at the federal level. The Criminal Code provision had become a "dead letter law," and Kelso had been conducting an active campaign, through petitions and in the press, for separate trials for young persons (Bain, 1955, p.82). The 1894 Act made it mandatory that persons under 16 years of age be tried separately from other accused persons, and without publicity, and provided for separate pre- and post-trial custody.

In the Senate, Senator Allen explained that certain sections of the Act concerning the role of the children's aid societies were restricted to Ontario because it was the only province with "the machinery . . . for carrying out these clauses" (Senate Debates, 1894, 10/05, p.349). A possible limitation to the notion of trials without publicity was suggested by Senator Kaulbach in that if the offence "were a very heinous one . . . a private trial would not be suitable for youthful offenders" (Senate Debates, 1894, 01/05, p.305; also Green, 1971; McDonald, 1965; Parker, 1969, p.196, 1970). In the House of Commons, Sir John Thompson indicated that "a great many magistrates from motives of humanity" were already conducting separate trials of juvenile offenders (House of Commons Debates, 1894, 24/06, p.4940). As well, the children's aid societies would not only investigate the home to determine whether the child should remain there but also would "carry out more effectively the system of suspended sentences with regard to children" (p.4941).

Although the latter allusion to probation may have been somewhat premature, the children's aid societies were actively involved with children accused of crimes, as indicated by the case of Maggie, from the Toronto Society's daily log: "April 20th, 1892 – Taken out of hands of a policeman and brought to Shelter by Miss Hamilton. Had been arrested for supposed attempted larceny. Was found in a terribly filthy condition" (Children's Aid Society, 1975, p.6). The reference to the prior initiation of separate trials was confirmed by Col. G. T. Denison (1920), a Magistrate in the Toronto Police Court, who later wrote that:

"In 1892 we instituted the Children's Court. It was not really a separate court, but we set apart a small room in the lower part of the City Hall, with a table and a few chairs, and I was accustomed to go down to that room to try all charges against children, in order to keep them out of the public court. . . . If I felt that punishment was necessary, I would send the child to the Children's Aid Society, or the Roman Catholic School for Children, for a few days, and give the culprits a scolding, and warn them to behave themselves in the future." (p.254; see also Kelso, 1908)

In spite of the distinction drawn between a separate "court" and a separate "trial," these developments, and Kelso's role in them, became the basis for claims that the juvenile court had a Toronto origin, and was therefore a "Canadian enterprise" that had been appropriated by "American social workers."[15]

Kelso was later somewhat disappointed that more recognition was not given to the pioneering work of the Ontario reformers in this regard. In a letter to Scott, he emphasized that "our Ontario work should not be overlooked as I advocated the Children's Court here twenty years ago, gave addresses in Chicago and elsewhere in favour of it and got the law passed here in 1893 . . . of course, the Denver and Chicago courts have far outstripped us but at the same time we gave them the inspiration that led to their present success" (Scott, 1906, 27/12; see also Scott, 1907, 04/07). The address to which Kelso specifically referred was given to the Waif-Saving Congress on October 11, 1893 (*Proceedings*, 1893; see also Flexner & Baldwin, 1914, pp.3-4; *Proceedings*, 1895). Kelso noted that "Judge Hurd consulted with me as to the drafting of the Juvenile Court following my address" and an article on his presentation appeared in the *Chicago Tribune* on the following day.

Thus, at the close of the 19th century, a comprehensive base of legislation had successfully been secured as authorization for child-saving ventures. In part because of inadequate financing, the two major institutions now associated with juvenile justice (a separate court and organized probation) were still in the formative stages. The links between neglect and delinquency (protection of, and from, children) had, in the context of the trial process, begun to place more emphasis on disposition than adjudication. The "trial" was to be part of the "treatment." Response to the delinquent behavior of children did not, for the child-savers, require a determination of "fault." Children "are what their surroundings have made them," wrote Kelso, "but they are still in the formative period, still capable of being put on the right path" (*Annual Report*, 1906, p.69). The ideal location for reformation was not in an institution but in a family home, be it natural or foster. This philosophy was not, however, uniformly accepted by all persons involved in crime prevention. In the context of an expanding bureaucracy, conflicts arose over which groups of professionals and volunteers would play the decisive role in dealing with delinquents. The dependent status assigned to children had left them open to the intervention of others. The final configuration of the system designed to respond to their situations and transgressions was the product of conflicts among those who had both personal and professional interests in the ultimate design of that system.

## A System for Juvenile Justice:
## Organized Probation and the Juvenile Court

In 1903, legislative recognition of probation was extended by an amendment to the Ontario Children's Protection Act. The amendment provided for the appointment of volunteer Children's Committees, whose agents, along with consenting officers of children's aid societies, could serve as probation officers in whose care a judge could place, without registering a conviction, a child under 16 years of age accused of a provincial offence. The probation officers, charged with the duty to take a "personal interest in the child . . . so as to secure its reformation," might be required to periodically report to the judge "concerning the progress and welfare of the child."

The idea of a probation *system*, manned by both volunteers and professionals, to "help the children before they become criminally disposed" was increasingly discussed (Kelso, 1907, p.107). In an address to the Sixth Canadian Conference of Charities and Corrections, Kelso gave this top priority: "Prevention work should begin when the children are small. . . . We want to bring about what is called the Probation System, following these children up from their first offence and never letting them get any further" (*Proceedings*, 1903, p.21). The probation officer would "frequently visit the home and insist on school attendance and proper moral instruction . . . [and], having a constant supervision of the child, would prevent his getting into trouble again" (p.21). Consistent with the related goals of protection and prevention, the methods used by probation officers would be based on "kindly advice and practical aid." These methods, furthermore, would be in direct contrast with those of the police, who, in the course of seeking convictions, were prone to use "force" and "punishment" in the "restoration" process (Kelso, 1907, p.107). Thus, according to Kelso, it was "too easy" simply to suspend sentence or to commit a child to an industrial school; and while some progress with probation had been made, "the machinery thus far provided is totally inadequate to meet the need that exists" (*Annual Report*, 1906, p.13).

Kelso was not alone in his advocacy of a children's court and probation. W. L. Scott, Local Master at Ottawa for the Supreme Court of Ontario and president of the Ottawa Children's Aid Society, attended the 1906 National Conference of Charities and Corrections in Philadelphia and found that the juvenile court and probation system were "looked upon as the highest and most important development of child-saving work yet reached" (*Annual Report*, 1906, p.69). On his return, Scott and John Keane, his co-delegate who was full-time secretary of the Ottawa Society, saw to the appointment of Mme. Bruchesi, a French Catholic, and Miss Cassady, an English Protestant, as probation officers "to cooperate with our regular agent in the endeavour to reform in their own homes children coming before the Police Magistrate for infractions of the criminal law" (Scott, 1907, 08/07). Scott later suggested that the choice of women as professional probation officers was based not only on the notion, popular among feminists of the time, that "women, intended by nature for motherhood, are better fitted for the work than men," but also because "a better class of women than men can frequently be got for the money available" (Scott, 1908, p.896; see also McClung, 1945, p.27; Morrison, 1971, 1976; Strong-Boag, 1972, p.viii).[16]

This latter issue, that of finances, was one of the three main concerns vocalized by Kelso and Scott during this period. Additional funds were needed to elevate "philanthropic work to the status of a profession and to encourage University graduates to become specialists in social and moral reform work" (*Proceedings*, 1905, p.8). In proposing that local counties and the Ontario government share the cost of salaries for probation officers, Kelso suggested that "the lack of paid agents I find to be the greatest drawback in the work today" (Scott, 1907, 04/01). A second concern was that although the Ottawa police had been cooperating with the local children's aid society to allow for probation, the probation offices were hampered in their work by a lack of "legislative recognition" (Scott, 1907, 02/01). And third, the existing Children's Courts were not "conducted by specially selected persons, and held in different premises from the ordinary legal Courts" (Kelso, 1908, p.164). This shortcoming, in particular the absence of special judges, was not consistent with the notion that the court "should undoubtedly be an educational rather than a police tribunal" (p.164). The remedy for these deficiencies, then, was to be sought in new federal legislation.

Early recognition of the proposed legislation came in the Speech from the Throne on November 23, 1906, with the mention of "a Bill to make better provision for dealing with juvenile delinquents" (House of Commons Debates, 1906, 23/11, p.5). This announcement was inserted by Senator R. Scott (father of W. L. Scott), who was then serving as Secretary of State. In doing so, the elder Scott failed to consult with the Minister of Justice, Mr. Aylesworth. Taking offence, Aylesworth refused to support the proposed legislation and it was over a year before he consented, under much pressure, to introduce the Bill to the House of Commons. However, Senator Scott was permitted to introduce the Bill to the Senate in April 1907 as a means of generating discussion, on the condition that it did not go beyond second reading (Scott, 1907).

Correspondence between W. L. Scott and Kelso towards the end of 1906 reflected the considerations that ultimately formed the basis of various provisions in the legislation. For example, Kelso asked whether "it is possible to have the offences of all children under sixteen classed as delinquencies so that they may be dealt with as neglected children under our Ontario Law rather than under the Criminal Code" (Scott, 1906, 21/11). Under the 1908 Juvenile Delinquents Act, the offence of "delinquency" included, for children under 16 years, violations of any federal or provincial statute or municipal by-law, or behaviors that created liability under any other act for committal to an industrial school or juvenile reformatory.[17] Scott later emphasized, however, that "the intention of Parliament was not to create a new class of offence, but to afford a means of dealing with offences, or evils, already in existence" (1927, p.7).

Scott, who admitted his unfamiliarity with criminal procedure (1906, 24/11), was assisted by Senator Beique, and Recorder Weir of Montreal, as well as Kelso, in drafting the Act (1907, 18/07). In the context of subsequent reactions to the proposals, three main groups may be discerned. The ultimately successful group, which advocated protection and prevention through probation and a special court, formed a powerful lobby that managed to rally considerable support among the public and among politicians. Information and copies of the Bill were distributed, petitions were circulated, letters were sent, and speakers, such as Judge Lindsay of Denver, and Mrs. Schoff of the Philadelphia Mother's Union, addressed various gatherings. Assistance was forthcoming from across Canada, and among those individuals and organizations that took action to indicate their support were Katherine Weller of the Montreal Women's Club; the National Council of Women; various chapters of the Women's Christian Temperance Union; F. C. Wade, president of the Juvenile Protective Association of British Columbia; C. J. South, superintendent of the Children's Protection Act of British Columbia; F. J. Billiarde, superintendent of the Winnipeg Children's Aid Society; and Premier Rutherford of Alberta. Petitions were received from several locations, including Medicine Hat and Claresholm in Alberta, and Canso, Guysboro, and Yarmouth in Nova Scotia. One Montreal petition had over 5 000 signatures, with many "prominent" people represented (Scott, 1907-1908). A circular that received wide distribution featured supportive statements from 12 judges, 10 senators, 3 clergymen, 2 police officers, and 10 others. Indicative of the extensive support generated for the proposals was the statement by Robert Borden, when Leader of the Opposition in the House of Commons, who wrote that while it was unusual for the opposition party to give advance assurances of support for legislation, "I am entirely in favour of the principle [of delinquency legislation]" (Scott, 1907, 20/02).

Opposition to the proposals was forthcoming, however, from two groups: those who were concerned with possible abuses of the proposed system and the resulting effects on the rights of children and their parents, and those who advocated a more "punitive" approach to delinquency. The former group's response was largely ineffectual. Its members, speaking independently, were more cautionary than critical, since they generally accepted the competence of those who advocated probation and a special court to act in the best interests of the child and society. For example, in a letter to Scott, Mr. Justice Anglin questioned the wisdom of removing safeguards against the arbitrary exercise of "very wide and largely discretionary" powers by judges and probation officers (Scott, 1907, 07/02). Scott, in reply, convincingly emphasized that "neither the Courts nor the probation officers will be anxious to take in hand cases where the child does not seem to be going wrong. Still it is desirable to have the definition wide enough to enable the Court to take hold of any case where the intervention of the Court seems desirable" (Scott, 1907, 08/02).

More significant opposition to the proposed legislation came from the second group, of which many members were actively working as police officers and magistrates with children, and in association with some children's aid societies. Their differences were more than philosophical: they considered their own continued involvement with child-saving in jeopardy. In the words of

R. E. Kingsford, a police magistrate in Toronto, "it would be a great pity if the notion got abroad that the police were so harsh in their dealings with juveniles that it was necessary to take from them that portion of work" (Scott, 1906, 20/12). The proposed juvenile court would replace the existing children's court. Probation might affect the use of other dispositions, such as dismissal, fine, committal to a children's aid society, or committal to industrial school,[18] and hence the personnel connected with them.

The police officials associated with the Toronto children's court, including Inspectors Stark and Archibald and Police Magistrates Denison and Kingsford, were most vehement in their attacks. They argued not only that the existing methods were both sufficient and less expensive, but also that the "harsh" attitude of the police had a deterrent effect by making an impression on children without resulting in the police being viewed as enemies (Scott, 1906, 20/12). The debate was often bitter, with Archibald (1907), in a report circulated to gain support for the police position, characterizing the new proposals as "child saving propaganda" and the advocates of these measures as "superficial and sentimental faddists" who, in the interests of their own "selfish ends":

"work upon the sympathies of philanthropic men and women for the purpose of introducing a jelly-fish and abortive system of law enforcement, whereby the judge or magistrate is expected to come down to the level of the incorrigible street arab and assume an attitude absolutely repulsive to British Subjects. The idea seems to be that by profuse use of slang phraseology he should place himself in a position to kiss and coddle a class of perverts and delinquents who require the most rigid disciplinary and corrective methods to ensure the possibility of their reformation. I would go further to affirm from extensive and practical experience that this kissing and coddling, if indiscriminately applied, even to the best class of children, would have a disastrous effect, both physically, mentally, morally and spiritually." (p.5)

In response to this criticism, Scott labelled Archibald a "person of very limited intelligence" (1907, 19/03), while Kelso called him "self-opinionated" and opposed to those who failed to treat him with deference (Scott, 1907, 14/05). Opposition from the Toronto police departments indicated to Scott that "the members feel the proposals are intended to supplant them and are a reflection on their past work" (Scott, 1907, 02/05; see also 05/05). Moreover, Archibald's particularly negative attitude was said to be based on the fact that he "had prepared all the legislation on the subject during the last forty years and . . . is apparently deeply offended that anyone else should have usurped this prerogative" (Scott, 1907, 16/04). For Scott, Kelso, and their supporters, probation was "the only effective method of dealing with young offenders," and the "trial [should take place] before a judge specially selected for his fitness for the work" (Scott, 1908, p.894). The police, they claimed, too often showed a "great lack of patience" with children, giving more weight to "the spirit of revenge . . . than consideration of a boy's future (*Proceedings*, 1903, p.5).

The children's aid societies in Toronto also opposed the proposals, although the Toronto Children's Aid Society eventually gave the new measures qualified approval. Kelso suggested that the "police officials have both our Societies hoodwinked" (Scott, 1909, 09/04). The St. Vincent de Paul Society were most vocal in their opposition, particularly as to probation, which would have "a troop of Probation Officers, women and men, shadowing . . .

[delinquent children] . . . through the Province'' (Scott, 1907, 11/04). Scott believed their opposition to be misconceived: ''What are the agents of the Children's Aid Societies but Probation Officers under another name?'' (1907, 11/04). Commenting on the situation in Ottawa with regard to dependent and neglected children, Scott noted that with the work of probation officers ''we have been enabled to place back an unusually larger number of children with their own parents during good behaviour'' (1907, 15/10). Extending probation work to delinquent children had allowed not only for supervision of those with suspended sentences but also for ''dealing with an increasing number of what may be called preventative cases . . . in which we are called in before the child actually gets into the hands of the police'' (1907, 08/07). And of at least equal significance was a further result of probation: ''to keep children in their homes who would otherwise go to the Industrial School'' (1907, 02/10).

The degree of success achieved by those who campaigned for special delinquency legislation was reflected in the overwhelming acceptance of the proposals in the House of Commons and the Senate. With few significant exceptions, the response of the less enthusiastic supporters of the legislation was characterized more by apathy than by opposition. In introducing the Juvenile Delinquents Bill to the Senate in 1907 ''in order to elicit an opinion on the subject,'' Senator Scott praised the work being done in Ottawa and elsewhere, quoting from the Preamble to emphasize that children should be ''guarded against association with crime and criminals, and should be subjected to such wise care, treatment and control as will tend to check their evil tendencies and to strengthen their better instincts'' (Senate Debates, 19/04, p.804). While some questions were raised as to the constitutional validity of the Bill, and Senator Ellis referred to ''considerable difference of opinion as to who shall take care of children, and how they should be taken care of'' (Senate Debates, 24/04, p.891), the discussion focussed on the causes of crime and its nature and extent in Canada. Senator Cloran best summed up the deliberations, and the mood of the Senate, by indicating that ''while other matters are contentious and are debated with some degree of feeling and sometimes hostility, there seemed to be but one opinion in the House as to the importance of this Bill and the humane and benevolent purpose which it is proposed to serve'' (p.896).

When the Bill was reintroduced to the Senate by Senator Beique in May 1908, Senator Coffey referred to ''the difference of view as to the means and methods whereby the best results may be achieved'' in reforming children, and explicitly dismissed the position of Inspector Archibald as being characterized by an outmoded ''spirit of rigidity and severity'' (Senate Debates, 21/05, pp.975-977). Even Senator Kerr, who came to Archibald's defence by characterizing him as a man to be commended for his work, indicated that he was glad the Bill was about to become law (p.981). Senator Wilson, however, questioned the broad powers given to probation officers. He was not convinced that it was in children's best interests to be effectively deprived, along with their parents, of certain rights:

''We are all desirous of making every child as it grows up a useful member of society, but we may differ as to the means of accomplishing that. Here we pass an Act to permit a child being taken away from its parents and put in other charge, and who is as solicitous for the welfare of the child as the parent? We put young children in the hands of an officer and that officer has absolute power and control over them. He may do anything under the Act and he is protected. I say that it is an unreasonable proposition to make, and I am fearful that instead of lessening the criminal juvenile class it will increase them." (Senate Debates, 1908, 04/06, p.1044)

These cautions appear to have gone unheeded, given Senator Scott's reply that he had "never heard of an instance where the whole community did not sustain the probation officer in the action he took" (p.1044). A second challenge to the Bill, on constitutional grounds, was defeated (Senate Debates, 1908, 16/06, pp.1152-1156).

In the House of Commons, Minister of Justice Aylesworth introduced the Bill by indicating that in Ontario "children's aid societies have felt the necessity of legislation of this character" (House of Commons Debates, 1908, 08/07, p.12400). The general attitude assumed towards this Bill may be gleaned from the critical statement of Mr. Lancaster, an Ontario lawyer, who expressed concern that:

"it is to be laughed through as a joke. Here is an Act respecting juvenile delinquents, a brand new law, brought in during the dying hours of the session by the Minister of Justice, containing thirty-five sections, and after midnight we are asked to pass but not consider it. It affects the liberty, the character and the treatment of every little child in this country." (pp.12400-12401)

Lancaster strongly defended the "rights" of children. He focussed on the failure to provide for the "protection" and defence of children by counsel, thus placing them "entirely at the mercy of a person called a probation officer," without an opportunity "to say he is not guilty if he is not guilty" (p.12402). Moreover, to justify depriving children of the "inherent right to trial by jury," it was not, according to Lancaster, sufficient to provide for lighter sentences and the avoidance of publicity: provision could be made for a less severe penalty without denying children or their parents, assisted by counsel, the right to elect for a jury (pp.12403-12405). In other words, the adjudication aspect of the trial should be kept separate from that of disposition. This position received no further support, however, and the Bill was passed.[19]

With enactment of the Juvenile Delinquents Act in 1908, the essential pattern for juvenile justice in Canada was established. The juvenile court was given exclusive jurisdiction in cases of delinquency, subject to a discretion to transfer certain cases to the ordinary courts. Trials were to be conducted by juvenile court judges, separately, and without publicity; and the proceedings might be "in the discretion of the judge, as informal as the circumstances permit, consistently with a due regard for a proper administration of justice." In addition to provisions for separate pre-trial detention and post-trial incarceration, several possible dispositions were set out, including commitment to a probation officer, and supervision by a probation officer in the child's natural or foster home.[20] Probation officers were assigned the powers of a constable, with their duties including conducting such investigation as required by the court; being present and representing the interests of the child in court; furnishing the court with such assistance or information as required; and taking charge of any child, before or after trial, as might be directed by the court. The underlying philosophy of the Act was expressed as follows:

"This Act shall be liberally construed to the end that its purpose may be carried out, to wit: That the care and custody and discipline of a juvenile delinquent shall approximate as nearly as may be that which should be given by its parents, and that as far as practicable every juvenile delinquent shall be treated, not as a criminal, but as a misdirected and misguided child, and one needing aid, encouragement, help and assistance.''

The drive to implement organized probation and special juvenile courts continued beyond the enactment of the 1908 Act. Concerned efforts were made to secure the necessary provincial legislation creating the recently authorized juvenile courts, and, not unrelated, to obtain sufficient funds from various levels of government to employ probation officers. In Ontario, this process followed a haphazard pattern (Ontario Law Reform Commission, 1974, p.8).

In November 1911, Reverend J. Edward Starr was appointed Juvenile Court Commissioner in Toronto. Archibald, who was then a Chief Inspector in the Toronto Police Department, had continued his active but unsuccessful opposition to the concept, maintaining that separate trial by police magistrates was sufficient (Bain, 1955, p.90). Both voluntary probation officers (Big Brothers) and professionals were used in Toronto during the ensuing years. There does not appear to have been a consistent trend or pattern in the number of juveniles being institutionalized over the next forty-odd years, and it is not clear how many juveniles were being placed on probation for what offences. There was, however, a significant increase in the size of the staff associated with the juvenile court. The number of judges (including deputy judges) increased from one in 1912 to four in 1950. The number of probation officers and other professionals increased nearly fourfold, from five in 1912 to 19 in 1950. And the number of other support personnel increased from one in 1912 to 10 in 1915. The period of most rapid expansion for all three categories was prior to 1930 (City of Toronto, 1912-1950).

Subsequent to the 1908 Act, a number of minor amendments to the provisions were adopted, largely at the request of those involved in the administration of the Act. A revised and consolidated Juvenile Delinquents Act was passed in 1929.

Thus, the origins of delinquency legislation in Canada may be traced to the perceived need to protect children and prevent crime through a system of probation and special court procedures and personnel. The primary emphasis of this system was on treatment, with only minimal attention paid to accountability. In the course of efforts to secure preferred methods for treatment, conflicts emerged between two competing groups, those who favored existing police methods, and those who advocated the expansion of probation and the creation of special courts. Only minor and largely ineffectual concern was expressed for the ''legal rights'' of children. The resulting procedural changes and innovations may best be viewed as evolutionary rather than revolutionary (cf. Lemert, 1970). In part because of financial constraints on the growth of professionalism, organizational development was gradual, in spite of the singular success of the ''reformers'' in securing the desired legislation.[21]

The philosophy of these reformers favored external support in a family context (through probation) over disruption of the family (through institutional commitment). The *extent* to which supervision by probation officers, as a frequently used disposition, resulted not only in a deemphasis of industrial schools but also in additional intervention in the lives of children who otherwise would have been discharged is not clear. From the reformers' own accounts it is apparent that although both of these effects were intended, there was a preference for probation. Further, with the creation of special juvenile court procedures there was a failure to distinguish between stages of adjudication and disposition, with the ''trial'' itself considered part of the treatment.

50

Hence, minimal attention was paid to ensuring recognition of legal rights for children at either stage of the process. There was, in this regard, a notable absence of organized support for such recognition, and children remained vulnerable to the protective intrusions, or assistance, of others. Only recently in Canada have the notions of nonintervention in the face of juvenile misbehavior (Barnhorst, Barnhorst & Thomson, 1976; Law Reform Commission of Canada, 1975; see also Schur, 1973) and recognition of rights for children during both the adjudication *and* disposition stages of the trial process (Thomson, 1973) received serious consideration.

**New Reflections on an Established Philosophy: Continued Dependency**
The former draft Young Persons in Conflict with the Law Act, currently revised as the draft Young Offenders Act, reflects a modification in the incidents of the child's dependent status. Rather than suggesting a radically new concept in Canadian juvenile justice, the "new reformers" have reaffirmed a philosophy of prevention through "the early identification of children who are experiencing conflict in their homes, schools and other areas," but with the appropriate services to be applied "before the child is brought within the juvenile justice process" (Solicitor-General's Committee, 1975, p.4). The Preamble to the Young Offenders Act continues a preference for supervision of the child within the family. While young persons are to assume responsiblity for their actions, the primary emphasis is not on holding them fully accountable, but on recognizing that "because of their state of dependency and level of development and maturity, young persons have special needs and require guidance and assistance."

Unlike their predecessors, however, the "new reformers" have purported to recognize and protect the rights and freedoms of young persons. They have approached their task with the realization that the present system has generated unintended and undesirable consequences. Thus, they have attempted to compromise the special "protective" treatments afforded juveniles with the provision of certain rights and safeguards. In this regard, their success in launching new themes in Canadian juvenile justice is limited (Catton & Leon, 1977).

The current draft Act specially proposes four such themes: the restriction of jurisdiction to federal offences (against the Criminal Code and other federal statutes) committed by young persons between 12 and 18 years of age (subject to provincial modification of maximum age to 16 or 17 years); the creation of screening agencies to divert young persons from the court process; the provision of special treatment that is subject to structured discretionary powers and possibilities for both judicial and administrative review; and the recognition of the need for certain safeguards in the trial process, including representation, a "beyond a reasonable doubt" standard of proof, and appeals.[22]

A basic implication of the historical development of delinquency legislation for the prospects of reform is that the dependent status of children has rendered them vulnerable to a variety of measures imposed by interested parties for protective purposes. Yet because at some point dependency translates into domination, children also may require protection from their "would-be protectors." It is the provision of this latter type of protection that remains problematic. There are limitations to the capacity and the ability of certain children to avoid protective domination. Thus, to assign "legal rights" to children, without addressing the difficulties faced in securing access to mechanisms for enforcement of those rights, leaves children to contend with those willing to act in the "best interests of the child."

In sum, two convergent approaches to delinquency legislation are required in a contemporary context. First, assumptions about children that are reflected in particular legislative schemes should be examined. Without denying the value choices involved in the selection of any given proposal, data from the social and psychological sciences can be used to minimize reliance on "untested" propositions concerning the behavior of children. Similarly, legislation that institutes currently experimental "treatment" programs, such as diversion, should be preceded by extensive evaluation. The object of this exercise would be to anticipate unintended consequences of intervention *before* an additional and possibly enduring structure is created.

Second, an ever increasing number of professionals, including social workers, lawyers, administrators, and researchers, have developed strong and frequently competing interests in attempting to influence the direction of Canadian juvenile justice. No single interest group can be assumed to objectively profess the "best" method for securing the child's "best interests." The effective assignment of certain "rights" to children may render it increasingly difficult to justify intervention in the life of a child that extends beyond meeting recognized needs engendered by dependency. Thus, significant opposition from those who anticipate curtailment of their roles in "child protection" may be forthcoming. Whether or not such opposition is congruent with the best interests of children requires consideration.

## Notes

Some of the historical data used in this paper were presented in preliminary form under the title, "Helping and Controlling: The Development of a Canadian Policy to Regulate the Delinquent Behaviour of Children" at the Annual Meetings of the Canadian Sociology and Anthropology Association, May 1975, Edmonton, Alberta. This paper is based on, and extends, the analysis formulated in two previous papers, Hagan and Leon (1977) and Leon (1977).

I would like to thank John Hagan and Mary Eberts for their comments on, and assistance with, previous drafts of this paper, although naturally the responsibility remains my own. The support of the Connaught Programme on Family Law and Social Welfare, Faculty of Law, University of Toronto, is gratefully acknowledged.

[1] Lord Chancellor Eldon in *Wellesly v. The Duke of Beaufort* (1827), 38 E.R. 236. While there was doubt as to whether the *parens patriae* jurisdiction could lie with a provincial juvenile court (*Report of the Department of Justice Committee*, 1965, p.63), the intention of those responsible for Canadian delinquency legislation was that the "spirit" of the juvenile court be "that of a wise and kind, though firm and stern father . . . [asking] not, 'What has the child done?' but 'How can this child be saved?' " (Scott, 1908, p.892). Assuming it to be a matter primarily related to criminal law, and hence within federal jurisdiction, the draftsmen defined "delinquency" as an "act" in order to make it an offence (Scott, 1927, p.1).

[2] Some early cases in this regard have been reviewed elsewhere (Mendes da Costa, 1957). Under the first Criminal Code of Canada, passed in 1892, a child under seven years of age could not be convicted of an offence; and a child between seven and 14 years could be convicted of an offence only if "he was competent to know the nature and consequences of his conduct, and to appreciate that it was wrong."

[3] Mr. Justice Hartt in *R. v. Haig* [1971], 1 O.R. 75 (Ont. H.C.).

[4] The following discussion deals with Canada in general, although the main focus of this and subsequent sections is on events that occurred primarily in Ontario. Ontario child-saving was most significant in the emergence of both the philosophy and the organizations that formed the basis of early Canadian juvenile justice.

[5] Several subsequent statutes authorized the establishment of reformatories in various provinces. Provisions dealing with reformatories in Ontario, Quebec, Nova Scotia,

and Prince Edward Island were consolidated in 1886 under An Act respecting Public and Reformatory Prisons, with provisions regarding reformatories in other provinces added to this Act in later years.

[6] The first Industrial School for boys in Ontario was opened at Mimico in 1887. The first such school for girls, Alexandria School, opened in 1891.

[7] With the enactment of An Act respecting Truancy and Compulsory School Attendance in 1891, a further category, "any child between eight and fourteen years of age, who has been expelled from school for vicious and immoral conduct," was added.

[8] Morrison (1976) suggested that "most feminists involved in child welfare and educational reform were married to professionals or businessmen" (p.46). Many women also assumed professional roles as social workers and nurses. Underlying their involvement in child-saving "was a belief that society would benefit in moral terms from an extension of woman's maternalism" (p.45). Thus, while the overall organization of reform efforts was carried out by men, women were involved in the daily administration of activities. With specific regard to the emergence of delinquency legislation, women generally assumed supportive roles, with the primary philosophical and organizational tasks initiated and conducted by men. However, after the enactment of the Juvenile Delinquents Act in 1908, women in various parts of Canada (such as Helen Gregory MacGill in British Columbia and Emily Murphy in Alberta, both of whom became juvenile court judges) assumed dominant leadership roles in the organization and expansion of the juvenile courts and the probation system (MacGill, 1955; Saunders, 1945).

[9] Among the elected officers of the Society were: Lieutenant-Governor Robinson (Patron), Mayor Howland (honorary president), Hon. S. H. Blake (vice-president), Prof. Goldwin Smith (vice-president), Rev. D. J. Macdonnell (vice-president), W. R. Brock (vice-president), Lieut. J.I. Davidson (treasurer), and J.J. Kelso (secretary). The balance of the council was composed of 14 men and 10 women.

[10] The definition of neglected children included children who, because of their parents' vices, their orphanage, or any other cause, were being exposed to "bad or dissolute life"; and children who were found begging or in the company of reputed thieves or prostitutes.

[11] Of the 85 boys committed to the reformatory in 1890, 55, or two-thirds, had been convicted of an offence involving some form of larceny. Of the 19 girls committed to the Industrial Refuge in 1889, 13, or more than two-third, were either "destitute and without a home" or "incorrigible."

[12] An Act respecting Truancy and Compulsory School Attendance (1891) made it compulsory for all children between the ages of eight and 14 years to attend school for the full term, subject to certain exceptions.

[13] Upon proof of the offence charged, the judge could order the child returned to his or her parents, guardians, or friends; authorize the officer to bind the child out; impose a fine; suspend sentence; or, in certain cases, send the child to an industrial school or to the provincial reformatory or refuge.

[14] A further provision in the Act authorized municipalities to pass by-laws stipulating a curfew time, after which children were prohibited from being in the streets without proper guardianship.

[15] See *Mail and Empire* (1933). These claims, as contrasted, for example, with those made for New York and Massachusetts, are less important for their factual accuracy than for their indication of close connections between Canadian and American child-saving efforts, and perhaps with those elsewhere as well (for early Australian developments, see Parker, 1976b). For example, Scott (1906) indicated to Kelso that in drafting an early version of the Juvenile Delinquents Act he "followed the Colorado and Illinois Acts . . . and . . . adopted from the Pennsylvania Act and from a bill now before the New York Legislature" (23/11).

[16] See footnote 8.

[17] By a 1924 amendment, the definition of "juvenile delinquent" was altered to include any child "who is guilty of sexual immorality or any similar form of vice." In spite of strong support for the amendment from those involved in child-saving, Arthur Meighen and Sir Henry Drayton questioned the advisability of making each individual judge "the arbiter of what constitutes a vice on the part of a juvenile delinquent" (House of Commons Debates, 1924, 23/06, p.3508). However, at a later stage of the debates Meighen reconsidered his objections, indicating that he "certainly would not like to be instrumental in disarming the organizations that have to do with the matters" (p.3512). Presumably, such behaviors had been previously dealt with under provincial child protection laws, again underscoring the links between delinquency and neglect.

[18] The actual impact that probation had on industrial school commitment is not clear, although it was the intention of Scott and Kelso "to save children going to those institutions . . . [even if] we can never hope to do without them entirely" (Scott, 1907, 12/05). In his correspondence, Scott emphasized that very few children had been sent to industrial school from Ottawa since probation had been initiated (Scott, 1907, 08/02, 11/04, 11/06, 8/07, 15/10, 1908, 10/01).

[19] Lancaster was confronted with the claim that depriving the child of the right to trial by jury was justified in that the Act was "for the benefit of the juvenile delinquent." His response, similar to that voiced by current advocates of "children's rights," was to ask: "How do you know it is?" (pp.12400-12405).

[20] Other dispositions available under the Act included adjournment; fine; commitment to a children's aid society or to the charge of the provincial superintendent of neglected and dependent children; or commitment to an industrial school. Later amendments gave the court the power to postpone or adjourn the hearing, or to impose "such further or other conditions as may be deemed advisable."

[21] There is no evidence that their success also served the larger interests of powerful industrialists, as suggested with regard to American delinquency legislation (Platt, 1974). This controversy is considered in Hagan and Leon (1977).

[22] There are several problems with these themes. For example, the limitations on jurisdiction will likely result in an increased number of children being dealt with under provincial child welfare laws that have generally failed to provide for or safeguard the "rights" of children. Diversion has been acknowledged as a limited but "healthy reform" (Wilson, 1976; Zimring, 1974). As recognized, adequate evaluation of the various possible models has yet to be conducted (cf. Barnhorst et al., 1976), and the possibility exists that unanticipated consequences may be generated. Further, the philosophy of diversion may not be significantly different from that of probation, which, in the words of Kelso, was intended to "secure the hearty cooperation of the boy or girl in his or her own reclamation" (1907, p.106). Moreover, to simply "entitle" a young person, in certain cases, to be represented by a lawyer should he or she retain one, without addressing questions related to availability, access, and the ability to understand the implications of representation, or the lack thereof, stops short of providing an effective "right" to counsel.

## References

*Annual report of the Department of Neglected and Dependent Children of Ontario*. Toronto: Warwick, 1906.

*Annual report of the Superintendent of Neglected and Dependent Children*. Province of Ontario, 1895.

Archibald, D. *Report on the treatment of neglected children in Toronto*. Toronto: Arcade, 1907.

Bain, I. The role of J. J. Kelso in the launching of the child welfare movement in Ontario. Unpublished Master's thesis, University of Toronto, 1955.

Barnhorst, R. F., Barnshorst, S. S., & Thomson, G. M. The Frontenac Diversion Program: Juvenile court committee guidelines. Kingston, 1976.

Becker, H. *Outsiders*. New York: Free Press, 1963.

Bready, J. W. *Doctor Barnardo: Physician, pioneer, prophet*. London: George, Allen and Unwin, 1930.

Catton, K. Models of procedure and the juvenile courts. *Criminal Law Quarterly*, 1976, **18**, 181-201.

Catton, K., & Erickson, P. The juvenile's perception of the role of defence counsel in juvenile court: A pilot study. Working paper, Centre of Criminology, University of Toronto, 1974.

Catton, K., & Leon, J. S. Legal representation and the proposed *Young Persons in Conflict with the Law Act. Osgoode Hall Law Journal*, 1977, **15**.

Children's Aid Society of Metropolitan Toronto. Summary of activities, 1875-1975. Toronto, 1975.

City of Toronto. *Annual reports of the Juvenile Court of the City of Toronto*. Toronto, 1912-1950.

Cousineau, D. F., & Veevers, J. E. Juvenile justice: An analysis of the Canadian Young Offenders Act. In C. Boydell, C. Grindstaff, & P. Whitehead (Eds.), *Deviant behaviour and societal reaction*. Toronto: Holt, Rinehart & Winston, 1972.

Denison, G. T. *Recollections of a police magistrate*. Toronto: Musson, 1920.

Djootes, I., Erickson, P., & Fox, R. G. Defence counsel in juvenile court: A variety of roles. *Canadian Journal of Criminology and Corrections*, 1972, **14**, 132-149.

Erickson, P. The defence lawyer's role in juvenile court: An empirical investigation into judges' and social workers' points of view. *University of Toronto Law Journal*, 1974, **24**, 126-148.

Erickson, P. Legalistic and traditional role expectations for defence counsel in juvenile court. *Canadian Journal of Criminology and Corrections*, 1975, **17**, 78-93.

Fiser, V. The impact of social change on organization of welfare services in Ontario, 1891-1921: Development of services for juvenile delinquents. Unpublished Master's thesis, University of Toronto, 1966.

Flexner, B., & Baldwin, R. *Juvenile courts and probation*. New York: Century, 1914.

Fox, R. G., & Spencer, M. J. The Young Offender's Bill: Destigmatizing juvenile delinquency. *Criminal Law Quarterly*, 1972, **14**, 172-219.

Fox, S. J. Juvenile justice reform: An historical perspective. *Stanford Law Review*, 1970, **22**, 1187-1239.

Goldstein, J., Freud, A., & Solnit, A. *Beyond the best interests of the child*. New York: Free Press, 1973.

Graveson, R. H. *Status in the common law*. London: Athlone, 1953.

Green, B. The disposition of juvenile offenders. *Criminal Law Quarterly*, 1971, **13**, 348-367.

Hagan, J., & Leon, J. Rediscovering delinquency: Social history, political ideology and the sociology of law. *American Sociological Review*, 1977, **44**.

Hart, H. H. (Ed.) *Juvenile court laws in the United States*. New York: Russell Sage, 1916.

Hodgins, J. G. (Ed.) *Aims and objects of the Toronto Humane Society*. Toronto: Briggs, 1888.

Houston, S. E. Victorian origins of juvenile delinquency: A Canadian experience. *History of Education Quarterly*, 1972, **12**, 254-280.

Houston, S. E. The impetus to reform: Urban crime, poverty, and ignorance in Ontario, 1850-1875. Unpublished doctoral dissertation, University of Toronto, 1974.

Isaacs, J. L. The lawyer in juvenile court. *Criminal Law Quarterly*, 1968, **10**, 222-237.

Johnson, G. The function of counsel in juvenile court. *Osgoode Hall Law Journal*, 1970, **7**, 199-212.

Juvenile court had Toronto origin. *Mail and Empire*, Oct. 4, 1933.

Kelso, J. J. Letter. *Toronto News*, Apr. 15, 1891.

Kelso, J. J. Delinquent children: Some improved methods whereby they may be prevented from following a criminal career. *Canadian Law Review*, 1907, **6**, 106-110.

Kelso, J. J. Children's court. *Canadian Law Times and Review*, 1908, **28**, 163-166.

Kelso, J. J. *Helping erring children*. Toronto: Warwick, 1909.

Kelso, J. J. *Early history of the Humane and Children's Aid Movement in Ontario, 1886-1893*. Ontario: King's Printer, 1911.

Kelso, J. J. Can slums be abolished or must we continue to pay the penalty? Toronto [n.d.]. (a)

Kelso, J. J. *J. J. Kelso papers*. Ottawa: Public Archives [n.d.]. (b)

Ketcham, O. The unfulfilled promise of the juvenile court. *Crime and Delinquency*, 1961, **7**, 97-110.

Langley, M. Juvenile justice: What is it? *Criminology Made in Canada*, 1975, **3**, 17-31.

Law Reform Commission of Canada. *Diversion*. Working Paper No.7. Ottawa: Information Canada, 1975.

Lemert, E. M. *Social action and legal change: Revolution within the juvenile court*. Chicago: Aldine, 1970.

Leon, J. S. The development of juvenile justice in Canada: A background for reform. *Osgoode Hall Law Journal*, 1977, **15**, 71-106.

Lou, H. H. *Juvenile courts in the United States*. Chapel Hill: University of North Carolina Press, 1927.

MacGill, E. G. *My mother the judge: A biography of Judge Helen Gregory MacGill*. Toronto: Ryerson Press, 1955.

Marks, F. R. Detours on the road to maturity: A view of the legal conception of growing up and letting go. *Law and Contemporary Problems*, 1975, **39**, 78-92.

Matza, D. Position and behavior patterns of youth. In R. L. Faris (Ed.), *Handbook of modern sociology*. Chicago: Rand McNally, 1964.

McClung, N. *The stream runs fast: My own story*. Toronto: Thomas Allen, 1945.

McDonald, J. A. Juvenile court jurisdiction. *Criminal Law Quarterly*, 1965, **7**, 426-433.

McGrath, W. T. The juvenile and family courts. In W. T. McGrath (Ed.), *Crime and its treatment in Canada*. Toronto: Macmillan, 1965.

McRuer, J. C. *Royal Commission Inquiry into Civil Rights*. Report 1, Vol.2. Toronto: Queen's Printer, 1968.

Mendes da Costa, D. Criminal law. In R. H. Graveson & F. R. Crane (Eds.), *A century of family law 1857-1957*. London: Sweet & Maxwell, 1957.

Mennel, R. M. *Thorns and thistles: Juvenile delinquents in the United States, 1825-1940*. Hanover, N.H.: University Press of New England, 1973.

Mnookin, R. H. Foreword to Symposium on Children and the Law. *Law and Contemporary Problems*, 1975, **39**, 1-7.

Morrison, T. R. The child and urban social reform in late nineteenth century Ontario. Unpublished doctoral dissertation, University of Toronto, 1971.

Morrison T. R. Reform as social tracking: The case of industrial education in Ontario, 1870-1900. *Journal of Educational Thought*, 1974, **8**, 88-110.

Morrison, T. R. "Their proper sphere": Feminism, the family, and child-centred social reform in Ontario, 1875-1900. *Ontario History*, 1976, **68**, 45-64.

Musgrove F. *Youth and the social order*. London: Routledge & Kegan Paul, 1964.

Noyes, A. D. Has *Gault* changed the juvenile court concept? *Crime and Delinquency*, 1970, **16**, 158-162.

Ontario Law Reform Commission. *Report on family law. Part V: Family courts*. Toronto: Queen's Printer, 1974.

Parker, G. E. Century of the child. *Canadian Bar Review*, 1967, **45**, 741-763. (a)

Parker, G. E. Some historical observations on the juvenile court. *Criminal Law Quarterly*, 1967, **9**, 467-502. (b)

Parker, G. E. American child-saving: The climate of reform as reflected in the National Conference of Charities and Corrections, 1875-1900. *University of Toronto Law Journal*, 1968, **18**, 371-393.

Parker, G. E. The appellate court view of the juvenile court. *Osgoode Hall Law Journal*, 1969, 7, 154-175.

Parker, G. E. Juvenile delinquency – Transfer of juvenile cases to adult courts – Factors to be considered under the Juvenile Delinquents Act. *Canadian Bar Review*, 1970, **48**, 336-346.

"Philanthropy." Care of our destitute and criminal population: A series of letters published in the *Montreal Gazette*. Montreal: Sallner & Ross, 1857.

Platt, A. *The child savers*. Chicago: University of Chicago Press, 1969.

Platt, A. The triumph of benevolence: The origins of the juvenile justice system in the United States. In R. Quinney (Ed.), *Criminal justice in America*. Boston: Little, Brown, 1974.

Prentice, A. The school promoters: Education and social class in mid-nineteenth century Upper Canada. Unpublished doctoral dissertation. University of Toronto, 1974.

*Proceedings of the Eighth Canadian Conference of Charities and Corrections*. Toronto, Ont., 1905.

*Proceedings of the Sixth Canadian Conference of Charities and Corrections*. Ottawa, Ont., 1903.

*Proceedings of the Tenth Canadian Conference of Charities and Corrections*. Toronto, Ont., 1909.

*Proceedings of the 22nd National Conference of Charities and Corrections*. New Haven, Conn., 1895.

*Proceedings of the Waif-Saving Congress*. Chicago, Ill., 1893.

Ramsey, D. P. The development of child welfare legislation in Ontario. Unpublished Master's thesis, University of Toronto, 1949.

*Report of the commissioners appointed to enquire into the reformatory system of Ontario*. Toronto: Warwick, 1891.

*Report of the Department of Justice Committee on Juvenile Delinquency in Canada*. Ottawa: Queen's Printer, 1965.

Sanders, W. B. (Ed.) *Juvenile offenders for a thousand years: Selected readings from Anglo-Saxon times to 1900*. Chapel Hill: University of North Carolina Press, 1970.

Saunders, B. H. *Emily Murphy: Crusader*. Toronto: Macmillan, 1945.

Schultz, J. L. The cycle of juvenile court history. *Crime and Delinquency*, 1973, **19**, 457-476.

Schur, E. *Radical non-intervention*. Englewood Cliffs, N.J.: Prentice-Hall, 1973.

Scott, W. L. *W. L. Scott papers*. Ottawa: Public Archives, 1906-08, 1912-28.

Scott, W. L. The Juvenile Delinquents Act. *Canadian Law Times and Review*, 1908, **28**, 892-904.

Scott, W. L. *The juvenile court in law and the juvenile court in action*. Ottawa: Canadian Council on Child Welfare, 1927.

Scott, W. L. *The juvenile court in law*. (4th ed.) Ottawa: Canadian Welfare Council, 1952.

Scott, W. L. The genesis of the Juvenile Delinquents Act, 1888-1908. Ottawa: Public Archives [n.d.].

Skolnick, A. The limits of childhood: Conceptions of child development and social context. *Law and Contemporary Problems*, 1975, **39**, 38-77.

Solicitor-General Canada. *Highlights of the proposed new legislation for young offenders*. Ottawa: Supply and Services Canada, 1977.

Solicitor-General's Committee on Proposals for New Legislation to Replace the Juvenile Delinquents Act. *Young persons in conflict with the law*. Ottawa: Information Canada, 1975.

Splane, R. *Social welfare in Ontario*, 1791-1893. *Toronto: University of Toronto Press, 1965*.

Stapleton, W. V., & Teitelbaum, L. E. *In defense of youth: A study of the role of counsel in American juvenile courts*. New York: Russell Sage, 1972.

Steinberg, D. M. The young offender and the courts. *Reports on Family Law*, 1972, **6**, 86-91.

Steinberg, D. M. Children's rights. *Chitty's Law Journal*, 1974, **22**, 238-243.

Stewart, V. L. The development of juvenile justice in Canada. Toronto, 1970.

Strong-Boag, V. Introduction. In N. McClung, *In times like these*. Toronto: University of Toronto Press, 1972.

Thomson, G. M. The child in conflict with society. *Reports on Family Law*, 1973, **11**, 257-263.

Wald, M. S. State intervention on behalf of "neglected" children: A search for realistic standards. *Stanford Law Review*, 1975, **27**, 985-1040.

Wald, M. S. State intervention on behalf of "neglected" children: Standards for removal of children from their homes, monitoring the status of children in foster care, and termination of parental rights. *Stanford Law Review*, 1976, **28**, 623-706.

Wang, K. The continuing turbulence surrounding the parens patriae concept in American juvenile courts (Parts I and II). *McGill Law Journal*, 1972, **18**, 219-245, 418-460.

Wilson, L. C. Diversion: The impact on juvenile justice. *Canadian Journal of Criminology and Corrections*, 1976, **18**, 161-167.

Zimring, F. E. Measuring the impact of pretrial diversion from the criminal justice system. *University of Chicago Law Review*, 1974, **41**, 224-241.

# Unmanageable Children in Ontario: A Legal Review

Karen Weiler/Ministry of the Attorney General, Ontario

The adventures of Tom Sawyer are read with delight by young people at both primary and secondary educational levels. It would probably come as a shock, however, if one were to point out that just for playing truant, as Tom Sawyer did, thousands of boys and girls in Ontario have been committed to correctional facilities known as training schools.[1]

Normally, children who present a behavior problem are dealt with privately by their parents, who will attempt to end the disturbing conduct by lectures, curfews, reducing the children's allowance, or ordering them to stay home on weekends and at night. Sometimes, a person outside the family – a school attendance counsellor, a psychiatrist, or a representative of a Children's Aid Society (CAS) – becomes involved with the children. In the past, continued concern about the children often led to their committal to training school, under Section 8 of the Ontario legislature's Training Schools Act, on the basis that they were beyond the control of their parents, or the parents were unable to meet the children's social, emotional, or educational needs (Revised Statute of Ontario, 1970, ch.467).

On May 5, 1975, Bill 64 repealed Section 8 of the Training Schools Act. However, this legislation was not proclaimed in force until January 1, 1977 and, although infrequently used in the interim, it was still possible to commit a child to training school as being "unmanageable."

The Toronto *Globe and Mail* (May 9, 1975) reported that the reason for the delay in enforcement was to ensure that care for those children who are already in the training school system under Section 8, together with those children who might otherwise be committed under the section, is available within the community. However, financial constraints on government funding to individual agencies has discouraged the community's willingness to accept problem children and to provide alternative residential care for them. Instead, the most common response has been to request that training schools continue to be used as a back-up resource for those problem children with whom it is felt an agency cannot deal. On occasion, committal to training school has been likened to sending a child to boarding school:

"Perhaps it may indicate something to you, I have visited private boys' schools. Private boys' schools such as St. Andrew's College and Upper Canada College and others; the boys are disciplined; they get up by a bell; they go to school by a bell; and they eat lunch by a bell and they recess by a bell and they go to bed by a bell. This is the same kind of thing as the training school. There are people there that are concerned with you . . . the people at the training school are not prison guards . . . don't walk into the training school thinking you are going to prison because you are not.'' (Weiler, 1974)

However, the word ''prison'' as defined in the Criminal Code includes an ''industrial school,'' a term commonly taken to mean training school. Similarly, a training school is also included in the definition of a prison. Therefore, in law, training schools have a direct penal nature.

Moreover, a committed child becomes a ward of the training school, and parental rights to care, custody, and control of the child are suspended for the duration of the wardship – indeed, are suspended after release until the child's 18th birthday unless terminated prior to that time by order of the Minister. Thus committal to training school carries with it serious implications for the rights of the child, and is very unlike the experience of boarding school.

In many ways Section 8 and its ancestor, the Industrial Schools Act, 1874, are a legislative example of a larger social movement that set as its goal the salvation of society. The ''child savers'' was the name given to a group of reformers who encouraged the removal of children from the criminal law process and the special handling of youthful misbehavior (Platt, 1969). They espoused the philosophy that children were not to be punished for their misdeeds but ''treated'' for their ''condition.''

The result was a change in the conception of the role of government and the function of social institutions. Attention was drawn to situations where, for example, no offence had actually been committed but a child was posing problems for some person in authority such as a parent, teacher, or social worker. This behavior was viewed as symptomatic of an underlying disorder either within the individual or in the social system, and was the occasion for intervention in the life of the individual.

The justification for such intervention was the exercise of the state's *parens patriae* power, based loosely on the court's equitable jurisdiction to protect the property of orphans and gradually extend it to a rather broad discretionary role over the guardianship and protection of children in general (Parker, 1967).

However, it is difficult to maintain the belief that, in committing a child to training school, the child is being *only* ''treated'' and not ''punished.'' Committal to training school results in a very real deprivation of liberty and that fact is not changed by refusing to call it punishment or because the good of the child is the objective.

This paper first reviews the use of Section 8 and in so doing makes apparent the reasons for its repeal. Most of the conclusions are based on data collected for a previous study (Weiler, 1974) in which 120 files of children committed to training school during 1969 were examined. More recent data, providing a valuable indication of trends in training school admissions up to and including 1975, are also included, thanks to Andrew Birkenmayer of the Research and Planning Branch of the Ministry of Correctional Services. Total committals to training school for 1977 show these trends have continued.

**Legislation**
Section 8 reads as follows:

''1. Upon the application of any person, a judge may order in writing that a child under sixteen years of age at the time the order is made be sent to training school where the judge is satisfied that,

(a) the parent or guardian of the child is unable to control the child or to provide for his social, emotional, or educational needs;

(b) the care of the child by any other agency of child welfare would be insufficient or impracticable; and

(c) the child needs the training and treatment available at a training school, and the order shall state the facts upon which the decision is based.

2. Where an application is made under subsection 1, the judge shall,

(a) hear the child; and

(b) hear the evidence of or on behalf of the person who has submitted the application and make adequate inquiry into the truth of such evidence.

3. The evidence shall be given under oath and shall be taken down and transcribed,

(a) by the court stenographer, where the court has a court stenographer; and

(b) by a stenographer appointed by the judge, where the court does not have a court stenographer.

4. The judge shall hear all cases coming before him under this Section *in camera*."

Because the status of Section 8 has implications for committals to training school under Section 9, it is important to consider that piece of legislation too. Section 9 reads as follows:

"The judge may order that a child be sent to a training school where,

(a) the child is at least twelve years of age and under sixteen years of age at the time the order is made; and

(b) the child has contravened any statute in force in Ontario, which contravention would be punishable by imprisonment if committed by an adult."

**Criteria of Section 8**

Under Section 8, the judge had to decide, first, whether or not the child was beyond the parent's control or the parent was unable to meet the specific needs of the child. Next, the judge determined that the child could not be cared for adequately or practicably by any other agency of child welfare. If these first two requirements were met, the judge then decided whether or not a training school could provide the treatment that the child needed when other attempts at control had failed.[2]

*"The parent or guardian of the child is unable to control the child or to provide for his social, emotional, or educational needs."*

Although Section 8 sought to deal with children's needs rather than focus on specific acts, children would be found to be beyond control when they engaged in certain types of conduct. However, the subsection gave only a vague indication of what conduct would be considered. A Central Toronto Youth Services (1975) study indicated that, "The most disturbing feature of the resulting data . . . is the poorly established evidence and relatively harmless behaviour which results in Section 8 committals." The most frequent reasons cited by judges in their orders for committal were truancy, running away, and staying out late or overnight, but swearing, disobedience to parents, temper tantrums, and undesirable associations were also given as reasons.

Section 8 was vague not in the sense that it required a person to conform to an imprecise but comprehensible set of standards, but rather that no standard of conduct was specified at all. Our pluralistic beliefs about child rearing do not lend themselves to a uniform interpretation as to when children are "beyond control" or when their "welfare" needs are not being met. The condition of being beyond control is a subjective one, which a person applying for a Section 8 order sought to ascribe to the child. It was not a property inherent in the behavior itself, because it depended on the applicant's definition of deviant behavior. The question of whether or not the child was beyond control was particularly subjective, because "for different groups the age of emancipation of the child – the time at which the parent ceases to identify the child with himself – varies and has much to do with whether or not the parent will seek outside sources of control. One group may be very much concerned with the misbehaviour of a 13-year-old which another may treat very lightly" (Robson, 1972, p.34). Toleration of a child's conduct may also be influenced by ethnic origins and social class. For example, as many writers have noted, truancy and under-age drinking are more prevalent and more tolerated amongst the well-to-do (Hobart, 1972; Ontario Interim, 1969; Shannon, 1964; Sidman, 1972). And, as discussed in the next section, there is often one set of standards for boys and another for girls.

*Sexual Conduct*. The subjectivity of Section 8 encouraged the blatantly discriminatory double standard of sexual mores espoused by society to be judicially enforced. Sexual promiscuity was the main reason why girls were committed to training schools, according to the Toronto Youth Services study (1975).

In their study of 464 wards committed to Ontario training schools, Lambert and Birkenmayer (1972) concluded:

"The differences between girls and boys found in these data suggest not only differences among the wards themselves but perhaps differences in society's views of acceptable behaviour for girls compared to that for boys. It appears that deviance on the part of girls, particularly sexual promiscuity, may have been less acceptable and because of this, girls sent to training schools reflect a much different phenomena than do boys."

Barbara Landau, a psychologist and Director of the Adolescent Treatment Unit of Queen Street Mental Health Centre, stated that,

"society reacts more with applause than condemnation to a boy who engages in normal intercourse and since there is a great deal more laxity in parental restrictions on boys (e.g., in curfews, choice of dates and friends, use of cigarettes and alcohol) there is far less chance of a boy being brought to court for the same reason as a girl. Also, the danger of venereal disease, pregnancy and adult prostitution arouse great public concern in the case of adolescent girls, but far less anxiety in the case of boys, even though the threat of V.D., parenthood and pimping could also be tied to boys' interest in heterosexual relations."

And often it is suspicion rather than proof that led to the committal of a girl.

*Parent–Child Conflict*. Children could also be sent to training school simply because their parents no longer wished to undertake the obligations associated with child rearing.

Any person could make application to have a child committed to training school under Section 8. In the 120 cases I studied, about one half of the applicants were parents. The system encouraged some parents to rid themselves of children who are troublesome. It was evident that, in several of these cases, there was serious discord between a step-parent and a step-child, and in one instance the natural parent stated bluntly to the court that the spouse she was about to marry would not support the child. In such instances shelter for the child was really the prime concern.

*Criminal Code Type Offences – Minimum Age.* Not all children sent to training schools under Section 8 were guilty merely of a status offence – that is, of conduct prohibited only because they are children. In almost half the cases in my study, I found that a charge of delinquency had been laid for breach of the Criminal Code, generally for theft, but either the child had been committed to training school under Section 8 or there was a Section 8 application and concurrent Criminal Code charge. In some cases the judge may have felt that Section 8 was a more accurate description of the child's problem. More often, the Section 8 committal appears to have been a deliberate attempt to avoid the age restrictions contained in Section 9, which require that a child be at least 12 years old before being sent to training school for an offence for which an adult could be imprisoned. Proportionately more boys than girls were committed prior to their 12th birthday. This may have been because a special facility within the training school system exists for the care of young boys and no such facilities exist for young girls.

As far back as 1916, the superintendent of neglected children stated in his annual report:

"It was never contemplated that any child under twelve years of age should be sent to these industrial schools [training schools] but there were quite a large number during the past year committed at the tender age of eight, nine and ten. . . . It is a great mistake . . . experience shows that when children of tender years are placed . . . with older or more experienced lads they learn the evil rather than the good, and choose as their heroes the boys who are daring and defiant rather than the ones who would be a benefit and inspiration to them. They also learn the fatal habit of depending upon others, and there are cases on record of some of these boys committed at an early age who for the rest of their youth have been a public burden owing to their indifference and lack of any willingness to care for themselves."

Although the lack of any minimum age was decried when Section 8 was before the legislature in 1965, an amendment to limit proceedings under the section to children 12 years of age or over was defeated, and the practice of committing young children to training schools, particularly boys, continued until the repeal of the Section (see Table 1).

In summary, meeting the first requirement of Section 8 was not difficult because anyone could bring any child within the criterion for behavior that is, at one time or another, engaged in by most children. Bearing this in mind, one would hope that strict proof of the second criterion would be required.

*"The care of the child by any other agency of child welfare would be insufficient or impracticable."*
My study indicated that judges have generally interpreted the term "any other child-caring agency" to mean the local Children's Aid Society, and, while

**Table 1/Training School Admissions of Children Under 11 Years of Age, 1973 to 1975, by Sex and Act and Section**[a]

| Year | Boys | | | Girls | | |
| --- | --- | --- | --- | --- | --- | --- |
| | Total | Sec. 8 | Juvenile Delinquents Act | Total | Sec. 8 | Juvenile Delinquents Act |
| 1973 | 34 | 30 | 4 | 1 | 1 | |
| 1974 | 11 | 6 | 5 | 2 | 2 | |
| 1975 | 17 | 5 | 12 | 2 | 2 | |

[a]From A. Birkenmayer, Trends in Training School Admissions, 1967 to 1975.

there may not have been a CAS resource that could meet the child's needs, no investigation was made to ascertain whether or not a local children's boarding home was available. This may have been because the CAS is not specifically charged with finding residential placement for the child. In fact, no one is – with the result that the second requirement has usually been met on the basis of an opinion that takes into consideration only a small number of resources in the immediate geographic area.

Although many of the alternate child-care organizations are licensed or funded by the Ministry of Community and Social Services (the same ministry that funds CASs), there is no provincially operated "clearing house" to assist the individual organizations across the province to place children according to their needs.

By contrast, once a child has been in training school and is ready to return to the community, the after-care staff of the Ministry looks at resources across the province if there is no suitable facility within the child's immediate geographic district.

The reason for the reluctance of some local CASs to seek alternatives for children outside their own resources may also be the cost. If a CAS is willing to intervene and the application under Section 8 is dismissed, the society then has the responsibility of caring for the child. Particularly in smaller centres where the CAS does not have any foster or group homes for teenage children, it may have to purchase, at great expense, care required for the child.

In a sense, then, legislation provided a financial incentive to a CAS to make application under Section 8 of the Training Schools Act. Children might end up being placed in a group home in the community. But it is also possible that they might be sent to a tight security institution, such as Hillcrest Training School at Guelph, where their room would be in a cell with bars. It is to be hoped that, in making a decision, a judge would weigh the risks to the child that a committal involved.

Finally, there were those children who had been placed in a CAS resource and who then proved too difficult for the society to handle. The local CAS representative may be of the opinion that a child who has failed in a CAS resource will not be apt to do well in other similar settings. The representative will therefore not seek them out. Furthermore, it is difficult to find a residential placement that will continue to "accept" children who continually break the rules or run away. Once committed to training school, however, these children would always be accepted into some program within the system no matter how difficult their behavior.

While acknowledging that children who have failed in CAS homes are poor risks, one judge recently held that, "the question is not whether [the child] will

64

succeed in another residential setting but whether he is more apt to succeed there than he is in training school."[3] This question was raised by the third requirement of Section 8.

*"The child needs the training and treatment available at a training school."*
Although the judge had to be satisfied that the child needed the training and treatment of a training school, in practice, once the first two criteria had been met, the decision tended to be automatic – although ignored the substantial evidence that, for status offenders at least, schools are seldom appropriate.[4]

*Perception of Committal.* Committal to training school imposes a stigma on a child because judges, police, and the ordinary public consider it to be the ultimate sanction that can be imposed (Green, 1966, p.417). The public often cannot distinguish between those children who were committed to training schools for serious Criminal Code offences and status offenders who represent no danger to the community. A report of the Department of Justice Committee on Juvenile Delinquency (1965) stated that children attach guilt to actions rather than situations. Regardless of the reason, children see committal to training school as punishment, and in this they are more realistic than the social workers and judges. A court order that seems out of proportion to the offence will seem unfair to the child. Moreover,

"the fact that such prohibitions are only occasionally enforced is little reason for solace. Sporadic enforcement frequently implies uneven or selective enforcement at the expense of those suspected of more serious infractions. Thus, both the existence of such statutes [regulating status offences] and the fact that they are only occasionally enforced may contribute to the delinquent's sense of injustice. The existence of the prohibition may violate the expectations of comparability [of treatment] whereas the sporadic enforcement does violence to the even more widespread expectation of consistency." (Matza, 1964, p.167)

In addition, by associating with hard-core delinquents, young persons may come to think of themselves as "a criminal" and to act accordingly (Grygier, 1973; Schur, 1973). The Honorable Mr. Potter, the then Minister of Corrections, implicitly acknowledged the danger when advocating repeal of Section 8:

"Our concern is that they are committed by a judge to a correctional institution or correctional service without ever having committed a crime and yet they are treated in the same way. Sometimes some of them are in the same institution as children who have committed crimes and we don't think that's right. A lot of people don't think that's right" (Legislature of Ontario Debates, Apr.24, 1975, p.1200).

*Research Findings.* The assumption that "treatment" in a training school is effective is open to serious question. While the scope of this paper does not permit a full discussion of specific types of treatment, it is worth while noting the conclusions of some who have done such evaluations.

After reviewing attempts to modify the behavior of delinquent and predelinquent children by intensive counselling, probation, community treatment, and institutionalization, Schur (1973) concluded,

"Much of the disenchantment with current delinquency policy arises from the simple fact that it doesn't work. As we have seen, neither the treatment reaction nor the reform response has provided any real basis for confidence that our measures are effective in preventing delinquent behavior or rehabilitating youthful offenders. Some programs do show more promise than others, but the impact of the specific successes on the overall problem of youth behavior is minimal. A traditional response to this situation has been to assume that the system merely needs improvement. Hence the call for more and better facilities, increasingly experimental rehabilitations schemes, further research – including evaluation studies and elaborate 'cost benefit' and 'systems' analysis. Naturally, it is possible by these methods to increase efficiency in juvenile justice and perhaps also to render the substance of the system somewhat more meaningful. Yet the conviction is growing that this kind of patching up will not suffice. Many observers are coming to believe that our present approach to delinquency and juvenile justice is basically unsound: that the underlying assumptions are wrong, and that present programs are not just ineffectual but positively harmful. This belief arises not only out of direct experience and research in the field of delinquency, but also from current thinking on the broader topic of deviant behavior and social control. Social scientists and, increasingly, laymen as well, are re-evaluating our society's response to rule violating behavior." (pp.153-154)

On the Canadian scene, Cousineau and Veevers, in their 1972 analysis of the Young Offenders Act, also discussed various kinds of treatment programs and concluded that "the available evidence suggests that the effectiveness of treatment has yet to be demonstrated conclusively" (p.255).

In Ontario, Lambert and Birkenmayer (1972) found two general types of patterns and training school wards. One group, to some extent recognizable at the time of admission, either showed emotional difficulties or came from a family experiencing serious problems. "These children were more likely admitted for reasons of unmanageability, truancy, running away, etc. . . . They were more likely to be girls than boys." For this group, Lambert and Birkenmayer concluded that, "The training school experience alone was not sufficient to prepare them to cope with the problems within the environment to which they are returned" (p.27).

Prior to this study, Grygier (1966) concluded that unmanageable children present a special problem: "They come to training school having been rejected by their parents as being 'incorrigible.' They continue their pattern of behavior in a training school and find that their behavior is unacceptable to the staff" (p.31).

Grygier noted that a high percentage of girls had been placed in training schools for unmanageable behavior such as sexual promiscuity and behavior that was not criminal in the first place. Since the behavior was an attempt on the part of these girls to assert themselves or to gain some of the recognition and affection of which they had been deprived, it was difficult to treat them in ordinary training schools. Moreover, although the pattern of conduct might remain unchanged, society lost interest as the girls grew older and ceased to punish the behavior. This and the other Ontario study both indicate that the type of child committed to training school under Section 8 would likely emerge unchanged.

Similarly, the results of my own study indicated that, even in those cases where the children were seen by the after-care officer as having made a satisfactory adjustment upon return to the community, their behavior was not necessarily modified. For example, those children who had been committed to training school for truancy and who were considered to be satisfactorily re-integrated into the community usually left school immediately upon return or within a few months. As the Director of Treatment at one training school told me about a girl committed for truancy: "Certainly . . . she can be forced to attend classes in the opportunity course, but what it is hoped there will be gained is highly problematical and she runs the very real danger of acquiring the self-image of a delinquent. . . . She will be in no better position to obtain employment after several months than she is at present."

Placing a child in a "secure" facility would therefore appear to be akin to merely "freezing" the behavior problem.

### *Summary of the Reasons for Repeal of Section 8*
From the preceding discussion, it is clear that the repeal of Section 8 is a step in the right direction.

To summarize, the lack of any clear definition as to what conduct was unacceptable led to a subjective and varying interpretation of the legislation; the lack of a minimum age restriction resulted in the institutionalization of very young children although the practice had been decried for years; fragmentation of the child-care system encouraged a community agency to pass on responsibility for a child and for different levels of government to avoid their responsibility to provide alternative residential accommodation; the stigma attached to training schools circumscribed a child's opportunities; being treated like a criminal could make the child develop feelings of injustice, and contact with hard-core delinquents could foster criminality. Finally, and perhaps most important, the theoretical basis of Section 8 – that committal of children to training school for non-criminal conduct would rehabilitate them – did not appear to be a valid one. The conclusion was obvious – Section 8 was abolished.

### Alternatives
Now that proclamation of the repeal of Section 8 has taken place, what has replaced it? I now discuss the various alternatives available under the two most relevant pieces of legislation, the Child Welfare Act and the Juvenile Delinquents Act, as well as mention other current and pending legislation.

### *The Child Welfare Act*
Under the Child Welfare Act "a child whose parent is unable to control him" and "a child who, without sufficient cause, habitually absents himself from his home or school" can be defined as a child in need of protection.[5] If running away, staying out late, playing truant, throwing temper tantrums, being disobedient, and swearing are indications that a child is out of control (as defined in Section 8 of the Training Schools Act), these criteria appear to fit equally well the definition of a child in need of protection. However, such a definition is open to the same criticism as Section 8 – it is too vague and subjective.

If a child is found in need of protection the judge may make one of three orders. The child may be returned to the parent or placed with some other person subject to supervision by the CAS – supervisory order. The child may be made a ward of the CAS for a period of up to one year and the order may be renewed for another year. Finally, the child may be made a Crown ward – i.e., committed to the care of a CAS until such wardship is terminated or the child attains the age of 18 years.

Responsibility for the children who were within the correctional system under Section 8 was transferred to the Ministry of Community and Social Services when the repeal of Section 8 was proclaimed. The transfer of responsibility for these children raises the question of what kind of supervisory or wardship order would be most appropriate.

*Crown Wardship*. On the surface, there appears to be little difference between an order for Crown wardship and an order making the child a ward under the Training Schools Act. A Crown wardship order has the advantage that a parent may apply to terminate it, and, upon attaining the age of 16, a child may apply for an order of termination. But the Crown wardship does not merely suspend parental rights to care, custody, and control of the child as in the case under the Training Schools Act; an order for Crown wardship *terminates* parental rights.[6] If it is felt to be in the best interests of the child, a Crown ward may be placed for adoption and, once notice of intention to adopt has been given, the parent's right to apply for termination of the wardship ceases. There is no requirement that notice of the intention to adopt be served on the child's parents. Therefore, if a training school ward under Section 8 had automatically become a Crown ward upon proclamation of the repeal, the child could be placed for adoption without his or her parents even knowing. In addition, unless a judge made an access order, it appears that a parent would not even have had the right to visit the child.

Perhaps because of these differences, the Provincial Secretary for Social Development told the Legislative Committee on Estimates on April 25, 1977 that it was decided to maintain the current Section 8 wards with the Ministry of Correctional Services (instead of making them Crown wards) and to move them out of training schools as quickly as possible.

Other alternatives open to a judge dealing with an unmanageable child under the Child Welfare Act are Society wardship and voluntary agreements.

*Society Wardship*. If the child is made a CAS ward, parental rights resume after a maximum of 24 months. At the end of 24 months, whether or not to apply for Crown wardship is considered on an individual basis. Quite possibly many of the children then have reached the stage where only a supervisory order is required.

The Act does not specify whether or not a supervisory order, which cannot be made for more than 12 months, can be renewed. Legislation should clarify this.

*Voluntary Agreements*. Instead of seeking an order under the Child Welfare Act, the child's parent may voluntarily place the child in the custody or supervision of a CAS. Since the behavior of an unmanageable child frequently centres around conflict involving the whole family, matters are seldom resolved simply by removing the child from the home.

The philosophy of the "child savers" was based on the assumption that it was necessary to remove the child from home to a reformatory or training school in order to attenuate the effects of parental neglect. However, the trend today is to encourage family cohesiveness by focussing on problems in the family setting. The provisions in voluntary non-ward agreements are an important tool that can be used to provide special services to a child in the home, thereby reinforcing the personal responsibility of the parents and children toward each other.

*Alternative Residential Care.* Nevertheless, the Ontario Association of Children's Aid Societies (1976) were of the view that in many instances it may be necessary to provide an alternative to home-care for the child. Existing resources are inadequate to care for seriously emotionally disturbed children and older, difficult to manage children. As can be seen in Table 2, between 1967 and 1973 the proportion of children sent to training school who had already had prior contact with a CAS rose steadily from 13.4% to 32.6%. Between 1973 and 1975, however, the proportion of these children remained relatively stable, while the overall number of admissions declined.

In terms of the actual number of admissions, 20 more children with prior CAS contact were admitted to training school in 1975 than 1972. One possible interpretation of the data would be that CAS attitude in dealing with the unmanageable child has remained unchanged while that of society as a whole has grown more tolerant. In line with this, some CASs might be continuing to use committal to training school as a method of shifting child-care costs. Another explanation advanced by the CAS is that the number of teenagers coming into care has greatly increased as a result of the repeal of Section 8. They therefore argue that further funds are necessary. Between 1972 and 1975, the number of teenage children in care rose from approximately 6,000 to 6,900 (Ontario Association of Children's Aid Societies, 1976) but, spread over 50 societies in the province, this increase does not appear to be unduly large.

It is also important, particularly in a time of budget constraints, to maximize the efficiency of child-care resources providing alternate residential care for children. The CAS requests for more funds must be closely examined in the light of a report by the Task Force on Community and Social Services (1974), which states,

"It is not an outrageous exaggeration to say that standards in the field of child welfare practice do not exist. Simply no means have been developed for measuring the effectiveness of the various types of services provided. As a result, it is not possible to choose between alternatives on the basis of cost effectiveness. Also, there are no ways of determining for a geographic area what the needs are in terms of service requirements. . . . What is true of the system generally holds equally for individual Societies, as was clearly and appropriately pointed out in the report that Urwick Currie made in 1969 on the managerial effectiveness of the Societies." (p.63)

The hodge-podge of statutes administered by a number of ministries has exacerbated the problem of effectively offering alternative residential services to children.[7] This situation has resulted in group homes being funded by different ministries at different rates and even at differing rates within the same ministry.

The Report to the Minister of Public Welfare (1961), the Report of the Ontario Legislature's Select Committee on Youth (1967), the Report of the Commission on Emotional and Learning Disorders in Children (1969), the Report on Selected Issues and Relations (1974), the Report on Central Toronto Youth Services on Control Problems and Alternatives to Section 8 (1975), and the Anderson report (1976) have all pointed out the need to coordinate the

Table 2/Training School Admissions of Children with Prior CAS Contact, 1967 to 1975, by Sex and Act and Section[a]

| | Males | | | | | | Females | | | | | | Total N with CAS Contacts | % of Total Admissions |
|---|---|---|---|---|---|---|---|---|---|---|---|---|---|---|
| | Section 8 | | Section 9 | | Juvenile Delinquents Act | | Section 8 | | Section 9 | | Juvenile Delinquents Act | | | |
| Year | N | % | N | % | N | % | N | % | N | % | N | % | | |
| 1967 | 59 | 42.1 | 34 | 24.3 | | | 38 | 27.1 | 9 | 6.4 | | | 140 | 13.4 |
| 1968 | 52 | 37.1 | 35 | 25.0 | | | 48 | 34.3 | 5 | 3.6 | | | 140 | 12.0 |
| 1969 | 74 | 42.5 | 39 | 22.4 | | | 50 | 28.7 | 11 | 6.3 | | | 174 | 13.1 |
| 1970 | 56 | 36.1 | 41 | 26.5 | | | 50 | 32.3 | 8 | 5.2 | | | 155 | 11.0 |
| 1971 | 69 | 34.2 | 58 | 28.7 | | | 58 | 28.7 | 17 | 8.4 | | | 202 | 15.4 |
| 1972 | 69 | 24.7 | 72 | 25.8 | | | 112 | 40.1 | 26 | 9.3 | | | 279 | 20.6 |
| 1973 | 101 | 26.1 | 118 | 30.5 | 5 | 1.3 | 134 | 34.6 | 28 | 7.2 | 1 | 0.3 | 387 | 32.6 |
| 1974 | 61 | 17.1 | 127 | 35.7 | 11 | 3.1 | 119 | 33.4 | 36 | 10.1 | 2 | 0.6 | 356 | 35.3 |
| 1975 | 25 | 8.4 | 140 | 46.8 | 25 | 8.4 | 61 | 20.4 | 36 | 12.0 | 12 | 4.0 | 299 | 34.5 |

[a]From A. Birkenmayer, Trends in Training School Admissions, 1967 to 1975.

various acts and to develop comprehensive guidelines for licensing and funding group homes.

It is unlikely that there will ever be enough money to meet all the needs that those who care for children believe to exist. Indeed, the first Industrial Schools Act was passed in 1874 partly because there were *no* alternative child-care resources. This is not the case today. Moreover, to allow training schools to continue to absorb those children whom the community feels unable to cope with scarcely encourages the responsible development of coordinated solutions by municipal councils. In fact, the province has increased its share of the cost of funding CASs from 60% in 1973 to 80% today, thereby reducing the proportionate cost burden on municipalities. In addition, where the budget of a CAS is subject to approval by the Minister of Community and Social Services, either the society or municipality can request that the estimated amount be referred to a child welfare committee when disagreements arise.

*Closed Facilities.* Apart from services to children within their own families or within a group home in the community, those seeking a substitute for Section 8 may feel there remains a need for a locked facility (in other words, a sort of prison) once training schools are no longer available as a "back-up" resource.

The Child Welfare Act contains no specific provisions allowing a child in need of protection to be detained in a locked facility. This is in accordance with the fundamental principle of our society that no person shall be involuntarily detained without due process of law. At the same time, a parent or person standing in place of the parent is justified in restraining or confining a child in his or her care. It has been suggested by the Ontario Association of Children's Aid Societies (1976) that the Child Welfare Act should be amended to enable a child to be locked up for a period of 30 days. It is unclear whether or not such a period of confinement would be renewable.

Such an amendment would in part make the repeal of Section 8 a matter of form rather than substance. It ignores both the evidence as to the inefficacy of such a measure in dealing with unmanageable children and the damage that may result from feelings of injustice. Paradoxically, "security" for the young person, one of the objectives the CAS has most in mind in suggesting a young person who runs away be locked up, is seldom provided in training school.

These days, most of the schools are quite open, and a young person can easily run away from all but the most secure settings.[8] However, the real point is that if the behavior is non-criminal and does not lead to criminality, why treat it in a correctional-like setting? With children who have a history of discipline problems at school, some hope is offered by the early school leaving regulation, recently passed by the Ministry of Education, whereby a child 14 years of age or more may forgo attendance in the classroom on a full- or part-time basis to engage in a supervised work experience.

*Other Provincial Legislation.* If the reason for intervening in a child's life is that the child is emotionally disturbed, he or she can be admitted to a Children's Mental Health Centre. Since health facilities are funded for 100% of approved operating costs by the government, no child-care costs are incurred by a CAS or by the parent. Indeed, many children who were formerly in CAS care because their parents could not afford the high costs of treatment are now being cared for in Children's Mental Health Centres.[9]

If it is considered necessary to detain children who present a danger to their own safety or that of others, the children can be committed under the provisions of the Mental Health Act to a mental hospital. Rarely, however, are children committed against their own wishes or those of their parents. This reluctance, I understand, stems partly from a desire to avoid stigmatizing the children. There is, however, but one designated Children's Mental Hospital for the entire province. Most provincial mental hospitals do not have adolescent units with special programs for young people.

With proclamation of the repeal of Section 8, an obvious solution for seriously disturbed children would be to upgrade adolescent treatment programs on a regional basis and to insert some special protections and rights for children so detained.

*The Juvenile Delinquents Act*
Even with the proclamation of the repeal of Section 8, training school is still available as a back-up resource. The pattern of training school admissions shown in Table 3 clearly indicates this situation. As the table shows, some children, especially boys, who were charged with delinquency based on Criminal Code offences but formerly committed under Section 8 are now being committed under Section 9 or dealt with directly under the Juvenile Delinquents Act.

**Table 3/Training School Admissions of Children, 1967 to 1975, by Act and Section[a]**

| Year | Section 8 | | Section 9 | | Juvenile De-linquents Act | | Total N |
|------|-----|------|------|------|------|------|---------|
| | N | % | N | % | N | % | |
| 1967 | 453 | 43.3 | 594 | 56.7 | | | 1047 |
| 1968 | 539 | 46.3 | 624 | 53.7 | | | 1163 |
| 1969 | 603 | 45.2 | 730 | 54.8 | | | 1333 |
| 1970 | 603 | 42.9 | 803 | 57.1 | | | 1406 |
| 1971 | 582 | 44.3 | 731 | 55.7 | | | 1313 |
| 1972 | 613 | 45.2 | 744 | 54.8 | | | 1357 |
| 1973 | 504 | 42.5 | 673 | 56.7 | 9 | 0.8 | 1186 |
| 1974 | 326 | 32.4 | 634 | 63.1 | 45 | 4.5 | 1005 |
| 1975 | 139 | 16.1 | 608 | 70.2 | 119 | 13.7 | 866 |

[a]From A. Birkenmayer, Trends in Training School Admissions, 1967 to 1975.

Despite the fact that Sections 8 and 9 of the Training Schools Act were intended to regulate all children sent to training school, it was held by the Court of Appeal in 1973 that Section 20 of the Juvenile Delinquents Act, under which a judge has discretion to order committal to training school, is independent of, and not restricted by, the provisions of the provincial act. Thus a judge may commit a child found to be a "juvenile delinquent" directly to training school without having to comply with the two restrictions contained in Section 9 – namely, that the offence be one for which an adult may be imprisoned and that the child be at least 12 years of age. Although the federal act requires that (1) an attempt must first be made to reform a child under 12 "in his own home or in a foster home or in the charge of a Children's Aid Society," (2) it be in the best interests of a child, and (3) the welfare of the community require such committal, a child under the age of 12 may be committed under the Juvenile Delinquents Act, 1970.

Overall, the number of boys under 11 committed to training school in 1975 was half the 1973 total, although three times as many were committed under the Juvenile Delinquents Act in 1975 compared with 1973. Despite the lack of any special facilities for young girls, one or two are being committed annually under Section 8. With the proclamation of the repeal, it is possible that they, too, will be committed under the Juvenile Delinquents Act or, better yet, dealt with in the community.

The definition of a juvenile delinquent includes not only a child who has committed a Criminal Code offence but also a child who is guilty of "sexual immorality or any similar form of vice" or one who has violated any provincial statute or municipal by-law. For example, under the Education Act, 1973, a child is required by law to attend school and one who refuses to do so or who is habitually absent without legal excuse may be dealt with as a juvenile delinquent and thereby committed to training school.

Sexual promiscuity was the reason given for committing the majority of girls to training school under Section 8. Now, some of these are probably being committed under the "sexual immorality" provisions of the Juvenile Delinquents Act. However, there has been a significant overall decrease in the proportion of girls committed to training school. "This one aspect would lead to the conclusion that the underlying cause in the declining use of Section 8 is a change in the societal norms regarding girls rather than legislative action"[10] (see Table 4). Statistics sent out by Chief Judge Andrews indicate that the trend of committing fewer girls to training school has continued inasmuch as only 124 girls were committed in 1977. The number of boys committed also declined to 567.

Another possible explanation that would lead to such a decline in committals is an increase in the number and use of community resources for girls. Unlike the restricted scope of Section 8, which allows a judge either to commit a child to training school or dismiss the application entirely, the Juvenile Delinquents Act gives the judge a broad discretion as to placement. First, a judge may order that a child be committed to the care of the CAS. In some cases this is done even when the CAS has indicated it does not wish to intervene. By virtue of the Child Welfare Act, this type of committal automatically makes the child a CAS ward. Although the CAS may apply to terminate wardship at any time, it is unlikely that the same judge would allow it to do so immediately. It is important to note that, if later the child commits another "offence," the CAS may bring the child back before the judge under the Juvenile Delinquents Act and the judge may make a further disposition – such as committing the child to training school.

Second, the judge may commit the child to the "care or custody of a Probation Officer or any other suitable person" and may also stipulate that the costs of such care be paid for by the municipality. Such support orders were held to be valid even when the child is a ward of the CAS. However, I would agree with His Honor Judge George Thomson that even in such cases,

"the delinquency charge is being used simply to finance the costs of care. Unless the delinquency charge is laid as a result of a decision which is not connected to the Society's reluctance to care for the child, I think the *Juvenile Delinquents Act* is being used improperly. This is my opinion, although I do feel that such an approach might have to be taken in appropriate cases for the benefit of the child who is in serious danger."

Increasing use of this option strained municipal budgets and resulted in a

**Table 4/Training School Admissions of Children, 1967 to 1975, by Sex and Act and Section[a]**

| Year | Males | | | | Females | | | |
|---|---|---|---|---|---|---|---|---|
| | % Under Section 8 | % Under Section 9 | % Under Juvenile Delinquents Act | Total N | % Under Section 8 | % Under Section 9 | % Under Juvenile Delinquents Act | Total N |
| 1967 | 34.8 | 65.2 | | 797 | 70.4 | 29.6 | | 250 |
| 1968 | 35.1 | 64.9 | | 832 | 74.6 | 25.4 | | 331 |
| 1969 | 33.8 | 66.2 | | 920 | 70.7 | 29.3 | | 413 |
| 1970 | 31.3 | 68.7 | | 953 | 67.3 | 31.3 | | 453 |
| 1971 | 31.2 | 68.8 | | 917 | 74.7 | 25.3 | | 396 |
| 1972 | 29.7 | 70.3 | | 893 | 75.0 | 25.0 | | 464 |
| 1973 | 27.8 | 71.5 | 0.8 | 796 | 72.6 | 26.7 | 0.8 | 390 |
| 1974 | 20.0 | 74.5 | 5.5 | 689 | 56.5 | 38.3 | 2.2 | 316 |
| 1975 | 8.0 | 78.0 | 14.0 | 659 | 41.5 | 45.4 | 13.0 | 207 |

[a]From A. Birkenmayer, Trends in Training School Admissions, 1967 to 1975.

74

challenge to the legislation in the Regional Municipality of Peel and Viking Houses.

In upholding the legislation, the court also held that the phrase "any other suitable person" must be read *ejusdem generis* with probation officer and that the corporate entity involved could not so qualify. The result of this decision was a series of meetings between municipal representatives and the Ministry of Community and Social Services, wherein an acceptable municipal–provincial cost-sharing formula for those children committed to group homes was worked out.

The Juvenile Delinquents Act gives the judge a number of further options. The judge may suspend final disposition, adjourn the hearing, impose a fine of up to $25, place the child on probation, or cause the child to be committed to a foster home.

In summary, the broad dispositionary powers a judge has under the Juvenile Delinquents Act still allow commitment of the unmanageable child to training school. So long as the act remains in its present form, proclamation of the repeal of Section 8 will not eliminate the use of training school for status offenders.

It is generally conceded that the present definition of "juvenile delinquent" contained in the Juvenile Delinquents Act is too broad in scope and that the use of the criminal law power should be restricted to violations of the Criminal Code or other federal acts.[11] The proposed Young Offenders Act embodies this view. That the minimum age for criminal responsibility would be 12 would mean that very young children could no longer be sent to training school. A parent, CAS, or school attendance counsellor would no longer be able to charge the child. Only the Attorney General or his agent would be empowered to proceed. If the proposal is enacted, it would no longer be possible to commit the unmanageable child or status offender to training school.

This proposed legislation, together with proclamation of the repeal of Section 8, has created pressure for further alternatives. If and when the federal Young Offenders Act is passed, the province could still pass its own legislation to deal with status offenders.

If we assume that, having repealed Section 8, the province would not re-enact legislation committing youngsters to a locked facility for a status offence, the effectiveness of a court appearance in dealing with unmanageable children, particularly truants, is seriously being questioned. "It's clear that juvenile court is not working for truancy, we have to start working on alternatives," said Mr. Chumak, chairman of the Toronto Board of Education's Committee on Young Offenders (Juvenile court, 1978). Social services aimed at juvenile delinquents are not effective in keeping them out of further trouble, a recent Hamilton study showed (Services useless, 1977).

The ineffectiveness of both the social services and juvenile court systems in dealing with children, according to its critics, results at least in part from the fragmented system of delivering child care services within the province. To meet this criticism, the Children's Services Transfer Act, 1977, transferred administrative responsibility for all group homes and facilities under the Children's Mental Health Centres Act, the Children's Mental Hospitals Act, the Training Schools Act, and the operation of observation and detention homes under the Provincial Courts Act to the Ministry of Community and Social Services. Besides the Child Welfare Act, this Ministry also continues to have responsibility for administering the Children's Boarding Homes Act, Charitable Institutions Act, and Home for Retarded Persons Act. Now that the hodge-podge of statutes has been transferred under one roof there remains the difficult task of coordinating the differing funding rates for similar programs under the various acts, along with the development of comprehensive guidelines for licensing and staffing. Hand in hand with this task must go the evaluation of the effectiveness of current programs and the development of new ones to meet the needs of the children the system is intended to serve.

## Notes

The author has generously agreed to supply further details of her thesis and fully comprehensive legal references regarding the statutes she has researched. Readers needing additional sources of information should contact Mrs. Weiler at the Ministry of the Attorney General, 17th Floor, 18 King St. East, Toronto.

[1] The Industrial Schools Act, containing a provision for the committal of a child beyond the control of a parent to be sent to an Industrial School, was enacted in 1874, S.O. 37. Vict. ch.29.

[2] Procedural requirements of a hearing under Sec. 8 are omitted from the discussion in this paper but are dealt with in Ch.VI of Weiler, 1974.

[3] In the Matter of: The Training Schools Act of Ontario and Patrick B., unreported decision, His Honor Judge G. M. Thomson, Provincial Court (Family Division) County of Frontenac, Mar. 13, 1975. See generally Weiler, 1974, Ch.V.

[4] For a collection of excerpts on this topic, see Family Law II Casebook, ed. Judge G. M. Thomson, University of Western Ontario.

[5] The Child Welfare Act also provides in S.43 that a boy or girl under 16 years of age who is found loitering in a public place between 10:00 p.m. and 6:00 a.m., and who is unaccompanied by a parent or adult person, can be given a warning. If this warning is ignored, the child may be dealt with as a child apparently in need of protection. R.S.O. 1970, ch.64.S.20 (i), (viii), and (ix).

[6] Parental rights as such are not completely terminated. Parents may apply to terminate the order of Crown wardship under S.32, and Crown wards are capable of inheriting from their parents.

[7] The "hodge-podge of statutes" refers to:
The Children's Institutions Act. R.S.O. 1970, ch.66.
The Charitable Institutions Act. R.S.O. 1970, ch.62.
The Children's Boarding Homes Act. R.S.O. 1970, ch.65.
The Homes for Retarded Persons Act. R.S.O. 1970, ch.204.
The Children's Mental Hospitals Act. R.S.O. 1970, ch.69.
The Children's Mental Health Centres Act. R.S.O. 1970, ch.68.
The Provincial Courts Act. R.S.O. 1970, ch.369.

[8] See [3]. Also from conversation with Andrew Birkenmayer.

[9] According to the Children's Services Branch of the Ministry of Community and Social Services, the number of children in care declined in 1971 from 1027 to 866 because of the Children's Mental Health Centres Act's (R.S.O. 1970, ch.68) taking over financial responsibility for children formerly cared for by the societies.

[10] By the term "proportion" is meant here the rate of the number of girls committed under Section 8 to the total number of girls as compared with the rate of boys committed under Section 8 to the total number of boys (see Table 4).

[11] The report of the Department of Justice Committee on Juvenile Delinquency (1965) stated: "It seems clearly to have been intended . . . to give a uniform quality to all juvenile misconduct, serious and minor alike, in order to further the general objective of the Act. These objectives were to minimize any attribution of criminality to a child's conduct and to focus attention, not upon the offence as such, but upon the underlying behavioural problem that gave rise to it. To put the matter differently, the existing provisions carry to its logical conclusion the principle that treatment must suit the

offender, not the offence. It is now apparent that a competing interest of public policy, namely the protection of the individual against undue interference by the state requires some limitations upon the unrestricted applications of this principle, and that a change in the law is intended'' (pp.67-68).

## References

Birkenmayer, A. C., & Madden, P. G. *Statistical report dealing with selected variables concerning wards of Ontario training schools 1967-1972*. Toronto: Planning and Research Branch, Ministry of Correctional Services, Ontario, 1973.

Central Toronto Youth Services. Control problems and alternatives to Section 8, Ontario Training Schools Act. Toronto, 1975.

Cousineau, D. F., & Veevers, J. E. Juvenile justice: An analysis of the Canadian Young Offenders Act. In C. Boydell, C. Grindstaff, & P. Whitehead (Eds.), *Deviant behaviour and societal reaction*. Toronto: Holt, Rinehart & Winston, 1972.

Department of Justice Committee on Juvenile Delinquency. *Juvenile delinquency in Canada*. Ottawa: Queen's Printer, 1965.

Green, B. Trumpets justice and federalism. An analysis of the Ontario Training Schools Act of 1965. *University of Toronto Law Journal,* 1966.

Grygier, T. Social adjustment, personality and behaviour in training schools in Ontario. Research report, Department of Reform Institutions, 1966.

Grygier, T. The concept of the state of delinquency – An obituary. *Journal of Legal Education,* 1973, Vol.18.

Hobart, C. W. A study of attitudes and behaviour. In C. Boydell, C. Grindstaff, & P. Whitehead (Eds.), *Deviant behaviour and societal reaction*. Toronto: Holt, Rinehart & Winston, 1972.

Juvenile court – to many children it's a chuckle. Toronto *Globe and Mail,* May 13, 1978, pp. 1, 45.

Lambert, L., & Birkenmayer, A. *An assessment of the classification system for placement of wards in training schools*. Toronto: Planning and Research Branch, Ministry of Correctional Services, Ontario, 1972.

Landau, B. The adolescent female offender. *Ontario Psychologist,* **5,** 2.

Matza, D. *Delinquency and drift*. New York: Wiley, 1964.

Ontario Association of Children's Aid Societies. Regarding the effect of repeal of Section 8, the Training Schools Act, on Children's Aid Societies. Feb.6, 1976.

Ontario Interim Research Project on Unreached Youth. June 1969.

Parker, G. The century of the child. *Canadian Bar Review,* 1967, **45,** 741-763.

Platt, A. M. *The child savers: The invention of delinquency*. Chicago: University of Chicago Press, 1969.

Robson, S. M. *Can delinquency be measured?* Patterson, N.J.: Smith, 1972.

Schur, E. M. *Radical non-intervention*. Englewood Cliffs, N.J.: Prentice-Hall, 1973.

Services useless for delinquents study shows. Toronto *Globe and Mail,* Apr. 29, 1977.

Shannon, P. H. (Chairman). One million children: A national study of Canadian children with emotional learning disorders. 1964.

Sidman, L. R. The Massachusetts Stubborn Child Law: Law and order in the home. *Family Law Quarterly,* 1972, **6,** 33-58.

Task Force in Community and Social Services. Report on selected issues and relationships. Jan. 1974.

Weiler, K. M. Section 8 of the Training Schools Act. Unpublished thesis, Osgoode Hall Law School, York University, 1974.

# A Critique of the Institutional Response to Juvenile Delinquency in Ontario

Dennis Conly/Carleton University

Juvenile delinquency is both behavior and a perception of behavior. To argue that it is solely the former is to deny that definitions of right and wrong are historically, culturally, and politically specific. However, to argue that delinquency exists only in the eyes of the beholder is to suggest that "meaning" is monopolized in the reaction, and the action itself is neutral and arbitrary. In my view, the development of the juvenile justice system in Canada can best be understood by synthesizing these positions. Behavior commonly seen and treated as delinquent has been rooted in dehumanized social conditions and as such is meaningful as an action. Delinquency is evidence that a lack of fundamental provisions (proper health and nutritional care, emotional and physical affection, respect, etc.) can affect behavior, sometimes making it careless and destructive. At the same time, interpretation of behavior and the response to it have often been value-specific. In this context the use of correctional institutions to confine juvenile delinquents, exemplified by the Ontario training school system, presents an example of how individual needs can be distorted and neglected in the service of broader organizational imperatives. This paper examines some of the major problems associated with institutionalizing delinquent children and concludes with a proposal to abolish the training school system.

It is in terms of fundamental premises that one must begin a critical examination of the institutional response to delinquency. In his examination of the Swedish juvenile justice system, Elmhorn (1974) concluded, "The main reason treatment of individuals in isolated environments has proven to be a failure lies in the fact that the real problems are to be found in the interaction between the individual and the environment and the social structure to which the individual has to adapt himself." Implicit in the act of removing a child from the community and placing the child in an institution such as a training school is the presumption of an individual pathology. The individual is seen as representing the "core" of the problem, a problem that can best be treated in a special, "structured" environment.

Similarly, the cause of juvenile delinquency in Ontario was defined in the 19th century as moral pathology. Over time it came to be seen as mental pathology, mysteriously rooted in the individual's psyche, understood only by professionals. However, youths enrolled in training schools frequently share a number of significant social characteristics, as exemplified by the 462 juveniles (Lambert & Birkenmayer, 1972) committed to training school for the first time in 1966-67.

The data of Table 1 suggest that children who end up in training schools

78

**Table 1/Background Characteristics of Boys and Girls in Training School (%)[a]**

| Background Characteristic | Boys | Girls |
|---|---|---|
| Living with both parents | 58 | 53 |
| Living with one parent | 27 | 21 |
| Living with relatives, foster home, group home, or other | 14 | 26 |
| History of criminality in nuclear family | 29 | 39 |
| History of drinking problems or alcoholism in nuclear family | 32 | 42 |
| History of mental illness in family | 8 | 8 |
| History of chronic physical disease or handicap in family | 28 | 41 |
| No employment in family | 22 | 27 |

[a]From Lambert and Birkenmayer, 1972.

do not compose a random sample of their age group. They are most often from families experiencing difficulty and hardship. Their most common characteristic is poverty. Of the sample in the table, 93% came from poor, working-class families. Although poverty alone does not cause delinquency, it is the most predictive variable for a child to be admitted to training school. A report by the National Council of Welfare (1975) concluded, "There seems little evidence that poor kids are disproportionately bad kids, but it may be that they are disproportionately treated that way." The "class bias" of the training school system is not the sole responsibility of those who administer it. Certainly, the informality of juvenile court proceedings has tended to encourage the passing of moderate dispositions for those children whose families are able to draw on more resources for resolving the problem. For example, a recent study (Erikson, 1975) demonstrated that private lawyers in juvenile court tended to see such things as "keeping the juvenile out of training school," "getting the child off," and "speaking to the disposition" as more consistent with their roles than did duty counsel lawyers.

An example of the way informal court proceedings have worked to victimize poor and minority-group children was detailed in a recent Ontario Supreme Court decision (*Globe and Mail*, Oct. 10, 1975) that concluded that a 14-year-old native girl from Kenora was treated unjustly by the juvenile court. The girl had been sentenced to an indefinite period in training school for allegedly setting fire to a house. However, in reviewing the case, Justice Samuel Grange stated that the accused girl should not have been convicted. He noted that the only evidence linking the accused with the commission of the offense was a statement obtained from her by a provincial police officer. The young girl denied her statement and proclaimed her innocence in court. Justice Grange concluded that the statement should not have been allowed as evidence because no relatives or counsel were with her when she made it and that she was "clearly of limited academic and intellectual attainment." The justice also noted that the lawyer "took very little part" in examining the admissibility of evidence and that the training school sentence in his view was unjustifiably harsh. Unfortunately what makes this case unique is not that the girl was convicted but that her conviction was reviewed in a higher court.

Training schools have consistently absorbed those children who are least wanted and most powerless. Rather than being "specialized treatment facilities," training schools have in fact earned a reputation as places to dispose of society's unwanted. In his "Youth at the Crossroads" series, Valpy (1973) argued that the "unstable and emotionally disturbed children committed to Ontario training schools pass through the institutions like water through a pipe – unchanged, unchecked, unhelped, the experience valueless to them. Why? Because the system is a dumping ground for every community's unwanted kids. Its primary tool for rehabilitation is the teaching of middle class virtues. And that has nothing to do with the unscrambling of messed-up psyches." In truth, however, even if the training schools were completely dedicated to the "unscrambling of messed-up psyches," they would still be off the mark. There is little doubt that a girl who has been raped by her father needs extra-sensitive counseling, but how could that ever happen to a child incarcerated in the artificial, chaotic, inherently insensitive environment of a training school?

Living in a custodial institution with literally dozens of other disruptive children, supervised by three different shifts each day, obviously does not enhance positive growth. Characteristically, a basic adversarial stance, based on manipulation and threat, underlies the relationship between young people and the staff of training schools. At the training school where I was employed for almost a year (Grandview for girls),[1] the staff were addressed formally to their face (by regulation) and called "goof" when their backs were turned (in defiance). Behavior modification techniques and solitary confinement were used as the main means of internal control.[2]

As a result of this authority structure the outlawed use of items such as tobacco becomes a major obsession in the social world of the training school. Smoking plays a primary role in both the day-to-day social life of the children and the rule-enforcement duty of the staff. Similarly, unusual sexual dynamics emerge within the confines of the institutional setting. For instance, nearly every girl at Grandview was "going with" another. There was a constant secret exchange of "love letters"; and the predictable instances of "broken hearts" would often occur, leading to loss of appetite, crying, or disruptive behavior. Girls who looked most like boys were prized. This was often the most frightening aspect of training school to Grandview newcomers. Once accepted and joined, however, this pattern became a major aspect of most girls' training school social life. The corresponding phenomenon in boys' training schools does not exhibit the same degree of overt sexuality. Rather, it is an on-going process of establishing and rating "toughness." The "rock of the house" is a training school term for the toughest boy in a particular living unit. Reports of staff actually using this social phenomenon for their own benefit, as an internal mechanism of social control, are not uncommon.[3]

Another disturbing institutional phenomenon in girls' training schools is the occurrence of self-mutilation. Tattooing and "carving" (scraping and cutting of arms with sharp objects) are common problems. This self-destructiveness becomes associated with status among other inmates and as a result girls who appeared to be coping comparatively well in the training school environment would suddenly show up with self-inflicted wounds on their arms.

These kinds of institutional dynamics frequently become overwhelming factors in the incarcerated child's social life and identity. The young people begin to define themselves in terms of their social environment. Being labeled deviant by a social audience, or by an agency of social control, can change one's conception of self and possibly lead to a situation where, even if there is no initial commitment to deviation, there may be a progressive turn to such commitment. Although labeling theory has tended perhaps to ascribe too much significance to social reaction as a behavioral determinant, certainly as Schur (1971) pointed out, the institutional environment does seem highly susceptible to both the giving and taking of labels: "[institutions] are among the most sig-

80

nificant of the direct reactors or labelers, for they implement the broader and more diffuse societal definitions through organized structures and institutionalized procedures."

Consequently, training school experience increases a young person's tendency either to break rules upon release or to embark on a criminal career. The fact that over 50% of the men at the Millhaven maximum security federal penitentiary were once in an Ontario training school indicates that the "process" is a difficult one to escape.[4] Similarly, a 1972 Ministry of Correctional Services study (Lambert & Birkenmayer) found that, within 18 months of first release from training school, 34% of the children had been convicted of another offense and 48% had either been returned to training school or were institutionalized elsewhere. A more recent study (Shortt, 1975), which followed the careers of Hillcrest training school boys, found, "Of the 532 wards, 357 (67.1%) were convicted of further offenses prior to termination of wardship. Of those having further offenses, 188 (53%) were sentenced to adult institutions. Only 58 (10.9%) of the wards were terminated under circumstances that were not clouded by further illegal activities or further dysfunctional behavior."

This evidence suggests that the institutional response to delinquency represents unjustifiable intervention into the lives of individual young people. But what about the community? Does society benefit from being able to remove disruptive children for a certain length of time? It can be argued, for instance, that if the training school does anything, it at least keeps young people in a controlled situation, and as such they are less likely to inflict damage on the rest of society. The child's need for a "structured environment" is often used to rationalize a training school committal. However, while it is true that training schools offer securely locked facilities, it does not follow that the children are always willing to cooperate. When I worked at Grandview, AWOL'ing, as it was called, was a major problem. The Ministry of Corrections reported in 1974 that there were 303 children AWOL from their training schools. For the most part, these children escape without anything, and sometimes in their nightclothes. Predictably, they are forced to steal, solicit, or prostitute themselves in order to survive. The "secure facility" aspect of training schools is to a large extent a myth.

Another common argument on the behalf of training schools is that they are used only "as a last resort" and that much more emphasis is placed on working with children in community-based settings. This argument is not consistent with even the most recent Ministry of Corrections' budget allocation. For 1976-77, $35.6 million was established as the total figure of the Ministry's juvenile program (Corrections estimates, 1976-77), with a breakdown as shown in Table 2.

Over 56% has been allocated to the training school system for which the taxpayer is required to pay the best part of $25 000/annum/child at the expense of other programs.

On a practical, political level, the training school system is well entrenched, providing jobs and a raison d'être for many of those employed by it. Some of the smaller towns where training schools are situated (e.g., Alfred) are extremely dependent economically on the continued existence of a training school in their local area. As a result, from the perspective of electoral politics, it has never been politically expedient to suggest major adjustments, let alone radical change.

On a broader level, the existence of the training school system allows the perpetuation of politically non-threatening myths regarding the nature of crime

**Table 2/Ministry of Correctional Services' Budget Allocations for Juvenile Programs in 1976-77**

| Program | Allocation (in millions) | No. of Clients (1975-76) |
|---|---|---|
| Training schools | $20.0 | 900 |
| Probation | $ 6.0 | 6 600 |
| Group homes | $ 3.6 | 200 |
| Foster homes | $ 1.4 | 200 |
| Other | $ .9 | |
| Administration | $ 3.7 | |

and delinquency. Imprisonment, even of young offenders, serves a functional role within the context of the prevailing social structure. Thomas Mathieson (1974), a Swedish sociologist and leader in Scandinavian penal reform, delineated four aspects of this role: an expurgatory function, which removes "unproductive" elements of society from the labor market – in part this is done by "criminalizing" certain activities; a power-draining function, in which rebellious elements are placed in locked facilities, thereby dispersing and nullifying their potential disruptive power; a divertive function, whereby, as the result of separating and disarming unproductive or rebellious elements, vastly exaggerated evils can be attributed to them – e.g., petty crimes can be characterized as a major threat to our way of life, thus diverting attention from the vastly more significant activities of those who monopolize and abuse power; finally, a purely symbolic function that enables us to stigmatize some elements of society as "bad" and consequently to see ourselves as on the side of "good." It is self-reaffirming to know that those who are not on "our" side are imprisoned. These social-psychological functions of imprisonment are exhibited in their purest form in adult imprisonment but the training school system fulfills part of its function as a "farm system" for adult prison systems.

While the idea of using custodial institutions for disruptive children has never generated public enthusiasm, euphemistic terminology and the mystique of clinical treatment have been used quite successfully to create the needed "smoke screen." They had to become "training schools" instead of "jails," "treatment" instead of punishment, "quiet rooms" instead of solitary confinement. For such reasons, rethinking the delinquency problem demands both an unveiling of myths and a reappraisal of what causes delinquency. Schur (1973) argues that "crime and delinquency, along with other problems, are integral features of our social order and hence cannot be explained by reference to some 'external' or 'abnormal' phenomena or occurrence" (p.11). In an earlier work (1969), he is highly critical of those who would "compartmentalize" delinquency as a problem unto itself, and he suggests that "the prime focus of crime policy must move away from law enforcement (and even treatment) towards general efforts at prevention and control. And the key to such efforts lies not in dealing with potential criminals, but rather in direct action against crime-encouraging elements" (p.6).

The continued existence and financial support of the training school system in Ontario represent a formidable stumbling block toward the development of such a policy. What is called for is the abolition of those responses to delinquency that are by their very nature coercive and based on premises that implicitly "excuse" the social conditions out of which delinquency emerges. The goal should be to cut off the channels for this type of response, not to replace them. Mathieson (1974) emphasizes both the "ideology" of abolition, as well as the dangers inherent in designing "finished" alternatives.

"Existing order changes in structure *while* it enters the new. The first political question then becomes that of how this 'while' should be started, how the sketch should be begun, how it should be mobilized. The second question, which is politically almost as central, is that of how the sketch may be maintained as a sketch, or at least prolonged in life as a sketch. An enormous political pressure exists in the direction of completing the sketch into a finished drawing, and thereby ending the growth of the product. . . . Through both of these questions, abolition runs like a red thread. Abolition is the point of departure." (p.13)

Mathieson's work, based on the Scandinavian penal reform movements KRUM (Sweden), KROM (Norway), and KRIM (Denmark), suggests that it would be a vast mistake to construct a finished alternative to the training school system prior to its abolition:

"By demanding 'alternatives' before a change in the established order is implemented, it is made certain that the framework for discussion becomes the question of attaining whatever objectives the established order already has. In this way, the demand for 'alternatives' has a conserving effect: the demand contributes to the maintenance of the establishment's objective, so that – if anything – only the means to reach the old objective are changed. In itself, this is a crucial limitation on the change which may be carried out." (p.84)

To work effectively toward delinquency prevention and treatment in Ontario is to work against those structural aspects of our society that, by virtue of their existence, predetermine delinquent behavior. No social or cultural group can be helped by training schools.[5] Our children are not going to be passive and non-violent as long as five or six thousand of them are brutally beaten every year by lonely, secluded, and, most often, poor parents.[6] They are not going to respect the norms and values of a society that does not allow them meaningful political and economic participation, and that distributes rewards, rights, and privileges in an inequitable manner. Delinquency prevention and treatment will not be achieved by institutions such as training schools, which are inherently repressive and more rooted in social control imperatives than constructive analysis.

### Notes

Assistance from Bob Crook, Andrew Jones, Martin Loney, and Sandra Ross in helping me with this paper is gratefully recognized.

[1] During recent budget estimates of the Ontario provincial government, the Minister of Corrections announced that the closure of Grandview as a juvenile institution is forthcoming. It is to become an adult correctional institution, and the girls at Grandview will be dispersed to other training schools, including Oakville.

[2] For an account of the use of solitary confinement in Ontario training schools, see Weitz (1976).

[3] For several case histories that illustrate this point see Watson (1976).

[4] This figure comes from an internal survey of 143 inmates done by Howard Brown (inmate of Millhaven).

[5] A large percentage of the training school population is made up of children with native backgrounds. A staff member of Cecil Facer T.S. (Sudbury) once told me that up to 75% of the inmates of that particular institution have native backgrounds.

[6] For a detailed report of child battering in Canada, see VanStolk (1972).

## References

Bellomo, J. Upper Canadian attitudes towards crime and punishment. *Ontario History*, 1972, Vol.14.

Elmhorn, K. Juvenile-Justice-Sweden. *UNSDRI Report*, 1974.

Erikson, P. Legalistic and traditional role expectations for defense counsel in juvenile court. *Canadian Journal of Criminology and Corrections*, 1975, **17**(1).

Faust, F., & Brantingham, P. (Eds.) *Juvenile justice philosophy*. St. Paul: West, 1974.

Francis, R. P. The training schools act. *Saskatchewan Bar Review*, 1966, Vol.31.

Galper, J. *The politics of social services*. Englewood Cliffs, N.J.: Prentice-Hall, 1975.

Green, B. Trumpets justice and federalism: An analysis of the Ontario training schools act of 1965. *Canadian Journal of Criminology and Corrections*, 1966, **8**(4).

Houston, S. Victorian origins of juvenile delinquency: A Canadian experience. *History of Education Quarterly*, Fall 1972.

*Kelso papers*. Vol.6. Ottawa: Public Archives of Canada.

Lambert, L., & Birkenmayer, A. *An assessment of the classification system of placement of wards in training schools*. Toronto: Ministry of Correctional Services, Ontario, 1972.

Mathieson, T. *The politics of abolition — Scandinavian studies in criminology*. London: Martin Robertson, 1974.

Milliband, R. *The state in capitalist society*. London: Quartet, 1969.

National Council of Welfare. *Poor kids*. Ottawa: The Council, 1975.

Ontario Ministry of Correctional Services. Annual reports, 1973-74, 1974-75, 1975-76, 1976-77.

Platt, A. *The child savers — The invention of delinquency*. Chicago: University of Chicago Press, 1969.

Schur, E. *Our criminal society — The social and legal sources of crime in America*. Toronto: Prentice-Hall, 1969.

Schur, E. *Labeling deviant behavior: Its social implications*. New York: Harper & Row, 1971.

Schur, E. *Radical non-intervention — Rethinking the delinquency problem*. Englewood Cliffs, N.J.: Prentice-Hall, 1973.

Shortt, R. *Abstract of a follow-up of Hillcrest graduates*. Toronto: Ministry of Correctional Services, Ontario, 1975.

Sinclair, D. Training schools in Canada. In W. T. McGrath (Ed.), *Crime and its treatment in Canada*. Toronto: Macmillan, 1965.

Splane, R. *Social welfare in Ontario 1791-1893*. Toronto: University of Toronto Press, 1965.

Sutherland, N. *Children in English-Canadian society: Framing the twentieth-century consensus.* Toronto: University of Toronto Press, 1976.

Taylor, I., Walton, P., & Young, J. *The new criminology.* London: Routledge and Kegan Paul, 1973.

Valpy, M. Youth at the crossroads. *Globe and Mail* (Toronto), Feb.12-17, 1973.

VanStolk, M. *The battered child in Canada.* Toronto: McClelland & Stewart, 1972.

Watson, G. The farm system. *Like It Is*, 1976, **2**(1).

Weitz, D. We still lock up children. *Toronto Life*, May 1976.

Young Persons in Conflict with the Law. Report of the Solicitor-General's Committee on proposals for new legislation to replace the Juvenile Delinquents Act, 1975.

# Educational Issues

# Student Rights in Canada: Nonsense upon Stilts?

Romulo F. Magsino/Memorial University of Newfoundland

"Right," the utilitarian philosopher Jeremy Bentham (1962) insisted, "is a child of law: from real laws come real rights; but from imaginary laws . . . fancied and invented by poets, rhetoricians, and dealers in moral and intellectual poisons, come imaginary rights."

If true, this statement should render us suspicious of the claims to rights made by or on behalf of Canadian students. Since there is a dearth of laws guaranteeing student rights in this country, what are we to think of such assertions that students have a right to freedom of speech and assembly in schools and classrooms, a right to study the subject matter they find relevant, and a right to participate in the determination of school policies? Are they not, together with claims to a host of other student rights that lack support in positive laws, imaginary claims because based on imaginary rights?

The thrust of Bentham's utterance is clear: a claimed right is not a right if it lacks legal recognition and sanction. Its implication for student rights in this country is equally obvious: students do not have rights unless these rights are duly enacted and sanctioned by appropriate authorities.

In this paper, I argue that Canadian students are entitled to a number of rights presently denied them. I believe, however, that recognition and sanction of student entitlement to these rights have not been achieved, partly because attempts to justify them have been confused. Accordingly, I distinguish between two kinds of rights that students might claim for themselves, and then attempt to show how each kind might be properly justified. Further, without agreeing with Bentham that rights are rights only when accompanied by sanctions, I suggest that if they are to be enjoyed by Canadian students, student rights should be institutionalized. I also explore briefly some modes of institutionalization to ensure for them such rights.

## A Comparative Perspective

A perspective on student rights in Canada might emerge more sharply by noting the recent developments in the area of student law in the United States. Since both Canada and the United States have their legal traditions deeply imbedded in the common law, and since in both countries education is a provincial or state concern, we might expect to see certain similarities in the rights enjoyed by students there.

Unfortunately, the anticipated similarities are largely missing. While in both countries the drive for the establishment of student rights has been strong during the last decade,[1] the cause of student rights in the United States seems to have succeeded; in Canada, it seems to have failed.

Any vestige of doubt about the legal status of student rights in the United States is dispelled by at least three landmark cases disposed of by the Supreme Court in recent years. The first case, *Tinker v. Des Moines Independent Community School District* (1969), unequivocally affirmed that fundamental constitutional rights available to adults are also available to students. Noting that neither teachers nor students shed their constitutional rights to freedom of speech or expression at the schoolhouse gate, the court said:

"School officials do not possess absolute authority over students. Students in school as well as out of school are 'persons' under our Constitution. They are possessed of fundamental rights which the State must respect. . . . In the absence of a specific showing of constitutionally valid reasons to regulate their speech, students are entitled to freedom of expression of their views." (p.511)

With this ruling and other libertarian cases in mind, Berkman (1970) concluded his study of the trends in the American law related to student freedoms with this comment:

"While courts might attempt to whittle down to the size of impetuous children the persons created by *Tinker*, it is clear the big change has already occurred: students have become active determinants of educational purpose both in law and in fact." (p.595)

So far, however, no such whittling has happened. On the contrary, the view that students are constitutional persons has been strengthened further by the U.S. Supreme Court. In the second case, *Goss v. Lopez*, the court gave its stamp of recognition to students' right to procedural due process. Here, the court ruled that schools are required to set up hearing procedures for students before they can be suspended. School suspension procedures, the court declared, should include a statement of the charges of wrong doing, presentation to the students of the evidence if they request it, and the opportunity for the students to present their side of the conflict. Should the students be subject to a longer period of suspension – longer than 10 days – or expulsion, something more than rudimentary procedures will be required (see Anson, 1975; Cary, 1975; MacFeeley, 1975).

As if a sequel to *Goss v. Lopez*, *Wood v. Strickland* held school officials liable for damages if they abridge the civil rights of students. The court ruled that school board members may be personally liable for damages if they knew or reasonably should have known that the action they took within their sphere of official responsibility would violate the constitutional rights of the student affected, or if they took the action with the malicious intention to cause a deprivation of constitutional rights or other injury to the student. Ignorance of the student's constitutional rights is no excuse for their violation, the court further asserted (see Anson, 1975; Cary, 1975).

Altogether, these three cases spell out the operative principle that American educators have to abide by in the conduct of their schools: unless there are valid reasons (which finally have to be determined by the court in its interpretation of the Constitution), students shall be allowed to exercise their constitutional rights. This contrasts with the operative principle in Canadian schools, namely, the school boards' control of student conduct inside (and, to some extent, even outside) schools. This principle springs mainly from a determining provision in the British North America Act, which reads: "Section 93: In and for each Province the Legislature may exclusively make Laws in relation to Education." By virtue of this provision, provinces have passed school acts granting schools the power to control the conduct of pupils.

Insofar as school boards are administrative agents for effecting provincial control of education, and insofar as they act, within the framework of delegated authority, as local legislatures in educational matters, the policies formulated by such boards have the force of law and constitute part of the legal framework within which schools operate (Bargen, 1961, p.10). Unfortunately for student rights, however, school boards have exercised their control of education in a context dominated by the doctrine of *in loco parentis*. The *Corpus Juris* states that:

"As a general rule a school teacher, to a limited extent at least, stands in loco parentis to the pupils under his charge and may exercise such powers of control, restraint, and correction over them as may be reasonably necessary to enable him properly to perform his duties as a teacher and accomplish the purposes of education subject to such limitations and prohibitions as may be defined by legislative enactments. . . . If nothing unreasonable is demanded, he has the right to direct how and when each pupil shall attend to his appropriate duties and the manner in which a pupil shall demean himself." (Bargen, p.114)

Whether the exercise of power results from the delegation of authority by parents or from the need to maintain order in and about the school, or from both, the net effect is indisputable. Whatever rights students may enjoy in Canadian schools depend on the judgments of school boards officials or their delegated authorities.

Nevertheless, provincial jurisdiction over education is insufficient, by itself, to explain the lack of student rights in Canada, since education in the United States is similarly a state jurisdiction. Some other reason must therefore be found, and the American experience seems to suggest one possibility. It is important to note that the explicit and uniform establishment of the constitutional rights of students has been undertaken by the American Supreme Court in its interpretation of the U.S. Constitution, particularly its Bill of Rights. During the last 20 years, the Supreme Court has actively utilized the process of judicial review not only to safeguard but also to strengthen the citizens' civil and political rights.[2] Court action has not spared the schools in its attempt to oversee social reform, resulting, as we have seen, in the various rulings made on student rights.

No such thing has happened in Canada. In 1960, high hopes were raised with the passage of the Canadian Bill of Rights. It was thought that the Bill would provide the courts in Canada with an instrument to increase judicial effectiveness in preserving various individual civil and political rights. Yet since then, the Bill has remained a "paper tiger" in the courts (Weiler, 1974, p.195). Thus, as late as 1968, Pierre Trudeau, then Federal Minister of Justice, could assert that,

"To date . . . there does not exist in Canada any form of guarantee (beyond those few contained in the British North America Act) which a provincial legislature or Parliament, as the case may be, cannot repeal as freely as any other statute it has enacted. In this sense, no Canadian has the benefit of a constitutional protection as exists in dozens of other countries." (p.11)

If the situation is this bleak for adult citizens, how can it be any better for students?

After Trudeau made this indictment of the Canadian situation, nothing much has happened to brighten the picture. In 1969, *Queen v. Drybones* excited civil libertarians when the court unmistakably exerted itself as protector of civil liberties (as outlined in the Canadian Bill of Rights) against parliamentary intrusion. So far, however, that decision has been an anomaly. In succeeding cases involving civil rights, such as *Queen v. Wray, Queen v. Osborn*, and *Attorney General of Canada v. Lavell and Bedard*, the court obviously shrank from the role (Weiler, 1974, pp.186-205). More recently, in *Hogan v. the Queen*, the court majority denied Chief Justice Bora Laskin's view that any evidence gathered by police as the result of denying any rights under the Canadian Bill of Rights should not be admissible in courts. Justice Ritchie, speaking for the court, contended as follows:

"Whatever view may be taken of the constitutional impact of the *Bill of Rights* . . . I cannot agree that, wherever there has been a breach of one of the provisions of that *Bill*, it justifies the adoption of the rule of 'absolute inclusion' on the American model which is a derogation of the common law rule long accepted in this country." (*Thomas Arthur Hogan*, 1974, p.8)

Here, it seems, is an expression of the firm commitment on the part of the Supreme Court to adhere to common law and to the standards and practices it sanctions – including those that have been traditionally followed in schools.

### Rights of Students in Canada
Cynicism has pervaded student quarters concerning student rights. Thus, the *Student Rights Handbook for Metro Toronto* (1972) acidly remarked that generally school rules do not protect or help students. People who sympathize with schools, however, do not see them as unregenerate institutions that brook no interference or that offer no help or protection to students in the exercise of their rights. What is raised then is an empirical issue: do schools recognize and enforce student rights?

In answering this question, it seems helpful to make a distinction between two kinds of rights, namely, option rights and welfare rights, a distinction suggested by Golding (1968). The dominant emphasis in option rights is freedom; in welfare rights, it is equality (Wise & Manley-Casimir, 1971, p.48). Option rights are based on the idea of sovereignty. In Golding's (1968) words, these rights cover "not only sovereignty over persons but also sovereignty over things and sovereignty in regard to oneself." One has a right to do various things with one's property aside from denying and extending its use to others. The right one has over oneself may be bounded by the sovereignty other persons may have over one, by the duties one has toward others, and by one's duties in respect of oneself. But, "outside of these boundaries . . . [one] may do many things at . . . [one's] option" (pp.541-542).

Welfare rights, however, are those "that are derived from the claims to the goods of life which are conferred by the social ideal of a community" (pp.542-543). They do not depend on one's options to exercise sovereignty over oneself, things, or people, or on one's possession of autonomy. While some writers would disagree, it seems possible to subsume the right to due process and reasonable care under this heading.

There are sufficient similarities between the two that hide from people their important distinctions. Both of them, as Golding (1968, pp.543-546) pointed out, give rise to questions of claimability and of waivability; both depend for their recognition and sanction on the ideals of the community or society where they are claimed. Yet they differ crucially in their justification and in the institutionalization they require.

### Welfare Rights of Canadian Students

Despite the many criticisms leveled against the Canadian systems of education for alleged denial of student rights, it is fairly clear that, at least in some areas, the record of these systems has not been disappointing.

1. *The right to education.* All provinces of Canada have statutory provisions requiring attendance of children in schools for differing numbers of years, and they oblige the provinces to provide facilities for the accommodation of qualified children (*Wilkinson*, 1928). Further, courts have determined that such statutory provisions are binding and decisive. This assures school-age children access to education, except those who are exempted for valid reasons.[3]

The compulsory nature of schooling in Canada has had an interesting history. In an early court decision, the judge saw compulsory education as an instrument of public interest (Bargen, 1961, p.48). The right to educational provisions thus strictly belonged to the society, and, by implication, children did not seem to have any inherent right to education on their own account. In later court decisions, however, a changing attitude toward children is reflected. Thus, the judge in the McLeod case pointed out:

"It is the Province which is directly and primarily responsible as the agency which enacted the legislation. In coming to a decision I am compelled to regard the interests of children as paramount. That is inherent in the *Public Schools Act*; and all its provisions . . . must be read in that light." (*McLeod*, 1952, p.566)

2. *The right to equal educational opportunity.* While the answer to the question of access to education is straightforward, the answer to the issue of equality of educational opportunity is much less so. In Saskatchewan, the court has ruled that where the trustees of a school district have made arrangements for the children's conveyance to and from school, they are bound to include all children in their district, not only a part of them (*Riding*, 1927). Yet this case addresses itself to only one small aspect of an immense problem being raised in education today. This problem, perhaps the most talked about both in the United States and Canada, raises the issue of resources and financing in education. Presumably, the right of students to equal educational opportunity is compromised by, among others, inequalities in educational resources and financing between public schools and separate schools (see Olthuis, 1972; Ontario Committee, 1972; Ontario Separate, 1972), between districts (especially between rural and urban ones) (see Humphreys, 1972), and between the "have" and the "have-not" provinces (Economic Council, 1972; Fleming, 1974).

There is no doubt that the problem is now widely recognized, and that both the provincial and federal governments are attempting to redress the imbalance (see Fleming, 1974), although it is not quite sure that anyone knows what equality in educational opportunity means,[4] and although recent nation-wide economic difficulties have blunted government attempts.

The problem of equal educational opportunity is increasingly seen to go beyond the question of government capacity to provide for equal plants and facilities, similarly qualified teachers, and equally enriched curricula. More and more it is placed in the context of a society characterized by inequalities. As *The Real Poverty Report* (Adams et al., 1971) insisted, "Equality of opportunity . . . is essentially non-existent in Canada" (p.81). So it is in education, if Porter (1971) is right, that the economic aspects of social class are a major factor in determining the educational prospects of students. According to him, whether a student will go on to higher education or not appears to be a function of a "set of interrelated sociological and psychological variables which make up the social class position of the family and thus influence the individual's chances in the educational system." Further, children from upper-class families

"will have a greater chance to complete their education and inherit parental status than children with parents of lower occupational status will have to improve their position. The lower-class family does not value education so highly because in part it is a privilege beyond their horizons of opportunity, and at the same time, lacking education themselves, they fail to appreciate its value and to encourage their children." (pp.179-180)

What all this suggests is that no amount of government support meant to equalize educational provisions will effectively solve the problem of inequalities in educational opportunity. The required remedy seems to call for a massive, fundamental restructuring of the socioeconomic order (see, e.g., Blackstone, 1969).

Altogether then, Fleming (1974) does not seem too far from the truth when he concluded his study of equality in Canadian education with these words:

"For those who feel that national self-compliments are in order, the Canadian record may be called commendable. For those whose aspirations and ideals are high, the shortcomings are easily found." (p.127)

3. *The right to procedural due process.* In light of the *Goss* and *Wood* decisions of the U.S. Supreme Court, the virtual absence of due process requirements in Canadian schools might well appear scandalous.

Schools Acts for various provinces grant schools the power to control the conduct of pupils. Typical, for example, is the provision for Ontario schools that "a pupil shall . . . submit to such disciplines as would be exercised by a kind, firm and judicious parent"; that the teacher and the principal are charged with the maintenance of school order and discipline; and that the principal is given the authority to suspend a pupil (Gilbert et al., 1973, pp.7, 27-28). The history of court litigation involving punishment of pupils is indeed a history of the affirmation of the principle that the law has granted educators the power of moderate correction and allows them to exercise their discretion within the limits of this grant (*R. v. Metcalfe*, 1927). On the whole, however, courts have been mainly concerned with examining whether the punishments that have been imposed on students have been meted out for just and reasonable cause; whether the teacher or school officials have acted on malice; whether the power exercised

94

has been abused; or whether the punishment has been rendered capriciously, excessively, or carelessly. Still, the courts have not attempted to impose on schools the requirements of due process that *Goss* has imposed on American schools. And there is not much evidence that schools or districts have, on their own, adhered to even the minimal procedures that form part of due process. Even recourse to courts would perhaps help but little. As Horne (1972) pointed out, "The success of an action involving due process . . . would be doubtful because of the . . . lack of any guarantee that a person in Canada, student or otherwise, has a right to due process" (p.188).

4. *The right to reasonable treatment or protection.* Nevertheless, despite the absence of the due process requirement in schools, it would be unfair to suggest that schools have uniformly disregarded their duty to treat and protect students reasonably. The right of the public school pupil to receive from teachers and school board officials the care that a judicious parent would give to the child is firmly established. In fact, it seems that the "degree of care owed to school children by school authorities is of a higher degree than that required of an invitor towards an invitee" because the child is a "compulsee" (Bargen, 1961, p.156). While the courts require that causal relationships must be shown to exist between the action of the defendant and the injury to the plaintiff (pp.140-142), teachers and school boards have been found wanting in the exercise of reasonable care and thus have been declared negligent and liable (pp.143-156; also Nemirsky, 1972; Perry, 1975a, 1975b). There seems some evidence that, further, the degree of care expected is greater where the teacher claims or possesses special skill. This principle seems to have been followed in a recent case, *Thornton v. Board of School Trustees of School District No. 57 & David Edamura* (Perry, 1975b).

While common law is largely settled with reference to the obligations of teachers and school officials toward the physical well-being of pupils, a new area of concern is emerging. Currently being researched in the United States, this area includes the right to be free from the adverse consequences of certain educational practices – the use of assessment and classification procedures for students based on standard intelligence tests, and the implementation of certain within-school practices such as ability grouping, special education placement, and the exclusion of "ineducable" children (see Kirp, 1974; Mercer, 1974). The question being raised in the United States is, can these practices be encompassed by the constitutional provisions for equal protection and fair treatment? Again, in Canada, the absence of an overriding Bill of Rights militates against any move to explore the same question. Yet any suggestion that it had best be forgotten in this country should prove disturbing.

*Option Rights of Canadian Students*
The option rights that have been claimed by and for students in Canada might be classified into two kinds: those that are usually referred to as civil and political rights, and those that have come to be known as "academic freedom." Under the first are the freedoms that American courts have inclined to grant students – the rights to symbolic expression, to written expression, to personal appearance, including the determination of dress and hair length, to public education free from religious overtones, and to privacy in one's person and property. Under the second are the rights to participate in the determination of school policies and to engage freely in the pursuit of knowledge and truth.[5]

It is doubtful that student protest in Canada made much impact at all toward the attainment of the rights just noted. Yet the matter is an empirical one, and in the absence of thorough research, any definitive judgment must wait.

Certainly students have netted a few gains over the last few years, especially with regard to hair, dress, and smoking in predesignated areas. Further, school administrators are known to have started bringing at least selected students into deliberative processes relating to academic, curricular, disciplinary, and other matters. Yet student enjoyment of academic freedom has been uneven among schools, because boards have taken different policies concerning them. Moreover, the rights – if we might call them that – that students have secured appear to be trivial. When students pressed for significant rights, such as those contained in the Student Bill of Rights proposed for the public secondary schools in the city of Toronto, neither the local boards nor the provincial government would listen.[6] Given the lack of regard for student rights in general, it should not be surprising that any survey of student option rights should be brief, for there are very few rights to be accounted for.

But whether students should be granted option rights or not – certainly a controversial matter – it may be said that for the proponents of students' rights, it is on the matter of changing attitudes that they can pin their hopes. Since rights are institutionalized based on the prevailing social views, a better attitude on the part of the public and of the educators themselves should mean much. Such an attitude was evident during the period of protest, and there are signs that the attitude is still there. A survey of educational literature would reveal some sympathy for student rights, and, in Newfoundland, the teacher association has published a short document outlining its official policy on the rights and responsibilities of students (NTA Policy, 1975). Attitudes alone will not do it, however. Just as legal positivists are wont to do, we also have to ask, how can we assure the enforcement of student rights in Canada?

**Justifying Student Rights in Canada**
Many claims made by or for students clearly do not have any basis in law, and thus there is a sense in which we can deny such claims. This point is not lost among the advocates of student rights in Canada. The thrust of their activities has therefore been to have appropriate authorities recognize their claims to certain rights and to have them fully legalized whether on the school board or the provincial level. It seems that for maximum effect, these activities must satisfy two steps: (1) the justification of the rights claimed, particularly if these rights go counter to established practice; and (2) the institutionalization of the rights, together with the sanctions appropriate to them. That nothing much has come out of present advocacies could perhaps be attributed, at least partially, to the confusion that attends the attempts to undertake both steps. In this section, I concentrate on the first step.

Generally, claims are advanced as if they were all of one piece – i.e., as if they had the same justification and as if they should be sanctioned in the same way. I am inclined to think that convincing the Canadian public as well as the proper authorities about the need to establish student rights requires different justifications, depending on the rights being sought.

At the outset, it should be obvious that while Canadian students have a dearth of legal rights, they can lay claim to other rights on non-legal grounds. Against the positivistic view that claimed rights are rights only if sanctions are available from the law, we can insist together with Benn and Peters (1965) that assertions attributing "rights" state or apply rules. If there are non-legal rules, then there can be non-legal rights. In their words, "it follows that there is no contradiction in saying that while 'X has a right to R' is invalid in law, it is valid in morals" (p.109). Rights and obligations arise not only in the law but also in morals. Student claims to rights may be seen, therefore, as claims that morally students are entitled to certain rights and that educators are under moral obligation to respect them.

Yet even if it is agreed that students may be said to have entitlements to rights in the non-legal sense, the problem is far from settled. Quite obviously, the rules that exist at any given time are usually determined by adults or are dependent on adult standards. In a traditionally conservative society, such as Canada (see Lipset, 1970), the existing rules may reflect the adult perception that students are not entitled to any extensive rights. Thus the advocates of student rights have to assume a posture not unlike that of crusaders. Their task becomes that of convincing the majority about the acceptability, and perhaps the superiority, of their position. It is, in other words, that of justification.

### Justification of Students' Welfare Rights

As "goods of life which are conferred by the social ideal of a community," welfare rights ought not to arouse much opposition. In fact, the force of social ideals in Canada, as in most civilized countries, has resulted in the institutionalization of the rights to education and to reasonable care and protection from harm. Unfortunately, the same social ideals have not sanctioned the rights to procedural due process and to protection from emotional or psychological harm, and the right to educational equality. A quick look into their justification seems in order.

1. *The rights to procedural due process and to protection from emotional or psychological harm.*[7] Whether the doctrine of *in loco parentis* is a sound one or not, a good cause can be made for some form of paternalism in schools. If defined as "the protection of individuals from self-inflicted harm, or their direction towards their own good or interests" (Downie et al., 1974, p.109), paternalism is not altogether an objectionable feature of schools, Canadian or otherwise. Clearly, expertise and informed judgment have to prevail in the determination of arrangements and policies in them.

Sadly, however, the working of schools in reality reveals educational policies or decisions that may not be for the good of students. Increasingly, such practices as suspension, expulsion, psychological punishments, streaming, exclusion of ineducable children, and special education placement are seen for what they sometimes are—decisions for students that have long-term harmful consequences for them. The call for due process, therefore, is not so much a challenge to educational authority as a recognition of the fact that, in some cases, authorities can be wrong. In such cases, the absence of due process provisions leaves almost completely locked any door for the redress of student grievances. There is thus some ground for instituting in Canadian schools certain minimal requirements of due process, similar to what *Goss v. Lopez* has imposed on American schools. Years before this landmark decision, Seavey (1968) put forward, in a rather impassioned manner, the case for student due process:

"At this time . . . when we proudly contrast the full hearings before our courts with those in the benighted countries which have no due process protection . . . our sense of justice should be outraged by denial to students of the normal safeguards. It is shocking that the officials of a state educational institution . . .

should not understand the elementary principles of fair play. It is equally shocking to find that a court supports them in denying to a student the protection given to a pickpocket.

For it must be noted that the harm to the student may be far greater than that resulting from the prison sentence given to a professional criminal." (pp.3-4)

2. *Equality of educational opportunity.* It might appear too hasty to assume the right to education in light of varied views about the basis of that right (see, e.g., Crittenden, 1973; Melden, 1973; Olafson, 1973). Nevertheless, while they do have varying emphases, a common claim among them is that education is a good (at least instrumentally) that individuals need in order to further their pursuit of other social goods. I do not think that the case for education, as a welfare right, has to be pushed farther than that. Perhaps naively, I am also inclined to believe that the theoretical justification for the equality of educational opportunities need not be a controversial one. In a democratic society dedicated, at least ideally if not actually, to the principle of egalitarianism, the case for the right to equality of educational opportunity (and also the right to equal protection from harm) derives from the principle of formal justice – defined by Perelman (1963) as that "principle of action in accordance with which beings of one and the same essential category must be treated in the same way" (p.16). Since it would be difficult to show differences between Canadian students that are relevant to their claim to the enjoyment of equal educational opportunities, presumption would seem to be in favor of equality.

The problems confound us, however, when we start asking the substantive question: what would constitute equality of educational opportunity?

A thoroughgoing response to this complex question could be pursued until opposing views are reached concerning our evaluative judgments on the nature of society and human life we ultimately incline toward, and concerning their ramifications for educational provisions. At this point, the notion of educational equality becomes too broad for us to grasp. In fact, it is not clear that, at this stage, we are talking of schooling at all. Without presenting an argument for it, it would seem advisable that the concept of equal educational opportunity be restricted in scope to exclude environmental factors that affect students' use of educational opportunities or provisions. It is not that the two are separable; it is only that unless we are to radically alter our socioeconomic and political arrangements, schooling in its present form is likely to be with us for a long while. In that case, good strategy suggests working for as much reform as possible within the present educational structures, even as society struggles to determine for itself the kind of society it wants to be. Given this, it does not seem inappropriate to accept Fleming's (1974) perception of the way in which equal educational opportunity is conceived in Canada:

"(i) the provision of facilities and programs of equal quality and variety for 'normal' individuals regardless of differences in physical location or social and economic circumstances; and (ii) the provision of special assistance to individuals with obvious intellectual, emotional, physical, or cultural handicaps to enable them to take advantage of educational opportunities." (p.125)

If this conception is granted, at least until we are prepared to accept more demanding conceptions,[8] we arrive at another crucial problem: how do we go about requiring that steps be undertaken to achieve equality of educational opportunities? If it is true, as Manley-Casimir and Housego (1970) pointed out, that "equality has not played an important operational role in the evolution of the Canadian political tradition," and that the recent enunciations of the federal government in Canada that the equalization of opportunity as one of its major responsibilities will most likely meet with strong resistance (pp.190-205), what would be the most effective means to bring equalization about?

## Justification of Students' Option Rights

The sphere of option rights, Golding (1968) noted, involves the exercise of one's sovereignty over oneself, over one's possessions, and over persons (and their things) who, because of valid agreements (e.g., contracts, promises), have surrendered at least part of their own sovereignty to one. John Stuart Mill (1961) lengthily argued the justification for these rights in establishing his view that:

"The sole end for which mankind are warranted individually or collectively, in interfering with the liberty of action of any of their number, is self-protection. That the only purpose for which power can be rightfully exercised over any member of a civilized community, against his will, is to prevent harm to others." (p.263) (See also Radcliff, 1966.)

This is not the place to carry on a defense of Mill's principle. The important point is that such an extremist in the matter of rights as Mill saw fit to deny freedoms to children or young persons below the age that the law may fix as that of manhood or womanhood. For him, those who are still in a state to require being taken care of by others must be protected against their own actions as well as against external injury. He goes on to say:

"Despotism is a legitimate mode of government in dealing with barbarians, provided the end be their improvement, and the means justified by actually effecting that end. Liberty, as a principle, has no application to any state of things anterior to the time mankind have become capable of being improved by free and equal discussion." (p.263)

There is no doubt that Mill requires of a free person the element of rational judgment as he speaks of his doctrine applying only to human beings who possess "maturity of their faculties." It is equally clear that he sees this rational judgment as instrumental when people make up their own minds with regard to truths, values, and styles of living.

It is also important to note that Mill's view about the need for mature rational judgments coincides with certain presuppositions in common law. The common law, O'Sullivan (1950) observed, "starts with man as he is . . . as a reasonable being: the reasonable man of the law." It might not correspond to our experience of human beings, but for the law, every individual is "a reasonable man" (pp.17-18).

Furthermore, this view underlies much of the accepted arrangements related to western penal law. It is by virtue of man's capacity for rational judgments that we ascribe to persons responsibility and mete out punishments. As Hart (1968) noted,

"In all advanced legal systems liability to conviction for serious crimes is made dependent, not only on the offender having done those outward acts which the law forbids, but on his having done them in a certain frame of mind or with a certain will. These are the mental conditions or 'mental elements' in criminal responsibility and, in spite of much variation in detail and terminology, they are broadly similar in most legal systems." (p.187)[9]

The granting of option rights therefore presupposes a prerequisite, namely, a presumed rationality on the part of those to whom the rights are granted.

Thus from the perspective of our moral–legal traditions, the position taken by the majority of the U.S. Supreme Court in *Tinker v. Des Moines* and in *Wood v. Strickland* should be disturbing. A general claim that students and children are also "constitutional persons" under the law in the sense that they have constitutional rights is not objectionable in itself. What is objectionable is the court's holding that, as constitutional persons, students are entitled to such option rights as freedom of speech, of assembly, and the like, and not only to such welfare rights as due process. If it is true that the exercise of option rights depends on one's possession of reason or autonomy, Justice Stewart appears to be on firmer grounds than the majority represented by Justice Fortas. While agreeing with the *Tinker* (1969) decision, Justice Stewart nevertheless insisted:

"I cannot share the Court's uncritical assumption that . . . the First Amendment rights of children are co-extensive with those of adults. . . . [A] state may permissibly determine that, at least in some precisely delineated areas, a child . . . is not possessed of that full capacity for individual choice which is the presupposition of First Amendment guarantees." (p.515)

In rendering his judgment, Justice Fortas commented that "the Constitution says that Congress (and the States) may not abridge the right to free speech. This provision means what it says." The principle enunciated here may be valid, but it seems it is applied in the wrong case. While Justice Stewart saw the issue, Justice Fortas missed it and, without much justification for a new doctrine, simply declared that children are in full possession of option rights. With the court having just rendered a contrary judgment (*Ginsberg v. New York* 360 U.S. 629) during the preceding term, it is not surprising that even Justice Stewart should be taken aback.

What is being said at this point is that in light of previous court decisions and of prevailing social arrangements, both of which make a distinction between children and adults in the exercise of option rights, a departure such as *Tinker*'s requires a thorough justification.

At least three justifications may be explored briefly in this regard.
1. The first would grant that the exercise of option rights might depend on the possession of rationality, yet would insist that the age of legal majority at which students are granted option rights is obsolete. The claim would be made that in our media-oriented society, formal education (through schools) and informal education (through the media, peer group, the community, etc.) have become so pervasive that younger people do mature mentally faster than they used to. If this is so, then they deserve option rights presently denied them.

Unfortunately, even if it were true that children mature early in our society, the argument does not justify the indiscriminate granting of option rights to children. All it could allow is the lowering of the age of majority. Yet even this more modest conclusion should be taken with caution in light of the available studies based on the views of Kohlberg (1968; Kohlberg & Turiel, 1971). If it is true that it is only during the latter part of adolescence that independent moral judgments are resorted to, then there can be genuine doubts about students' readiness for option rights. In view of the increasing complexity of the problems that confront each individual in the present time, the case for lowering the age of legal majority (let us say below 18) might well remain a controversial one.

2. A more radical justification rests on the claim that we ought to reverse the presumption of incompetence on the part of children. The ground for reversal would lie on the view that, on the one hand, we have underestimated children, and, on the other, have overestimated the quality of help we can offer them (Adams et al., 1971; Holt, 1974). The thesis, as Holt put it, is that "the rights, privileges, duties, and responsibilities of adult citizens be made *available* to any young person, of whatever age, who wants to make use of them" (p.1).

Without dealing extensively with Holt's presentation of his case, I might point out why his position is suspect: (a) As Hare (1976) showed persuasively, Holt cripplingly fails to make distinctions between crucial concepts such as judgment and intuitive guesswork, wants and needs, hurts and harms, and instinctive and learned curiosities; (b) with dramatic yet limited examples, Holt generalizes a good deal, as if his examples were sufficient to establish his generalizations; and (c) Holt assumes a fallacious either–or dichotomy when he says, "The only way we can fully protect someone against his own mistakes and the uncertainties of the world is to make him a slave" (1974, p.57).

Holt's position may be made palatable by holding that children are possessors of full civil and political rights, although their exercise will be regulated by the courts or other proper authorities (Rodham, 1973). The "regulation of their exercise" aspect of this modified position appears to take away the radical tinge in the Holt position. Nevertheless, it remains unacceptable because it begs the whole issue: why accept the assumption that children are possessors (or ought to possess) option rights?

3. Rather than insist that students are entitled to option rights, the third justification (which I am inclined to favor) would argue that students can justifiably claim rights comparable to the option rights of adults. These rights, however, are more properly called developmental rights.

The justification suggested here maintains that insofar as our society is committed to a democratic way of life, one of the primary aims of schools ought to be the development of rational and autonomous individuals. Insofar as our political system grants adults option rights, then it becomes imperative that our schools develop adults who can seriously and intelligently exercise those rights – who are, in short, the reasonable men and women of the law.

When the process of schooling is seen as working toward individuals who think and act as a result of their "own choices, deliberations, decisions, reflections, judgments, plannings, or reasonings,"[10] based on the best available evidence, every student may be seen in the appropriate light. "The student," as Strike (1973) observed, "may be regarded as an apprentice libertarian attempting to internalize the standards and practices of a certain political form of life."[11] In the internalization of such standards and practices, educators are under obligation to develop in students appropriate skills and knowledge. While this is an entirely empirical claim, it would seem that to achieve this goal, educators need to provide for conditions under which the skills and the knowledge can be exercised. But further, since the development of rational and autonomous individuals involves the predisposition or inclination to use knowledge and skills as situations require, educators must establish an atmosphere of freedom. Altogether, there seem to be good reasons to agree that, "If . . . students are to become citizens trained in the democratic process, they must be given every opportunity to participate in the school and in the community with rights broadly analogous to those of adult citizens" (American Civil Liberties Union, 1969, p.9).

It is, however, important to stress that the rights are merely broadly analogous to the option rights of adult citizens. The developmental rights demanded for students in this paper differ from option rights in at least three ways. (a) Developmental rights will be limited in their scope or expression. As Green (1971) pointed out, "The institutions of teaching . . . embody some elements in the behavior of civilized men, and they do describe some indispensable ingredients of any society that seeks to civilize its people" (p.224). Therefore, schools are, or ought to be, deliberative institutions that function by virtue of reason. If this is so, could there be a place in them for armbands, placards, picketing, sit-ins, demonstrations, and the like, each of which is a practice "which tests not reason and integrity but strength and desire" (pp.223-224)? (b) Developmental rights, unlike option rights, may not be granted in a wholesale manner. The determination of just what rights may be given to students depends, to a large extent, on empirical considerations, i.e., on whether the rights to be granted would on balance achieve the formation of the autonomous person. (c) Finally, the implementation of developmental rights will depend to a great extent on the vision and enlightenment of educators themselves. In a very real sense, it will require autonomy on the part of educators to determine what is educationally the fitting thing to do. Obviously, this is quite consistent with the tradition of common law in Canada.

## Institutionalizing Student Rights in Canada
The enforcement of student rights in this country is best understood in the context of a society in which basic rights are being claimed as guaranteed rights without much success. The ineffectiveness of the Canadian Bill of Rights as a judicial instrument for securing individual rights has prompted Trudeau (1968) and like-minded legal scholars to propose what is known as "entrenchment" of the Bill. This would serve, as he sees it, "to withdraw certain subjects (i.e., rights) from the vicissitudes of political controversy, to place them beyond the reach of majorities and officials, and to establish them as legal principles to be applied by the courts" (p.11). While it does not have a standard usage, "entrenchment" would consist of one or more constitutional amendments that would place the human rights so designated (e.g., the Canadian Bill of Rights) in those parts of the constitution most difficult of subsequent amendment (Smiley, 1975, p.89). It would prohibit either the federal parliament or any provincial legislature in the future from passing legislation taking away certain defined rights (Scott, 1968, p.24). As Smiley (1975) pointed out, "most provisions related to human rights . . . would necessarily be expressed in general language conferring on the courts of law the responsibility of defining and ranking rights in an ongoing process of judicial review of the constitution" (p.90). The net effect would be, as in the United States, a more active role for the judiciary, particularly the Supreme Court, in the establishment of rights not only for the population at large but also for students.

The case for and against judicial review has been extensively debated in the United States (see, e.g., Bickel, 1962; Forte, 1972; Levy, 1967) and in Canada. Whatever direction the debate has taken, there are two points that have to be made with reference to student rights. The first point should note that entrenchment of the Canadian Bill of Rights alone will perhaps not achieve our expectation that student rights will be enshrined as inviolable. The American experience is instructive in this regard. The denial by the Supreme Court that the right to educational opportunity is covered by the equal protection clause of the Fourteenth Amendment caught expectant reformers by surprise, and it was indeed a shocking letdown for egalitarians. If the student right to equal educational opportunities is to be assured, the present Canadian Bill of Rights has to be amended such that the right becomes explicitly embodied in the bill in a way that precludes subsequent doubt or need for interpretation about its meaning. No doubt, attempting to do so will occasion the need to determine the dimensions of this right – i.e., the conception we should give to it – and thus debate that will touch the core of Canadian values will have to to be undertaken.

In light of the previous discussion about the justification of option and welfare rights, the next point to be made is that perhaps it is best to include in the entrenched Bill of Rights only the welfare rights of students. (This is, of course, if entrenchment comes about at all.) The reason for this is roughly analogous to the reason given by Trudeau for the entrenchment of certain human rights. It is that such basic rights as the right to protection from harm and the right to educational opportunity provided in an equal manner should be withdrawn from vicissitudes or circumstances that are beyond student control, but are nevertheless within the realm of social action. However, it is not so obvious that certain option rights (such as civil and political ones) are crucial to students, whether as children or as students. In fact, as I showed earlier, there are good reasons for withdrawing from them such rights. Moreover, insofar as students have claim to rights roughly analogous to civil and political rights (we have referred to them as developmental rights), the determination of such rights is best left to those whose training and expertise allow them to make the most appropriate judgments possible.

It does not mean, however, that we are to leave student developmental rights to the whims and caprices of school officials and teachers. Insofar as the educational process is aimed at, among other things, the development of autonomy in students, then a measure of the good teacher is the teacher's capacity to contribute to that development; a measure of the good school is the degree to which it provides opportunities that are conducive to the autonomy of the student. In this regard, there is no reason why a move for more accountability should not produce teachers and school officials who are sensitive to and capable of meeting the need to provide for the developmental rights of children. Furthermore, possibilities exist by which students, teachers, and school officials can sit together to draw up statements outlining the rights and responsibilities of students.[12] These statements can then be made part of any school board's rules and regulations. Insofar as these rules and regulations have the force of law, they bind teachers, students, and officials alike – in a way most conducive to a civilized, cooperative atmosphere because everyone participated in their formulation. Should controversy arise in their implementation, recourse to the courts of law should be available. This, it seems, is as far as we need to go in the pursuit of students' developmental rights.

In the area of basic rights – including students' welfare rights – perhaps we require a much stronger approach. It is the nature of these rights that they have to be distributed in as equitable and as liberal a manner as possible. In a society that has pretensions to democratic principles and yet is characterized by undemocratic practices and institutions (Porter, 1971), more decisive and more reform-oriented action seems called for. In this light, entrenchment of rights becomes an attractive possibility.

## Notes

[1] The extent of student protest in the United States is common knowledge. In Canada, attempts have also been made to indicate the depth and breadth of this phenomenon (McGuigan, 1968; Reid & Reid, 1969).

[2] This point has been strongly emphasized by observers of the U.S. Supreme Court (Bickel, 1970; Cox, 1967).

[3] Typical among reasons for exemption are those acceptable in Alberta: (1) efficient instruction at home or elsewhere; (2) attendance in a private school; (3) mental or physical unfitness; and (4) special education needs, as determined by the school superintendent, that cannot be met by regular attendance (Nemirsky, 1971).

[4] The issue of what would constitute "equality of educational opportunity" is unresolved. Wise (1972) listed several definitions of this concept and examined whether the equal protection clause of the Fourteenth Amendment of the U.S. Constitution may be held to require substantial equalization of educational opportunities within the American states.

[5] A comprehensive study that attempted to draw a distinction between students' civil freedoms and academic freedoms was undertaken by myself several years ago (Magsino, 1973).

[6] An example of a serious attempt to have student rights legislated is the "Student Bill of Rights Proposed for the Public Secondary Schools in the City of Toronto: An Act Respecting the Rights and Responsibilities of Students."

[7] The two rights are treated here as one since legal research may yet reveal that they are similarly covered by the Fourteenth Amendment.

[8] A more stringent demand, for example, is the equalization of educational opportunity based on the equality of educational outcomes.

[9] It does not mean, of course, that the absence of the "mental elements" is sufficient for acquittal from charges. There are cases that fall under the doctrine of strict liability.

[10] Dearden (1972) has characterized the autonomous man. The phrase quoted in the article is borrowed from him.

[11] I have taken the liberty of using the terminology of Strike (1974) to refer to the freedoms I would provide students in schools.

[12] Student participation in the formulation of such statements is quite consistent with my view that enlightened educational practice aimed at autonomy of students should involve them not only in the determination of academic matters affecting them, but also in the framing of school rules and regulations.

## References

Adams, I., et al. *The real poverty report*. Edmonton: Hurtig, 1971.

American Civil Liberties Union. *Academic freedom in the secondary schools*. New York: The Union, 1969.

Anson, R. J. The educator's response to *Goss* and *Wood*. *Phi Delta Kappan*, 1975, **57**, 16-19.

Bargen, P. F. *The legal status of the Canadian public school pupil*. Toronto: Macmillan, 1961.

Benn, S. I., & Peters, R. S. *The principles of political thought*. New York: Free Press, 1965.

Bentham, J. Anarchical fallacies. In John Bowring (Executor), *Works of Jeremy Bentham*. New York: Russell & Russell, 1962.

Berkman, R. I. Students in courts: Free speech and the functions of schooling in America. *Harvard Educational Review,* 1970, **40**, 567-595.

Bickel, A. *The least dangerous branch*. Indianapolis: Bobbs-Merrill, 1962.

Bickel, A. *The Supreme Court and the idea of progress*. New York: Harper Torchbooks, 1970.

Blackstone, W. T. Human rights, equality, and education. *Educational Theory*, 1969, **19**, 288-298.

Cary, E. *What every teacher should know about student rights*. Washington, D.C.: National Education Association, 1975.

Cox, A. *The Warren court*. Cambridge, Mass.: Harvard University Press, 1967.

Crittenden, B. *Education and social ideals*. Don Mills, Ont.: Longman Canada, 1973.

Dearden, R. F. Autonomy and education. In R. F. Dearden et al. (Eds.), *Education and the development of reason*. London: Routledge & Kegan Paul, 1972.

Downie, R. S., et al. *Education and personal relationships*. London: Methuen, 1974.

Economic Council of Canada. Trends and regional differences in education. In H. A. Stevenson et al. (Eds.), *The best of times/the worst of times*. Toronto: Holt, Rinehart & Winston, 1972.

Fleming, W. G. *Educational opportunity: The pursuit of equality*. Scarborough, Ont.: Prentice-Hall, 1974.

Forte, D. (Ed.) *The Supreme Court in American politics*. Lexington, Mass.: D. C. Heath, 1972.

Gilbert, V. K., et al. *A hard act to follow*. Toronto: Guidance Centre, Faculty of Education, University of Toronto, 1973.

Golding, M. P. Towards a theory of human rights. *Monist*, 1968, **52**, 521-549.

Green, T. *The activities of teaching*. New York: McGraw-Hill, 1971.

Hare, W. Calling a halt. Paper presented at the Conference of the Canadian Society for the Study of Education, Quebec City, June 1976.

Hart, H. L. A. *Punishment and responsibility*. Oxford: Clarendon Press, 1968.

Holt, J. *Escape from childhood*. New York: Ballantine, 1974.

Horne, N. D. The education issue in the 1980's will be student rights. *British Columbia Teachers*, 1972, **51**, 186-188.

Humphreys, E. H. Equality? The rural-urban disparity in Ontario. In H. A. Stevenson et al. (Eds.), *The best of times/the worst of times*. Toronto: Holt, Rinehart & Winston, 1972.

Kirp, D. Student classification, public policy, and the courts. *Harvard Educational Review*, 1974, **44**, 7-52.

Kohlberg, L. The child as a philosopher. *Psychology Today*, 1968, 7, 25-30.

Kohlberg, L., & Turiel, E. Moral development and moral education. In G. Lesser (Ed.), *Psychology and the educational process*. Chicago: Scott Foresman, 1971.

Levy, L. W. (Ed.) Judicial review and the Supreme Court. New York: Harper Torchbooks, 1969.

Lipset, S. M. Revolution and counterrevolution: The United States and Canada. In O. Kruhlak et al. (Eds.), *The Canadian political process*. Toronto: Holt, Rinehart & Winston, 1970.

MacFeeley, R. W. The nuts and bolts of procedural due process. *Phi Delta Kappan*, 1975, **57**, 26.

Magsino, R. F. The courts, the university and the determination of student academic freedom. Unpublished doctoral dissertation, University of Wisconsin, Madison, 1973.

Manley-Casimir, M. E., & Housego, I. E. Conclusion: Equality of educational opportunity as social policy. In C. A. Bowers et al. (Eds.), *Education and social policy: Local control of education.* New York: Random House, 1970.

McGuigan, G. F. (Ed.) *Student protest.* Toronto: Methuen, 1968.

*McLeod v. Board of School Trustees of School District No. 20 (Salmon Arm)* 1952, 2 D.L.R. 562.

Melden, I. A. Olafson on the right to education. In J. F. Doyle (Ed.), *Educational judgements.* London: Routledge & Kegan Paul, 1973.

Mercer, J. A policy statement on assessment procedures and rights of children. *Harvard Educational Review*, 1974, **44**, 125-141.

Mill, J. S. On liberty. In M. Lerner (Ed.), *Essential works of John Stuart Mill.* New York: Bantam Books, 1961.

Nemirsky, J. Under the Act: Compulsory attendance of students. *Alberta School Trustee*, 1971, **41**, 18.

Nemirsky, J. A point of law: A question of liability. *Alberta School Trustee*, 1972, **42**, 17.

Newfoundland Teacher Association policy on student rights and responsibilities. *Newfoundland Teacher Association Bulletin*, 1975, **19**, 1.

Olafson, F. A. Rights and duties in education. In J. F. Doyle (Ed.), *Educational judgements.* London: Routledge & Kegan Paul, 1973.

Olthuis, J. A. A place to stand: A case for public funds for all public schools. In H. A. Stevenson et al. (Eds.), *The best of times/the worst of times.* Toronto: Holt, Rinehart & Winston, 1972.

Ontario Committee for Government Aid to Jewish Day Schools. Brief to Premier John Robarts. In H. A. Stevenson et al. (Eds.), *The best of times/the worst of times.* Toronto: Holt, Rinehart & Winston, 1972.

Ontario Separate School Trustees' Association. Equal opportunity for continuous education in separate schools in Ontario. In H. A. Stevenson et al. (Eds.), *The best of times/the worst of times.* Toronto: Holt, Rinehart & Winston, 1972.

O'Sullivan, R. *The inheritance of the common law.* London: Stevens, 1950.

Perelman, C. *The idea of justice and the problem of argument.* London: Routledge & Kegan Paul, 1963.

Perry, M. The legal status of the teacher in Newfoundland – the legal responsibilities of teachers for classroom supervision. *Newfoundland Teacher Association Bulletin*, 1975, **19**, 5. (a)

Perry, M. The legal status of the teacher in Newfoundland – supervision on school premises. *Newfoundland Teacher Association Bulletin*, 1975, **19**, 6. (b)

Porter, J. Social class and education. In B. Blishen et al. (Eds.), *Canadian society: Sociological perspectives.* Toronto: Macmillan, 1971.

Reid, T., & Reid, J. (Eds.) *Student power and the Canadian campus.* Toronto: Peter Martin, 1969.

*Riding v. Elmhurst School District No. 2*, 1927, 3 D.L.R. 173.

Rodham, H. Children under the law. *Harvard Educational Review*, 1973, **43**, 487-514.

Russell, P. Judicial power in Canada's political structure. In M. L. Friedland (Ed.), *Courts and trials*. Toronto: University of Toronto Press, 1975. Pp.75-88.

Schmeiser, D. A. Disadvantages of an entrenched Canadian Bill of Rights. *Saskatchewan Law Review*, 1968, **33**, 249-252.

Scott, F. R. Human rights in Canada. In, Discussions on human rights. Provincial Conference on Human Rights sponsored by the New Brunswick Human Rights Commission, Fredericton, Mar. 25-26, 1968.

Seavey, W. A. Dismissal of students: Due process. In J. W. Blair (Ed.), *Student rights and responsibilities*. Ohio: S. Rosenthal, 1968.

Smiley, D. Courts, legislatures, and the protection of human rights. In M. L. Friedland (Ed.), *Courts and trials*. Toronto: University of Toronto Press, 1975. Pp. 89-101.

Strike, K. A. Philosophical reflections on *Tinker v. Des Moines*. Paper presented at the 1974 Philosophy of Education Society Conference, Boston, Mass.

Tarnopolsky, W. S. A constitutionally entrenched charter of human rights – why now? *Saskatchewan Law Review*, 1968, **33**, 247-249.

Tarnopolsky, W. S. *The Canadian Bill of Rights*. Toronto: McClelland & Stewart, 1975.

*Thomas Arthur Hogan v. Her Majesty the Queen*. June 1974.

*Tinker v. Des Moines Independent Community School District*, 393 U.S. 503 (1969).

Toronto Alternate Press Service. *The student rights handbook for Metro Toronto*. Toronto: The Press Service, 1972.

Trudeau, P. E. *A Canadian charter of human rights*. Ottawa: Information Canada, 1968.

Weiler, P. *In the last resort*. Toronto: Carswell/Methuen, 1974.

*Wilkinson v. Thomas,* 1928, W.W.R. 700.

Wise, A. *Rich schools, poor schools*. Chicago: University of Chicago Press, 1972.

Wise, A. & Manley-Casimir, M. E. Law, freedom, equality – and schooling. In V. F. Haubrich (Ed.), *Freedom, bureaucracy and schooling*. Washington, D.C.: Association for Supervision and Curriculum Development, National Education Association, 1971. Pp. 46-73.

# School Discipline and Corporal Punishment: An American Retrospect

Donald R. Raichle/Kean College of New Jersey

A few years after the end of World War II, H. D. F. Kitto (1957) wrote in despair that, "The training in virtue, which the medieval state left to the Church, and the polis made its own concern, the modern state leaves to God knows what" (p.75). Perhaps he should have said to God and the public school, for the modern state has designed the school as its own instrument to transmit both its moral and its intellectual heritage to the next generation.

As modern heir to the responsibility of cultural transmission, the public school encounters dilemmas on several fronts. First, the institutions of family, church, and community, which previously shared this responsibility, have never yielded ground easily. Thus the school carries out its task in alternating accommodation and conflict with other institutions. Further, in a pluralistic society cultural conceptions of what is worth preserving and developing in the child necessarily differ.

Training in virtue has never been easy and when the societal view of virtue is undergoing rapid changes, and the society itself produces no easy consensus in evaluating those changes, the task becomes monumental. The modern state's implicit assumption of the existence of a common cultural heritage, readily accessible to the agents of its transmission, does not fit well with what occurs in the school. Indeed, the school necessarily reflects and responds to the values and experiences of many often incongruous social groups.

Shifting visions of child nurture, linked to different social experience and cultural values, have generated different theories and strategies of school discipline. Conflicting social and economic classes, religious denominations, and ethnic groups have all demanded the right to develop schools according to their own aspirations. Under the impact of these forces, in more than three centuries of American experience the image of the child and patterns of nurture and education have undergone considerable transformation. In addition, school discipline is further determined by the character of the teacher, who has not always been the community's ideal in knowledge, wisdom, or stature. The result is a varied rather than uniform history of educational ideals, particularly of school discipline.

A basic conflict of values exists in liberal society between the inculcation of its cultural heritage and the development of the child as a free individual. If the child is to be free, then coercion seems out of place. But passing on intact a moral and intellectual heritage requires limitations on freedom. The earlier traditional approaches to school discipline assumed that the child was to be fitted at all costs to the society, including the school. That we are confronted with a history of truancy, absenteeism, and child rebelliousness suggests that this approach engendered significant resistance and led to frequent confrontation. Thus the history of school discipline is in part a history of warfare with the child, and ideas of school nature as well as child nature must be explored to understand this war.

## The Colonies
The fierce passions of Calvinism have often been credited with making colonial New England schools grim places. Calvinists saw the child as a vessel of sin, "unspeakably wicked, estranged from God," whose independent will was in obstinate conflict with divine will. Therefore, they considered beating just, both as punishment and as a way to "break the will" in its resistance to the Lord. But New England churches also preached love for the child, and declared that to withhold love was to offend the Lord. Corporal punishment might be enjoined by Scripture, but Scripture also taught that the child was to be won by kindness. "Puritan education was intelligently planned, and the relationship between parent and child which it envisaged was not one of harshness and severity but of tenderness and sympathy" (Morgan, 1966, pp.103-108). Still, the Puritan approach provided sanction for corporal punishment even though accompanying constraints have sometimes been overlooked. Clearly, Calvinists were as ambivalent about the role of love and fear in child nurture as we are today. Moreover, the liberal use of corporal punishment in the colonies was far more widespread than Calvinism. Thus, we must turn to the general character of 17th- and 18th-century society and the shortcomings of the early American teacher to explain harsh disciplinary practices.

Among other things, 17th- and 18th-century society was hierarchical. We Americans have so long rejoiced in our egalitarian society that we sometimes forget that there was nothing egalitarian about social classes in the colonies. Although no titled aristocracy emerged in English America, a man of the lower orders (a servant, for example) did not equate himself with the owner of a freehold, who was worthy of the title "Goodman," and still less with one of "quality," entitled to a "Mr." before his name to betoken wealth, power, and position. Time and the American Revolution shook this hierarchy but did not destroy it. Indeed, in Massachusetts as well as in Virginia, the hierarchy lived on well into the national period, dictating that however broad the qualifications for the franchise and however widely the vote was used, people knew and accepted their place and did not presume to seek political office unless they had some claims to the status of the higher orders. "Go into every village of New England," wrote John Adams, "and you will find that the office of the justice of peace, and even the place of representative, which has ever depended only on the freest election of the people, have generally descended from generation to generation, in three or four families at most." This "deferential society" did not disappear until the Jacksonian upheaval (Pole, 1962). Until then, differences in status reflected reverence, respect, and even awe of birth and family.

As well as being hierarchical colonial society was coarse, not yet won over to gentility from its unruly medieval past or its frontier present. Even the godly Puritans could speak with a frankness that their Victorian descendants would have found scandalous (Morgan, 1966, p.63). That Shakespearean schoolboy "with his satchel and shining, morning face" might have worn a sword, and used it too, to threaten his schoolmaster. Schools in Europe collected arms from their charges at the door, but even this did not eliminate riots (Ariès, 1962, pp.315-

328). Like their parents who introduced slavery and the slave trade to America, 17th-century youths had strong stomachs. The gallows, the branding-iron, the pillory, and the whipping-post awaited the criminal, and the lash bit the bare backs of women as well as men. If one had intractable servants, one beat them. This was not merely punishment: it pointed up the relationship between the parties. Submission to a beating symbolized general submission to one's betters; humiliation served to remind inferiors of their station in life. The master swung the lash secure in the knowledge that all he asked was obedience, little enough because to deny it would shake the very order on which society was built. So it was with children, who owed no less obedience than servants. In both Massachusetts and Connecticut the law followed the Mosaic code in prescribing capital punishment for disobedient children, although the record does not show that it was ever actually implemented (Bailyn, 1960, p.23; Morgan, 1966, p.78). Presiding over schools were "schoolmasters," who, like all masters, had the responsibility of exacting obedience from their charges. And school methods did not soften the climate. Learning by rote was the mode. The pupil was either right or wrong: this was a moral as well as an intellectual distinction. The pupil who was wrong was at the same time guilty and a taste of the birch was the suitable punishment to lead to righteousness in the future.

Not only the rod but also numerous devices such as whispering-sticks, yokes, and unipods, one-legged stools on which miscreants balanced themselves (Chrisman, 1920, p.413), were employed to purge the offender of evil. The disciplining arm of the schoolmaster was further strengthened by psychological techniques: name-calling, the dunce-cap, and other means of shaming were standard. Fear prevailed in the classroom, on the plantation, on the ship, in the prison, in the army, and in the servants' quarters, and it was not unknown between parents and their children.

**The Early 19th Century**
In the national period, schools changed their character little at first. The Revolution may have weakened the hierarchical basis of this society but had not overthrown it (Greene, 1946, pp.313, 317-318; Main, 1965, pp.218-219). Deference to the higher orders continued well into the 19th century. The overt class system extended into the schools. Each church set up its own, and these schools divided as much as they united society. Nowhere did they have adequate public funds for their support. Free schooling was for paupers; the more well-to-do paid "rates" for the education of their children (Welter, 1962). Often dissolute, inebriate, and shiftless, the teachers in this society had low status, inadequate training, and little pay (Elsbree, 1939, pp.179-180, 272-282).

The second quarter of the 19th century saw the old social order demolished. The older generation had, wrote Horace Mann (1867),

"brought into active life strong hereditary and traditional feelings of respect for established authority, merely because it was established, – of veneration for law, simply because it was law, – and of deference both to secular and ecclesiastical rank, because they had been accustomed to revere rank. But scarcely any vestige of this reverence for the past now remains. The momentum of hereditary opinion is spent." (p.168)

Mann voiced here the malaise that lay behind so much Jacksonian reform. The expansion of the economy, industrialization, the growth of the wage-earning

110

class, the movement to the cities, the frontier, and a flood of immigration sapped the old order. The inauguration of Andrew Jackson symbolized the aspirations of the common man breaking old bounds. No longer content with the work of church and charity schools, the new America turned part of its energy toward building public schools. Where Jefferson had called for schools to *preserve* liberty, the newly articulate called for schools to *extend* liberty, to abolish class distinctions, and to guarantee social and economic equality. However, the aims of various dominant groups frequently differed. Businessmen wanted better educated and more orderly, disciplined workers; humanitarian reformers and societies thought schools could eliminate crime and poverty; church groups relied on the development of a common school to inculcate Christian morality and to teach the Bible (Welter, 1962). Mingled with these aims was the pervading anxiety of conservatives who had less and less confidence that the old institutions, such as family and church, could keep the fabric of society whole.

The character of the American schoolteacher changed along with the society. Less concerned with differences in status than their predecessors, most were young and viewed teaching as a temporary career. The men went on to what they regarded as more promising futures while the women gave up their teaching after they married. A Swedish observer of American antebellum schools, Per Adam Siljeström, thought these young people taught remarkably well, largely because of their warm feelings for children: they became elder brothers or sisters to the pupil (1853, p.184). Siljeström reminds us that teaching to the tune of the hickory stick was only one pattern. The informality, the spontaneity that characterized the family and other institutions in the United States (Calhoun, 1960, Vol.2, pp.51-56; Tocqueville, 1898, Vol.2, pp.233-239) also infiltrated the school. No doubt the harmony in relations between teacher and pupil would have extended further had not so many young teachers, tense and insecure because of their lack of training, relied on coercion simply because they did not know an alternative.

While remembering that writers on teaching theory do not provide precise pictures of classroom practice, we may assume that the social and intellectual ferment of the first half of the 19th century (Tyler, 1944) had an impact on the classroom. Early American writers on education were profoundly influenced by Locke, Rousseau, and Pestalozzi, who sought not only to mold the child but also to set him free. Such notions conformed with the humanitarian strivings of the time and were heard in the schools as elsewhere. Samuel Read Hall in 1829 pioneered the new approach, which finally dominated 20th-century education. Hall saw two kinds of teachers: the "pleasant and obliging," the "affable and condescending," the "affectionate and kind" as opposed to the "morose and ill-humored." Good teachers governed uniformly, firmly, and impartially. They did not act hastily, speak angrily, lose countenance in the face of an "insult from an inferior," or use "corporeal" punishment except as a last resort. The literature reminded beginners who were tempted to imitate the classroom despot that they were there not for their own benefit but for the children. "Think your way through it," commanded Hall (1832). "Endeavor to ascertain by what means you are to gain that ascendancy over your pupils, which is necessary, in order to confer on them the highest degree of benefit" (pp.31-45). The exhortation was authoritarian, but at the same time offered the teacher alternatives to severity.

But weakening of the formal trappings of social hierarchy in the early 19th century by no means spelled the end of class discrimination. Reference to common schools as "seminaries of vice" and the comment "he learned it at school" betrayed suspicion of the antecedents of some of the children who attended the common school (p.14). There is no reason to believe that teachers ordinarily dispensed the even-handed justice that Samuel Hall proposed. It would be idealizing to suppose that the ragged little boy from the working-class immigrant family received all the kindness bestowed on the tidy little girl with blonde curls whose origin was not only middle class but also "Anglo-Saxon" and Protestant.

Beyond class, ethnic, and religious concerns, the unspoken element in the debates about corporal punishment was the characteristically liberal idea that republican doctrines called for child nurture that would produce a free person, a free individual. However, Jacob Abbott, one of the most popular of the ante-bellum writers on child nurture, still laid it down as the first duty of the teacher "to obtain the entire, unqualified submission of his school to his *authority*" (1831, p.6). One need not adopt the "*tone and manner* of authority"; one might go about the business "in the easiest and pleasantest way you possibly can, but ... *make them obey*" (1834, p.16). Abbott's message was that the teacher had two simultaneous duties: to instruct and to govern. "It is this double attention which makes his life a weary one." Abbott's emphasis on the need to coerce illustrates the lack of solidity in the alliance between school and family. Abbott knew parents who did not require anything from the child "except what the child could understand and feel right," that is to say, parents who were led in their child-rearing more by the vision of the free individual than by a system of absolute values. This conflict tended to align school against home in the corporal punishment debate. As David Page (1838) pointed out, parents had an easier time with discipline than did teachers. Parents are absolute despots from whose sentence there is no higher court of appeal. From the family despot stemmed a threat not only of the rod but also of solitary confinement, even a diet of bread and water. Moreover, the despot had leisurely evenings as well as the day to devote to the business. Against this, the teacher's "authority ... is somewhat questionable." Usually restricted to a single room, he had no prison for solitary confinement and his writ did not run beyond school hours. Not for him the authority to dispense or withhold bread and water. And whatever his sentence, it was subject to challenge by the parent (pp.18-19). So went the argument.

The upshot was that school and family suffered the usual frictions of even the most successful alliances and often tended to take different sides of the corporal punishment argument. In Boston the teachers showed their strength by putting down attempts to abolish corporal punishment in the schools. New Jersey, where the teachers had comparatively little strength, abolished corporal punishment in 1867 in all schools, public and private, as a gesture to the protection of the family (Raichle, 1974). This is not to imply that the law was enforced or was even intended to be.

Hall, Abbott, and Page illustrate the softening approach to school discipline. Although they do not condemn corporal punishment, they begin to direct attention to the child's sensitivities, feelings, and interests. Obedience was still primary but might be won by kindness. People more favorable to the use of the rod perceived a parental tendency to permissiveness and thus they were suspicious of the new, liberalized, non-sectarian Protestant morality that came to dominate the common schools. Almost no one opposed corporal punishment absolutely, they opposed abuses of it. Writers on pedagogy in the 19th century, from Hall on, attacked the discipline that relies primarily on fear, shame, and ridicule, but they did not reject the rod as a last resort. Page carefully described the kinds of punishments that were improper but, typically, gave carefully measured approval to corporal punishment. Anathema he reserved for indignity against the person, such as wringing the nose, pulling the hair, tweaking the ear, snapping the forehead, scolding; punishments that betrayed a love for prolonged torture, such as holding weights at arms length or keeping the body in awkward positions for sustained periods; and, finally, ridicule.

Page had observed a teacher catch a child in a proscribed act without the child knowing that she had been seen. Calling her to the front of the room, the teacher asked the child what she had done. With all the innocence of the accused who counts on acquittal through lack of evidence, the child responded that she had done nothing. Then the heavens opened. In the presence of visitors the teacher very softly informed the child that she was shocked to learn that the child was a liar, that now all her classmates knew she was a liar, that in the teacher's judgment none of the other children would care to have anything more to do with her, and, finally, that the teacher should not be surprised if all the children were to point their fingers at her and hiss. Which, of course, the children enthusiastically proceeded to do. The terror, the panic, and the utter alienation of the child, Page (1867) persuasively argued, was far more traumatic than would have been the case had she been subjected to corporal punishment (pp.179-189). Cruelty, then, drew the attack, rather than what was deemed to be a discreet use of the rod of correction. Moreover, as in this case, the literature focused on the child's reaction, forcing the teacher to consider the child's feelings. The more the teacher identified with the child, the less likely it was that the child would be abused. This was most important. Mann (1867) claimed that adults typically had little empathy with children's complaints about corporal punishment. Adults thought of punishment lightly, spoke of it with amusement, and inflicted it liberally (p.357). There was a widespread adult attitude that child nurture was not an altogether serious business.

But for writers on educational theory it was, and the development of normal schools helped to disseminate their views more widely. Cyrus Peirce, first principal of the first state normal school in the country, taught his charges to exclude not only "all appeals to fear" but also to premiums or emulation (Barnard, 1851, p.61). The very idea of instruction in teaching opened up alternatives to corporal punishment; the missionary spirit of the normal schools tended to align them with the "soft-line educators"; Pestalozzi and object teaching shifted the thinking of the teacher to the humanity of the child (Woody, 1929, Vol. 1, p.476).

With the rise of the normal school, women began to replace men in the schoolroom early in the 19th century and they depended less than men on physical punishment in their classes. Writers on child nurture in the 1830s and 1840s stressed the need for "a new mother" who should lovingly implant all that is "sublime in morals" in the child (Wishy, 1968, p.28). In this context the schoolmistress was enjoined to serve as the loving mother surrogate. As boys seemed more in need of whipping than did girls, so stalking the classroom with rod in hand seemed less befitting to "delicate females" than to men. The trend was to emphasize what Barnard called "the silken cord of affection." Moreover, the attempt to extend family love to the school, the idea of a "family school," affected not only public schools but all-male establishments like boys' boarding schools (McLachlan, 1970, pp.86, 116-117).

Of course, theory outran practice. To know a better way is not necessarily to practice it or even to be able to practice it. Mann thought the discipline of the school should include self-discipline, that the school should be a training ground for self-government. "He who has been a serf until the day before his twenty-one years of age," he wrote in 1845, "cannot be an independent citizen the day after; and it makes no difference whether he has been a serf in Austria or America. . . . The fitting apprenticeship for self-government consists in being trained to self-government" (Welter, 1962, p.98). Jacob Abbott (1833) heartily approved the use of republican forms in the schools, but only forms; he warned against delegating any real authority (p.60). The Abbott formula won out in the high school in Hartford, Connecticut, where Siljeström reported that a court was established to be run by the students. The real power, however, remained with the teacher, who exercised an absolute veto. Whether or not this was *training* in self-government, self-government it certainly was not. As with so much theory militating against corporal punishment, circumstances dictated practice, and circumstances were often compelling.

Despite the powerful impact of humanitarianism, Mann showed why corporal punishment could not be eliminated entirely. The great mass of children "scooped up from all places" who flooded the common schools and the capacity of teachers "in the present condition of things" combined to make it impossible to keep the peace without punishment (1867, p.338). Mann (1845) summarized the "present condition of things" neatly in his final school report. He estimated that six years earlier in Massachusetts, 300 to 400 schools had been "broken up" either by the insubordination of scholars or by the incompetence of teachers. At the same time he announced with some pride that in the school year 1843-1844, only 43 schools were closed because of teacher incompetence and *only* seven by insubordination (p.67). As Massachusetts had established the first state normal school in 1839, and presumably had the best-trained corps of teachers in the country, the testimony forcefully suggests not only the low state of the teaching profession, but also the fury that the teacher faced on the other side of the desk. Small wonder that corporal punishment survived and that strict, almost military, discipline was often maintained. Pupils in at least one school changed from shoes to slippers inside the schoolhouse to ensure quiet. (The practice also kept the floors clean.) Extreme examples of insubordination on the part of pupils are matched by equally extreme punishments. But the liberalizing of religion, the strength of the desire to adjust child-rearing to the principles of a free society, and growing humanitarianism in the treatment of the physically and mentally afflicted and even of the criminal pointed the direction in tempering harsh discipline. The analogy between the family and the school attested the new direction. More could be done with love than with threats or force. Faced with anxiety about changes in society itself and about the relationship of the child to that society, the family offered the best model for the school to emulate. Educators in Upper Canada, for example, evidenced American influence in envisioning the family as the repository of the ideals the schools needed (Prentice, 1972). William A. Alcott summed up the new mood in 1843 in an article in *The Mother's Assistant* that he called "There is no School Like the Family School" (a title that, written a century later, might have been put to music).

## The Later 19th Century
After the Civil War people clung to their belief in the certainty of moral values and in the necessity to develop in children the free individualism that was equally, and paradoxically, part of the national heritage. True, the sanction for moral values was less conspicuously religious among the writers on child nurture, who increasingly turned to science for authority (Wishy, 1968, pp.106-107).

114

Francis Wayland Parker, called by John Dewey "the father of progressive education," illustrated the further development of the "soft line" when the school board of Quincy, Massachusetts, appointed him superintendent of schools in 1873. Abandoning the old curriculum and texts, Parker started children on words and sentences in place of the rote alphabet, taught arithmetic through material objects rather than abstract rules, and began geography with trips around the countryside (Adams, 1879). Whatever the final judgment on the "Quincy system" – and it has not lacked for critics – it did not make for routine use of the rod. And Parker's schools were not alone in the approach. Others appeared, such as Dewey's own Laboratory School; the schools of Menomenie, which influenced Canada's rural schools; and Marietta Pierce Johnson's Organic School in Fairhope, Alabama. These subverted the rigid formality and rote instruction under which corporal punishment flourished (Cremin, 1961, pp.127-160).

But tension over school discipline persisted within the school community, as an 1887-1888 report from Louisiana showed. There the state board of education stated its preference "above all others" for teachers who successfully maintained order without the use of corporal punishment, which drew an immediate reply from the Superintendent of Schools of New Orleans that such a rule did not mean that a teacher should prefer anarchy. In 1889, at a teachers' institute in New Jersey, Professor Emerson E. White of Cincinnati, next to William Torrey Harris the most frequent speaker in the history of the National Education Association, expounded the "hard line." He proposed that corporal punishment should be promoted from a last resort to a first resort. And White was not certain that "the will of the child is never to be curbed or checked." He disallowed the same kinds of punishments as Page in his antebellum textbook, and continued the argument of submission to rightful authority. But Page had played a liberalizing role in his day; White was reactionary. He emphasized the restraints a child needed while others spoke for release. However, his concern about suspension from school cut across hard and soft lines (*Newark Daily Advertiser*, June 1, 1889; Wesley, 1957, pp.167-168).

Suspension from school had emerged as an alternate method of discipline. No child could be permitted to disrupt the learning of other children and the unruly were exiled. This punishment might be used instead of corporal punishment or along with it (U.S. Commissioner, 1889, p.161). For many, including White, suspension was intolerable because it deprived the child of moral shelter from the vices of the world. This was a reprise of an old theme; in 1834, Abbott had warned parents about their children in imperative capital letters: "KEEP THEM OFF THE STREETS." To cast the child, especially the poor child, into the streets was to bequeath a crop of criminals to the future (p.16).

For those who rejected both the rod and suspension, there was a third choice. The "incorrigibles" must be kept out of the classroom so that other children might continue to learn, but also they must be kept off the streets. Special schools were designed and provided with special teachers, schools for "incorrigibles." Usually ungraded, these schools were to serve the double purpose of punishment and rehabilitation. Under the watchful eye of a skilled disciplinarian, the "incorrigibles" or habitual truants would be taught the error of their ways and, after redemption, returned to their original classroom. Such schools by their very existence were threats to the potential miscreant, but were not necessarily cruel. In at least some instances both theory and practice emphasized rehabilitation (Newark *Evening Star*, Jan. 13, 1913; Newark *Sunday Call*, Dec. 3, 1911).

115

William Torrey Harris exemplified the new rationale for those who continued to see obedience as the first demand of the schools. Harris, consolidator of the pioneer work of Horace Mann in universalizing education and a spokesman for the urban order that demanded the preservation of the status quo, called for an education system that would "cause the pupil to love to obey the law for the law's sake." The *Annual Report* of the Bureau of Education for 1887-1888, which defined "true discipline . . . as cheerful submission on the part of the scholar to his instructor, not from fear, but from love," summed up Harris's view. Such discipline could be effected not by inculcating a theoretical view of right and wrong but by developing the will into ethical habits, so that the obedience of the schoolroom extended progressively to parents, to employers, to the government, and to the divine will. Harris still sought to develop the inner-directed person in such a way that freedom stood for little more than freedom to obey. He did attack the frequent and severe use of corporal punishment; but after all, no one defended its frequent and severe use, and Harris was cited as a leading educator who defended the practice (Harris, 1888; Newark *Sunday Call*, Mar. 3, 1895). He represented a conservative, essentially authoritarian approach to the problems of a rapidly growing urban school system, which seemed increasingly threatening. More and more children stayed longer and longer in schools; bigger boys tended to challenge the order of the classroom and the physical prowess of the teacher.

In contrast to Harris, G. Stanley Hall, pioneer in educational psychology and leader of the "child study movement," rationalized the new "soft" line. Like Harris and a host of predecessors, he cited religious sanction, but his shift to science was pronounced. Harris saw the school as preserving the ancient wisdom of the race, hence the necessity of fitting the child to the school. Hall proceeded from a psychological stance that made the child the center of the school and argued that the school must begin with a study of the child, based on the child's individual background and needs (Hall, 1901). The impact of this view on the American school strengthened the hand of Parker and other progressives and laid more groundwork for the philosophy that John Dewey later developed. Unswerving obedience in this context no longer took center stage. Teachers became "defenders of the happiness and rights of children." To teach children one must know and love them, in all their mysteries, not beat them. The choice between beating and suspension thus shifted to a debate between coercion and winning children by offering them a program suited to their needs, as well as renewed emphasis on motivation through approval from both teacher and peer group.

Meanwhile, a new problem had emerged toward the end of the 19th century, as the country made its first attempt to cope with the large-scale education of black children. Educators cited experience with these children in Reconstruction schools to show that corporal punishment was unnecessary in any school. Reverend J. F. Ware, in charge of Freedman's Schools in Maryland, reported that "in dealing with a degraded race we took at once a stand *against the rod* and it worked" (Massachusetts Education Committee, 1868, p.29). As the quotation indicates, discipline was among the least of the problems with blacks, who were shortchanged among other things in teacher training, curriculum, and, of course, financing. Although black children increasingly stayed longer in school and expenditures for their education rose, the per capita expenditure for them was still about one-fourth that for whites in 1930. By that time, 20% of black children were in Northern cities, evidence of the first step in their large-scale migration (Woofter, 1934, pp.586-588).

Oppressed politically, economically, and socially in both the North and the South, blacks adopted a pattern of at least outward conformity, together with a healthy skepticism toward both the white world and those blacks who advocated resistance (Clift, Anderson, & Hullfish, 1962, pp.28-31). Before the vast changes that, although rooted in the early 20th century, took little overt form until after World War II, the black child was not a major discipline problem. In 19th-century Newark, New Jersey, for example, fewer whippings were administered per capita to black children in the colored school than to white children in the rest of the system. In the school year 1875-1876, teachers reported whippings of 9 408 white children out of an average daily attendance of 9 527. For the colored school, the figures were 72 out of 117.[1] A century later, black educators, discussing corporal punishment as it affects black children, point out that the threat facing black youngsters in the American South is not so much that they will be beaten as that they will be suspended or expelled, depriving them of the benefits of the school (*New York Times*, May 8, 1972). In other words, they repeat for black children the apprehension expressed for white children by every generation of educators since Horace Mann.

**The 20th Century**

Although corporal punishment continued into the 20th century, its scope, type, and severity contrast sharply with that of the late 19th. Mark Sullivan (1927) recorded some odious stories that public men told him of harsh school discipline they knew as boys in the 1880s. Former Associate Justice John H. Clarke of the Supreme Court of the United States held that the kind of discipline he knew as a boy would be "thought 'cruel and unusual punishment' in any school today" (pp.136-142). Better trained teachers, growing humanitarianism, an increased knowledge of the social situation and the psychology of the child, and family attitudes more critical of the school, all have tended to discourage swinging of the rod. Yet Judd (1934) went too far in his claim that by the 1930s "harsher forms of punishment [had] entirely disappeared from the school."

Openly and covertly, flogging continues today. Like their predecessors of the 19th century, today's teachers are unwilling to abandon corporal punishment. In 1961 the National Education Association favored it by a three-to-one margin. Since then, both teachers and the community have argued for greater severity. In the five years up to 1971 the number of schools using corporal punishment tripled, and the use of corporal punishment is even negotiated in teacher contracts (National Education Association, 1969, p.59). In such a climate, the movement to outlaw corporal punishment throughout the country has met little success. The U.S. Supreme Court has broken ground in upholding due process for students in disciplinary procedures, but has refused to outlaw corporal punishment in the schools.

Massachusetts lined up with New Jersey in 1972 as only the second state to ban corporal punishment in the schools by statute. Maryland has since passed similar legislation. More usually, where the practice is banned it is done by regulation of the board of education. Countering this is the upsurge in the use of corporal punishment in the last decade (Raichle, 1974).

In September 1975, Gene I. Maeroff wrote in the *New York Times*, "Dealing with disruptive pupils in a legal and educationally sound manner is one of the great challenges facing the schools in these troubled times." True this statement may be, but it is not new; it is as old as the public schools. Only the word "legal" has a current ring, reflecting the comparatively recent court advocacy of extending due process to children. This is one of the more hopeful signs. The uneasy alliance in child nurture between home and school shows increasing strains. Corporal punishment and suspension come under more and more criticism on grounds of both substance and procedure. Never were parents or teachers more litigious, and parents never more prone to press differences with schools through the courts. The new emphasis on due process for students, although complicating the immediate problem of school discipline, makes a real contribution to the education of free citizens and, in the end, minimizes the friction between parent and teacher. Also subject to increasing criticism are ineffective and inflexible school programs, the effectiveness of communication among school, parents, and community, and the capacity of the schools to serve the varying needs of the children in a pluralist society. These, too, must be weighed as factors that influence the disciplinary problems facing teachers. The school cannot in justice hold the child accountable unless the school itself is adequately designed and capable of carrying out its own mission. It has always been true that in the end the community itself must sanction whatever discipline is to characterize the public school. To win that sanction in a day when authority of every kind is under seige, when the problem of sheer mass seems to dwarf individual effort, when the community seeks to implement ideals of equality on a scale not hitherto attempted, when absolutism has been washed out of the truth in the moral heritage, the schools face a challenge greater than any they have known in the past.

## Notes

The author owes a considerable debt to Robert J. Fridlington for substantive suggestions and for incisive criticism of a preliminary draft.

[1] Newark Board of Education, Minutes in manuscript in the office of the Secretary to the Board, Oct. 26, 1876 reports the number of whippings in each school for the year ending June 30, 1876. Board of Education *Annual Report*, 1876, p.16 gives average attendance for the same period.

## References

Abbott, J. *A lecture on moral education*. Boston: Hilliard, Gray, Little and Wilkins, 1831.

Abbott, J. *The teacher: Or moral influences employed in the instruction and government of the young*. Boston: Peirce and Barker, 1833.

Abbott, J. *The duties of parents in regard to the schools where their children are instructed*. Boston: Tuttle and Weeks, 1834.

Adams, C. F., Jr. *The new departure in the common schools of Quincy*. Boston: Estes and Lauriat, 1879.

Adorno, T. W. *The authoritarian personality*. New York: Norton, 1950.

Anonymous. Suasion with a trunk-strap. *Literary Digest*, 1925, **85**, 33.

Ariès, P. *Centuries of childhood*. New York: Vintage, 1962.

Bagley, W. C. *School discipline*. New York: Macmillan, 1964.

Bailyn, B. *Education in the forming of American society*. New York: Norton, 1960.

Barnard, H. *Normal schools*. Hartford, Conn.: Case, Tiffany, 1851.

Barnes, E. Corporal punishment as a means of social control. *Education*, 1898, **13**, 387-395.

Calhoun, A. W. *A social history of the American family.* Cleveland: A. H. Clark, 1915-1918. 3 vols. (Reprinted New York: Barnes and Noble, 1960.)

Chrisman, O. *The historical child.* Boston: Gorham Press, 1920.

Clift, V. A., Anderson, A. W., & Hullfish, H. G. *Negro education in America.* New York: Harper, 1962.

Cobb, L. *The evil tendencies of corporal punishment as a means of moral discipline in families and schools, examined and discussed.* New York: Mark H. Newman, 1847.

Cremin, L. *The American common school: An historic conception.* New York: Teachers College, 1951.

Cremin, L. *The transformation of the school.* New York: Knopf, 1961.

Davis, H. H. Corporal punishment and suspension. *School and Society*, 1928, **28**, 632.

Elsbree, W. S. *The American teacher: Evolution of a profession in a democracy.* New York: American, 1939.

Falk, H. A. *Corporal punishment.* New York: Teachers College, 1941.

Goldstein, W. Discipline: For someone else's kid. *The Clearing House*, 1973, **47**, 455-458.

Greene, E. B. *The revolutionary generation, 1763-1790.* New York: Macmillan, 1946.

Hall, G. S. The ideal school as based on child study. *National Education Association Journal of Proceedings and Addresses*, 1901, pp.474-488.

Hall, S. *Lectures on schoolkeeping.* (4th ed.) Boston: Richardson, Lord and Holbrook, 1832.

Harris, W. T. *Moral education in the common schools.* Washington, D.C.: U.S. Government Printing Office, 1888.

Hess, W. L. Corporal punishment. *The school news of New Jersey*, 1914, **4**, 5-6.

Hofstadter, R. *Anti-intellectualism in American life.* New York: Knopf, 1963.

Judd, C. H. Education, President's Research Committee on Social Trends. *Recent social trends in the United States.* New York: McGraw-Hill, 1934. Pp.325-381.

Katz, M. B. *The irony of early school reform.* Cambridge: Harvard University Press, 1968.

Kitto, H. D. F. *The Greeks.* (2d ed.) Baltimore: Penguin, 1957.

Landon, J. *School management.* (2d ed.) Syracuse: C. W. Bardeen, 1903.

Main, J. T. *Social structure of revolutionary America.* Princeton, N.J.: Princeton University Press, 1965.

Mann, H. *Eighth annual report of the board of education together with the eighth annual report of the secretary of the board.* Boston: Ditton and Wentworth, 1845.

Mann, H. *Lectures and report on education.* Cambridge: Author, 1867.

Massachusetts Education Committee. *Reports on the abolition of corporal punishment in the public schools.* Document No. 35. Boston: Wright and Patten, 1868.

May, H. F. *The end of American innocence: A study of the first years of our own time.* New York: Knopf, 1959.

McLachlan, J. *American boarding schools.* New York: Scribner, 1970.

Morgan, E. S. The Puritans and sex. *New England Quarterly*, 1942, **15**, 591-607.

Morgan, E. S. *Virginians at home.* Charlottesville: University of Virginia Press, 1952.

Morgan, E. S. *The puritan family.* New York: Harper & Row, 1966.

Newark Superintendent of Schools. Minute book of committee on teachers.

National Education Association. *Bulletin,* 1969, **47**, 59.

Nye, R. B. *Society and culture in America, 1830-1860.* New York: Harper & Row, 1974.

Page, D. P. *The mutual duties of parents and teachers.* Boston: William D. Ticknor, 1838.

Page, D. P. *Theory and practice of teaching, or the motives and methods of good schoolkeeping.* (90th ed.) New York: A. S. Barnes, 1867.

Parker, F. W. *Talks on teaching.* New York: A. S. Barnes, 1883.

Parker, F. W. *Talks on pedagogics.* New York and Chicago: E. L. Kellogg, 1894.

Pole, J. R. Historians and the problems of early American democracy. *American Historical Review,* 1962, **68**, 626-646.

Prentice, A. Education and the metaphor of the family: The Upper Canadian example. *History of Education Quarterly,* 1972, **12**, 281-303.

Raichle, D. R. The abolition of corporal punishment in New Jersey schools. *History of Childhood Quarterly,* 1974, **2**, 53-78.

Rapson, R. L. The American child as seen by British travellers, 1845-1935. *American Quarterly,* 1965, **17**, 520-534.

Reisman, D., Glazer, N., & Denney, R. *The lonely crowd: A study of the changing American character.* (Rev. ed.) Garden City, N.Y.: Doubleday, 1953.

Siljeström, P. A. *Educational institutions of the United States.* London, England: John Chapman, 1853. (Reprinted New York: Arno Press, 1969.)

Stearns, L. E. The question of discipline. In A. I. Hazeltine (Ed.), *Library work with children: Reprints of papers and addresses.* White Plains and New York: H. W. Wilson, 1917. Pp. 223-228.

Sullivan, M. *Our times.* Vol. 2. *America finding herself.* New York: Scribner's, 1927.

Tocqueville, A. de. *Democracy in America.* New York: Century, 1898. 2 vols.

Tyler, A. F. *Freedom's ferment.* Minneapolis: University of Minnesota Press, 1944.

United States Commissioner of Education. *Annual Report 1887-1888.* Washington, D.C.: U.S. Government Printing Office, 1889.

Welter, R. *Popular education and democratic thought in America.* New York: Columbia University Press, 1962.

Wesley, E. B. *NEA: The first hundred years.* New York: Harper, 1957.

Wishy, B. *The child and the republic.* Philadelphia: University of Pennsylvania Press, 1968.

Woody, T. *Women's education in the United States.* Lancaster, Pa.: Science Press, 1929. 2 vols.

Woofter, T. J. The status of racial and ethnic groups, President's Research Committee on Social Trends. *Recent social trends in the United States.* New York: McGraw-Hill, 1934. Pp.553-601.

# A Case Study Approach to Discretion in School Discipline

Michael E. Manley-Casimir/Simon Fraser University

*"Report to the office!" The teacher's command cracks out like a rifle shot across the classroom. The unfortunate student, target of the teacher's wrath, rises, ambles towards the door, every action a statement of injured personality – eyes blazing indignation, lips smirking defiance, muscles taut with anger.*

Scenes like this punctuate the daily routine of schools and form the crucible of conflict for student rights. For it is in cases of student misbehavior that the latent conflict between students and adults, between individual aspirations and organizational expectations, erupts most dramatically. It is in these cases where students are dealt with by school disciplinarians possessing extensive discretionary power that the school's recognition or denial of student rights and interests assumes sharpest focus.

## The Problem of Administrative Discretion

The exercise of discretion – or making a choice among alternative courses of action – pervades alike the lives of presidents of corporations and school teachers. As Gulick (1933) noted:

"It is impossible to analyze the work of any public employee from the time he steps into his office in the morning until he leaves it at night without discovering that his every act is a seamless web of discretion and action. It is impossible to discover any position in government service, or in any other service for that matter, in which the element of discretion is absent except in the purely mechanical operations which will doubtless in time be entrusted to machines. What we have in administration is a continual process of decision-action-decision-action, like a man running after a high-batted ball." (p.61)

Discretion is thus vital to administrative decision-making. However, despite the vital and necessary role which discretion plays in decision-making, it does have a Janus-like quality that is too infrequently recognized. Discretion can be used benevolently or malevolently, reasonably or unreasonably, justly or unjustly. While it can ensure administrative responsiveness and flexibility, particularly in situations where formal policies provide inadequate or inappropriate guides to action, it can also allow for arbitrary and unjust treatment of individuals.

The scope of discretionary action thus needs to be limited in a way that preserves administrative flexibility and safeguards individuals from possible abuses. This is especially needed in the schools, where the doctrine of *in loco parentis* confers an extremely wide latitude of discretionary power upon school officials to discipline students in matters of formal pedagogy and conduct. The limiting of discretionary action requires first an examination of both its descriptive and normative/prescriptive dimensions. As Keith-Lucas (1957) observed:

"It is necessary not only to know to what influences, controls, or other impersonal factors an administrative official is actually responsive, but to what he should be responsive, and how this responsiveness can be made effective, if there is to be a minimum of arbitrary decision." (p.41)

The case studies reported in this paper were thus designed to explore how school officials exercise discretionary power on a day-to-day basis. The concluding section makes some suggestions as to how "good" discretionary action might be ensured in Canadian schools.

### Discretionary Justice

The conceptual framework of discretionary justice employed by this study accommodates the administrator's exercise of discretionary power in the disposition of a problem involving another individual.

"Without trying to draw precise lines, this essay [discretionary justice] is concerned primarily with a portion of discretionary power and with a portion of justice – with that portion of discretionary power which pertains to justice, and with that portion of justice which pertains to individual parties." (Davis, 1969, pp.5-6)

The approach is appropriate here for three reasons. First, school officials possess and exercise extensive discretionary power over a wide range of student behavior. Second, discipline is usually dispensed on a one-to-one basis in a closed context, i.e., one administrator deals with one student in a closed office, thereby increasing the possibility of inconsistency and arbitrariness. Third, school discipline is usually enforced through a system of rules and sanctions. Generally, rules are viewed as one end of a rules–discretion continuum. The more rules and the more specific the rules, the less the discretionary power.

Discretion is responsibly exercised not only when the administrator takes into account all relevant considerations and can elaborate reasons for the choice of a particular course of action, but also when the reasons themselves are defensible. When the reasons are not defensible, then the action taken may be considered the arbitrary abuse of power. Thus the crucial aspect of the exercise of discretion is the basis upon which the decision is made.

Justice is intimately related to the exercise of discretion. Here justice refers to the notion of "fairness" advanced by Rawls. Justice involves "the elimination of arbitrary distinctions and the establishment, within the structure of a practice, of a proper balance between competing claims" (Rawls, 1969, p.133). Inherent in the concept of a "practice" is the notion that individuals who are equally situated should be treated equally.

Substantively, justice is related to the exercise of discretion in terms both of the defensibility of the reasons underlying the selection of a particular course of action and of prevailing practices and standards. Procedurally, justice is related to the exercise of discretion in terms of the rights and interests of the affected party throughout all stages of decision-making. Clearly, assessing the defensibility of a discretionary action is difficult, especially since practices and standards tend to vary from place to place and to change from time to time. A solution to this difficulty is to assess the defensibility of any given course of action in terms of legal standards and educational considerations.

Three other notions integral to the concept of discretionary justice are confining, structuring, and checking discretionary power. Confining discretionary power means locating the boundaries of discretionary action and ensuring that discretion is exercised only within these limits. Structuring discretionary power means controlling the way in which discretionary power is exercised within the designated limits. Checking discretionary power involves the correction of arbitrariness or illegality.

## Case Study: Discretionary Justice at Integrated High School

To examine how school disciplinarians exercise their discretion, I conducted an exploratory study of the administration of discipline at Integrated High School in Chicago. The socioeconomically heterogeneous student body is 41% black and 58% white. There are two disciplinarians at the school: Mr. Foster (white) is responsible for boys referred to the discipline office, Mrs. Stanbury (black) for girls.

The school has a highly developed discipline system. Offences, procedures, and penalties are clearly specified and form an impressively articulated and coherent structure. A student receiving a major discipline (which generally means either breaking a school rule that involves the safety of other students or behaving in a way that challenges the authority of adults in the school) is automatically referred to Mr. Foster or Mrs. Stanbury in the discipline office. In this study, students receiving major disciplines are defined as trouble-cases.

The first set of data was collected between mid-March and the beginning of June 1971. Administrative files containing data on all students receiving major disciplines since September 1970 were also examined to provide an overall perspective. A 50% systematic sample yielded 152 usable trouble-cases. Background data on the students and complainants were obtained from other sources in the school and assembled with the trouble-case data to provide complete socioeconomic profiles. These then served as independent variables in the first stage of analysis, the "action taken" by the disciplinarian (non-suspension/suspension) being the dependent variable.

The second set of data was obtained from interviews with Mr. Foster and Mrs. Stanbury. The purpose of the interviews was to elicit information about the reasons governing the selection of the course of action in particular cases. Several criteria were used to select this sample of trouble-cases (12 with each disciplinarian). First, they were all drawn from cases occurring during the week of April 19. Second, the major referral form was inspected to get some feel for the gravity of the offence. Third, care was taken to include incidents involving both boys and girls, both black and white. Fourth, incidents were selected as they happened because they appeared to be "interesting." Finally, because I was both observer and interviewer, the choice of cases had sometimes to be made on grounds of expediency.

This procedure is open to criticism. No generalizations to other populations may be conclusively made from these data, even though the findings may be replicated in subsequent studies. The problems of representativeness of cases and bias in selection are real and acknowledged. *The real test is whether or not, given the exploratory nature of this study, the analysis of these data generates new concepts and explanations and identifies new facets of the problem for further research.*

## Discretion in Discipline Decisions

The role of discretionary power in the discipline system at Integrated High required some preliminary investigation. Analysis of documents and observational data showed that statute and board policy conferred substantial legal discretion upon the principal, Dr. Young, and that, in the years immediately preceding the study, the discipline system had evolved through three stages: from a system using unfettered discretion, through one with written guidelines mechanically applied, to the recognition of the need for the enforcement of rules with discretion. The analysis further showed that Dr. Young's delegation of discretionary power to Mr. Foster and Mrs. Stanbury was more a process of gradual devolution than explicit delegation. It showed that Mr. Foster and Mrs. Stanbury exercised their discretionary power at several stages in the disciplinary process but most prominently in deciding whether or not to suspend a student and, if so, for how long. And finally, it showed that there was no systematic way of confining, structuring, and checking the disciplinarian's discretionary power.

## Selective Enforcement

With this background it is now possible to consider the actual exercise of discretion by Mr. Foster and Mrs. Stanbury in the day-to-day administration of discipline at Integrated High. The analysis of administrative statistics demonstrates the persistence of a pattern of sex-linked selective enforcement. Table 1 shows this pattern clearly: Mr. Foster suspends boys receiving major disciplines significantly more often than Mrs. Stanbury suspends girls. This situation suggests that Mr. Foster does not use the discretionary power of leniency to the same extent as does Mrs. Stanbury, and such bias in enforcement penalizes boys by treating them more severely.

**Table 1/Relation Between Disciplinarian and Action Taken**

| Disciplinarian | % Not Suspended | % Suspended | No. of Cases |
|---|---|---|---|
| Mr. Foster | 33 | 67 | 99 |
| Mrs. Stanbury | 76 | 24 | 45 |

Corrected $x^2$ = 20.50 with 1 *df*, $p < .01$

In general, this pattern of selective enforcement persists even when other factors are taken into account. The analysis of student characteristics shows that the race, grade year, level of scholastic ability, and perceived social class of the student do not affect the pattern of selective enforcement. The analysis of complainant characteristics shows that sex, race, and years of experience at Integrated High do not affect the pattern but that the educational level of the complainant has a statistically significant effect on the pattern of selective enforcement for Mr. Foster but not for Mrs. Stanbury. The following propositions summarize the significant findings of the analysis:

1. Mrs. Stanbury suspends girls receiving major disciplines significantly less frequently than Mr. Foster suspends boys receiving major disciplines.
2. There is a significant, positive relationship between the likelihood of suspension for boys by Mr. Foster and the complainant's level of education.

124

3. There is a significant, inverse relationship between the likelihood of suspension for boys by Mr. Foster and complainant intercession.

The persistence of the pattern of selective enforcement is important for three reasons. First, although the complainant's level of education and complainant intercession begin to explain the differential rate of suspension between Mr. Foster and Mrs. Stanbury, these variables do not account for the entire pattern. Second, although they differ in rates of suspension, each seems to be consistently different, i.e., Mr. Foster appears to be consistent in his treatment of boys and Mrs. Stanbury appears to be consistent in her treatment of girls. This situation suggests that explanations of their enforcement practices may derive from differences in their values and attitudes toward students and toward discipline. Third, the existence of sex-linked selective enforcement in the administration of discipline at Integrated High raises the question of justice. Davis (1969) pointed out that "selective enforcement obviously may be just or unjust depending upon how the selections are made" (p.167). The critical factor is the basis of a particular decision – the "conscious choice" of the administrator in selecting one course of action rather than another.

Upon what bases, then, do Mr. Foster and Mrs. Stanbury make their decisions? The second stage seeks to develop a more complete explanation through a case-by-case analysis of the trouble-cases selected for intensive investigation. Given the limitation of the small number of cases, it is clearly indefensible to try to present a demonstrated conceptual model generalizable to other situations and administrators. What follows is an attempt to develop a plausible hypothesized model for Mr. Foster and Mrs. Stanbury in terms of the bases of their decisions.

## Mr. Foster: Decisional Premises

Mr. Foster's beliefs about cause and effect in the discipline process are threefold. The first is his belief in the deterrent value of punishment:

"Suspensions never help a student individually. I guess it's more of a threat than anything else. He does know we mean business."

"If there isn't some threat of penalty over extreme cases then the school will fall apart.

"If we let the students think they have a right to carry and pull knives on other students, then we're headed for trouble."

The last two statements, however, go beyond recognition of the deterrent effect by implying that the school must keep control of the student body. They foreshadow the second of Mr. Foster's concerns – the general welfare of the school as an institution. To my query, "What did you hope to achieve by invoking the maximum sanction allowable both by the rules of the Board of Education and by school policy?", he replied,

"You mean help for that young man? None at all. This was a decision made, I think, for the school itself. . . . I believe that type of student is a danger to the health and welfare of the student body. So you're not helping him one bit by throwing him out of school or suspending him for twenty days."

The impression conveyed is that Mr. Foster sees his role from an institutional perspective in terms of order maintenance, although, as the following statement suggests, he is aware of the personal or idiographic dimension of the administration of discipline.

"If you don't follow policy, then you have to use personal judgment – that leaves you open to charges of prejudice, but I think you have to do so to allow room for the human element."

This emphasis on institutional maintenance of order is especially evident in the third of Mr. Foster's decisional concerns – his commitment to supporting the teacher's authority regardless of circumstances.

"I respect the integrity and I'm saying this because she is a rather elderly woman. I don't think she's senile in any way. In other words, in my mind *I did side one hundred percent with the teacher on the story* she was telling. And I did have to choose, and the parent knew I had to choose, and the parent of course got extremely mad when she heard my choice."

What is instructive here is that even when he knows the teacher is a poor disciplinarian, Mr. Foster still supports her authority. He must, for he sees himself as the teacher's last resort.

Mr. Foster brings to his task considerable knowledge about the school and its community, teachers and their effectiveness, students and their family backgrounds. This knowledge provides a baseline of information about a particular student, which Mr. Foster draws upon when he handles a trouble-case. The data suggest that Mr. Foster makes major judgments about the student in three areas: he assesses the student's culpability, credibility, and educational commitment.

Mr. Foster's assessment of student culpability seems to involve three variables: the student's previous discipline record, attitude, and intent. However, the influence of the latter two on him is negligible compared, say, with the character of the offence.

The credibility of the student's story seems to depend for him on two variables: the presence of an adult witness and the inherent reasonableness of the student's version. In one particular case, Mr. Foster repeatedly notes the lack of an adult witness.

"Since there was no adult witness to the fight, and in most students' eyes it wasn't even a fight, it looked to me like a misjudgment. . . . Basically the boy with the knife was charged with possession of an illegal weapon and the follow-up charge was that he carried and took the weapon out in a threatening manner and used the knife to cut the other student across the face. We felt he acted without sufficient provocation even to justify this type of action. The student's defence of his action was that he was using it in self-defence because this guy was supposedly a karate expert. . . . But I think it's just kid's talk. And besides to me it sounded more like a way of trying to justify why he did what he did."

Evidently the student's justification for pulling a knife is indefensible. The interview data show Mr. Foster's concern with the reasonableness of the student's story in five separate cases.

The third judgment Mr. Foster makes concerns the student's educational commitment. He does this by looking for signs of improved behavior and academic application. Evidence that a student is making a conscious effort to improve his behavior encourages Mr. Foster to exercise his discretionary power of leniency. This was clearly demonstrated in three cases.

"I said normally, by going by the book, he should be on a fifteen or twenty-day suspension considering his entire past record. . . . I figured anybody who can go from six or even seven major disciplines down to the next year with four, and this year with two, is improving, and I figured I ought to take this into consideration. So I figured a five-day suspension was fair."

This analysis generated three plausible hypotheses about Mr. Foster's methods:

1. The more extensive a student's previous discipline record, the greater the likelihood of a longer suspension.
2. The more unreasonable the student's story, the less credibility ascribed to it (particularly in the absence of adult corroboration) and the greater the likelihood of suspension.
3. The greater the student's educational commitment (defined in terms of improved behavior and academic application), the greater the likelihood of leniency in determining the duration of the suspension.

Mr. Foster's willingness to respond to intercession by the complainant seems to be directly related to his commitment to support the complainant's authority and, more particularly, to the complainant's perceived control effectiveness. Evidence from five trouble-cases supports this observation. In one case Mr. Foster supported a biology teacher's wishes because he considered her a conscientious and capable teacher, career-oriented, with a great deal to offer students. Since she seldom wrote major disciplines and since he perceived her as having good control effectiveness, he was quite prepared to respect her wishes in not suspending the student. In another case, however, Mr. Foster reluctantly acceded to the complainant's wishes because he perceived the complainant as having poor control effectiveness. Finally, in yet another case, Mr. Foster refused to accede to a particular teacher's request for clemency because the complainant tended to undermine the enforcement system by issuing a major discipline and then interceding on behalf of the student to withdraw it. On the basis of this analysis, the following hypothesis seems plausible:

1. The better the perceived control effectiveness of the complainant, the more likely the complainant's wishes are respected in deciding whether or not to suspend a student.

The key feature influencing Mr. Foster's decision is the gravity of the offence. This is exemplified in a case where a student pulled a knife on another student. Although the other student was not seriously injured, the potential for a very serious and possibly fatal injury existed. After consulting with the principal, Mr. Foster invoked the full 20-day suspension. This analysis suggests the following hypothesis may be plausible:

1. The more culpable the student as measured by the gravity of the offence, the greater the likelihood of suspension.

Figure 1 incorporates the essential features of the preceding analysis and shows the hypothesized relationships in Mr. Foster's exercise of discretion. The model is, by its nature, designed to raise questions for subsequent testing. Some of the hypotheses may not withstand critical scrutiny or verification, but they seem sufficiently plausible to justify being included.

**Figure 1/Model of Hypothesized Relationships in Mr. Foster's Exercise of Discretion**

Decisional Premises      1st Order Variables      2nd Order Variables      Outcome

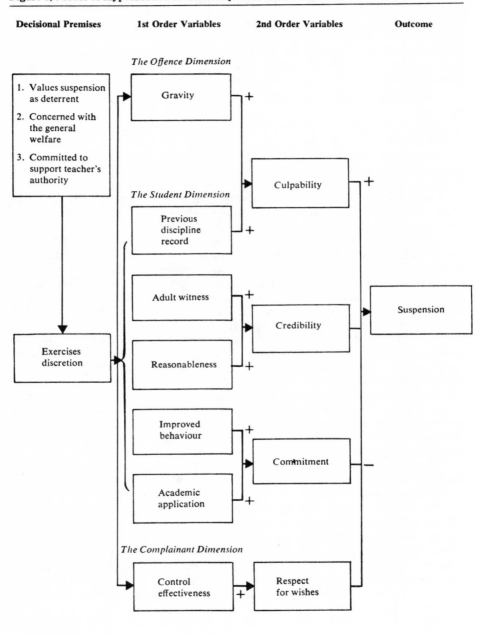

128

## Mrs. Stanbury: Decisional Premises

Three major decisional premises seem evident in Mrs. Stanbury's administration of discipline at Integrated High. The first premise, evident in three trouble-cases, is Mrs. Stanbury's belief in the deterrent value of punishment. To my question, "In the context, then, of this minor, what purpose do you see the three-day suspension serving?", she replied,

"To reinforce on L. that she cannot show belligerence to a teacher. . . . I'm not too much in favor of the exclusion, but there's nothing else. I felt if it had gone on – this bullying attitude – and if nothing was done when she was actually caught, then she would continue."

The second premise, closely related, is Mrs. Stanbury's commitment to upholding the teacher's authority, I asked, "How did the conference go?"

"As expected. The student apologized, and the teacher accepted the apology. I think she [the student] was a little dissatisfied because she really didn't think she had done anything wrong. But we must maintain this idea that the teacher must rule her classroom."

To further questioning, she identified the "we" referred to as "the administration, the establishment, something of that nature."

The third premise is reflected in Mrs. Stanbury's concern with maintaining the integrity of the enforcement process and is evident in three trouble-cases. She recognizes the need to establish and maintain the credibility of the discipline system in the eyes of the students and teachers down to the extent of sometimes overruling a teacher's recommendation.

Mrs. Stanbury makes two main judgments about the students referred to her: she assesses the culpability of the student and the cost of suspension to the student. Her assessment is based on the student's previous discipline record, attitude, and intent.

After reading the major to grasp the general features of the case, Mrs. Stanbury checks the student's discipline record. She does so to establish a perspective on the student, but the record is not by itself a crucial determinant of action. Similarly, the student's attitude, while important, is not an independent determinant of action.

The most potent of these judgmental factors is Mrs. Stanbury's assessment of student intent. One case involved the alteration of a report card letter grade. Mrs. Stanbury explained:

"The student admitted changing the red F and gave no particular reason except that she was sitting doodling and she hated her mother to see this red F glaring her in the face [a bit of a laugh in her voice]. She *could* have changed the F to an A by the drawing of one line. She didn't. We can only conclude from this that she had no definite intent to actually misrepresent her failure. Just soften it a little."

To my query, "Presumably, had the intent been there and had it been changed to an A, this would have been considered a more serious offence?", she replied,

"Oh yes! Even though this is *technically* forgery, if the grade had been changed it would have been actually forgery and that student would have ended up with a double major and a five-day suspension.''

On the basis of this analysis, the following hypothesis seems plausible:
1. The more extensive a student's previous discipline record and the more malicious her intent, the greater the likelihood of her being considered culpable and so suspended from school.

Mrs. Stanbury also considers the cost of suspension to the student, both in terms of educational needs and social vulnerability. In three cases Mrs. Stanbury's concern with the student's educational needs caused her to be lenient. In one case, she reduced the suspension to five days. In another, she did not suspend at all. And in the third, she considered the student's 16-day absence from school to be sufficiently damaging to the student's education that further suspension was unwarranted.

Furthermore, Mrs. Stanbury is concerned with the social vulnerability of students, particularly those classed Educable Mentally Handicapped (EMH). Speaking of EMH students, Mrs. Stanbury observed:

''We avoid suspension at all costs. There are two reasons for this: first, because the student is not used to an academic situation; second, because this student is more inclined to be taken advantage of. Other students use their houses for parties or as gathering places, and become a hindrance to the community in general. These students for the most part are unable to work alone academically, and there they are stuck in the house with no one to help them. There is really no advantage that I can see giving suspension to these students, for the most part.''

Although Mrs. Stanbury's concern for the EMH students may be viewed as maternalistic, she is more likely acknowledging their functional limitations.

This analysis yields the following plausible hypothesis:
1. The greater the perceived educational need and social vulnerability of the student, the greater the likelihood of leniency in dealing with a referred student.

As with Mr. Foster, Mrs. Stanbury's judgments are directly related to the wishes of the complainant and the confidence she has in the complainant's control effectiveness. She said,

''It's perfectly all right with me. I very seldom go against the recommendation of the teacher, only when there's an extremely weak disciplinarian will I go against it.''

Within the constraint of the complainant's wishes, Mrs. Stanbury makes two judgments: one concerns the teacher's intent and the other the teacher's control effectiveness. Mrs. Stanbury draws on her knowledge of the teacher and on her ''reading'' of the major discipline to infer the intent of the teacher. This process is evident in four cases.

''I noticed that the teacher did *not* write forgery, which means to me that she simply wants R. to be aware of the fact that this is wrong – that a student may not change anything regarding an official record – but that she does not necessarily want to charge the student with forgery. More than likely during the conference the student will be made aware of the fact that this is forgery and more than likely the major will be held.''

130

Here Mrs. Stanbury infers the teacher's intent from the written major, concludes that the teacher wants the student's awareness rather than punishment, and anticipates the likely outcome.

The frequency of awarding major disciplines also colors Mrs. Stanbury's perception.

"With a teacher who rarely writes a major, her major is looked at twice, perhaps three times, and you wonder *'What on earth happened?'* Perhaps this is unfortunate but with a teacher who is constantly writing majors, you feel that he has no other way to control the class. And this of course is unfortunate and harmful to the students. I am afraid it also colors the office. I know I tend not to be as strict with the student who received a major or minor as I am with one who received a major from a teacher who writes two a year."

The following conjoint hypothesis seems plausible on the basis of the data presented here:
1. The better the perceived control effectiveness and the firmer the perceived intent of the complainant, the more likely the complainant's wishes will be respected in deciding whether or not to suspend a student.

The parental valuation of education and the level of parental support for the school enter Mrs. Stanbury's deliberations when determining the culpability of the student.

"The mother is rather more difficult to understand. She doesn't seem to be the least bit worried by the fact that her daughter has lost so much time in school. . . . What we're really trying to do is to put pressure on the parents to perhaps see that they take better care of their youngsters, that they do get to school. Now if we felt that this was completely C.'s fault, she would have been dropped. With the drop form previously signed, on a 16-day absence, she would have been immediately expelled from school completely. But we do feel that there is parental neglect here."

Culpability is shared between student and parent, and Mrs. Stanbury's assessment of low parental concern seems to provide warrantable grounds for leniency. On this basis, the following conjoint hypothesis may be plausible:
1. The lower the perceived parental valuation of education and the lower the perceived level of parental support for the school, the less culpable the student and the greater the likelihood of leniency in dealing with a referred student.

Figure 2 collates the hypothesized relationships generated through the preceding analysis into one diagram. In a primitive way, this diagram constitutes an analogue model of Mrs. Stanbury's exercise of discretion.

**The Pattern of Selective Enforcement**
The data analyzed in the generation of the analogue models begin to account for the differences in enforcement styles between Mr. Foster and Mrs. Stanbury. Two particular explanations merit attention.

The first concerns the administrative style and decisional premises of each administrator. Mr. Foster seems to pay much more attention to the nature and gravity of the offence in assessing student culpability, whereas Mrs. Stanbury places more emphasis on student intent. Mr. Foster exercises his discretionary power of leniency only if the student demonstrates educational commitment, whereas Mrs. Stanbury exercises her discretionary power when

131

**Figure 2/Model of Hypothesized Relationships in Mrs. Stanbury's Exercise of Discretion**

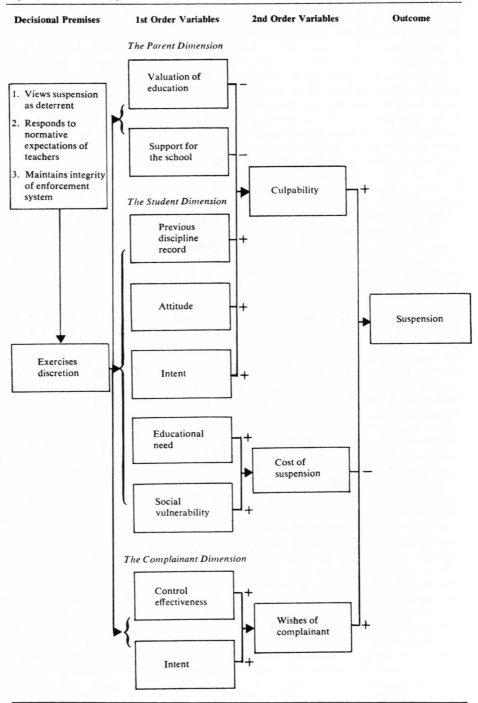

she considers the educational cost of suspension to the student to be too high. In sum, the two administrators, while preoccupied with order-maintenance and control, differ because their models of the world, their decisional premises, and their assumptions of causality are differentially complex. On the one hand, Mr. Foster's model is simpler than Mrs. Stanbury's; his decision-making style seems to be more administrative and institutional in orientation – he is more concerned with the discipline infraction in terms of order-maintenance and of the possible consequences for the school's general welfare. On the other hand, Mrs. Stanbury's decision-making style seems to be more judicial and personal in orientation – she seems more concerned with the discipline infraction in terms of individual treatment and of the possible consequences of action for the student's individual welfare.

The second explanation relates to the preoccupation of both administrators with order-maintenance and control of student conduct and is suggested by Mr. Foster's volunteered observation about the need to keep control of the student body lest institutional breakdown occur. Boys by virtue of their physical size and strength generally pose a greater threat to the good order of the school than do girls. This may explain Mr. Foster's practice of suspending boys more frequently than Mrs. Stanbury suspends girls.

These explanations, requiring further investigation as they do, seem plausible enough to be framed as hypotheses:

1. The more prominent the discipline administrator's concern with order-maintenance (control), the greater the likelihood of students being suspended.

2. The more prominent the discipline administrator's concern with individual treatment, the greater the likelihood of students being treated leniently and not suspended.

3. Boys, posing a greater threat to the security and good order of the school, are suspended more frequently than girls.

The third and last of the three main guiding questions is whether or not, in the light of the findings, the discretionary power of Mr. Foster and Mrs. Stanbury needs further confining, structuring, and checking. Analysis of this question requires that both the legal and educational defensibility of the decisions made by Mr. Foster and Mrs. Stanbury and the breadth of their discretionary power be examined.

Regarding the defensibility of their decisions in terms of legal principles, the conclusion is that sex-linked selective enforcement, constituting as it does *prima facie* discrimination on the basis of sex, violates the principle of fundamental fairness – that members of a class of persons who are similarly situated should be similarly treated – and so is indefensible. Further support for this conclusion is that Mr. Foster and Mrs. Stanbury seem to use different decision-making models and to place different weightings on factors associated with a given case, a situation that suggests that students who are similarly situated are not necessarily treated similarly. In procedural terms, however, the discipline procedure at Integrated High seems broadly compatible with the requirements of procedural due process as laid down by the U.S. Supreme Court in *Goss v. Lopez*. As for educational considerations, Mr. Foster's and Mrs. Stanbury's decisions appear to be defensible – they are primarily concerned with the law enforcement, housekeeping, and protection aspects of discipline, of necessary institutional control over student conduct.

With regard to the breadth of Mr. Foster's and Mrs. Stanbury's discretionary power, sex-linked selective enforcement argues the need for adopting the discretionary justice approach to discipline. This implies further confining, structuring, and checking of discretionary power.

## Implications for Canadian Schools

What then are the implications of the research reported here for discipline in Canadian schools and for students' rights in Canada? As Magsino points out elsewhere in this volume, there are important differences in the legal status of public school students in the United States and their counterparts in Canada. The landmark U.S. Supreme Court decisions of *Tinker v. Desmoines Community School District*, *Goss v. Lopez,* and *Wood v. Strickland* have dramatically affirmed the rights of students to constitutional protection, to procedural due process in school discipline proceedings, and to claim damages against a school board member for violating the constitutional rights of students (Manley-Casimir, forthcoming). No such development has occurred in Canada. In Canada, the regulation of student conduct and the making of rules and regulations fall within the purview of school boards and their officers. Since the Canadian Bill of Rights lacks constitutional force, recourse to its provisions is pointless; so the Canadian student is totally dependent on the discretion of local school authorities.

The chief implication of the absence of "rights" for Canadian public school students is that the fair use of discretion in school discipline proceedings becomes paramount – even more than in the United States, where at least students have judicial recourse if necessary. This, of course, is not to argue that Canadian students should not have "rights" – both option and welfare rights. They should. But in the absence of such protection, the responsibility placed upon school officials for the wise exercise of discretion is critical.

As I have argued elsewhere (Manley-Casimir, 1971), it is possible and desirable to conceptualize the administration of discipline as a problem of discretionary justice and, more broadly, to conceptualize "school governance" in the same way (Manley-Casimir, 1974). Such approaches, if adopted in schools of education and administrator training programs in Canada, would raise the awareness of professional educators about the exercise of discretion and its attendant problems.

A second implication of the research reported here is that we need more studies of the exercise of administrative discretion. How do school administrators exercise their discretion? What bases underlie their decisions? Is there evidence of selective enforcement? If so, on what bases are distinctions made? Are such bases defensible? Answers to these and related questions may generate the elements of a theory of administrative discretion.

There are, in addition, broader questions provoked by this study. Is the capacity of an administrator to exercise good judgment related to the administrator's effectiveness? If so (and I suspect it is), then perhaps we should be paying more attention to this dimension of administrative behavior both in research and preparation programs.

Finally, from a very practical viewpoint, provincial educational authorities and local school boards could immediately endorse the principle and practice of discretionary justice by requiring school principals and disciplinarians to confine structure and check their discretionary power. School officials can confine discretionary power through administrative rule-making, thus making it reasonably specific. For example, at Integrated High, the disciplinarians might use their administrative rule-making power to clarify "forgery" in terms like these:

"A student commits forgery when he or she willfully alters or knowingly uses an altered official school document, e.g., report card or hall pass, with the intention to deceive. In cases where this occurs, it is likely that a suspension will be invoked unless relevant extenuating circumstances are present. Circumstances conducive to leniency are evidence of improvement in behavior and academic application, or where the benefit of suspension is not defensible in terms of the educational cost to the student."

The precise phrasing might require refinement and periodic revision, but similar specifications could be applied to all offences, thereby clarifying them and confining discretionary power.

A second procedure is to develop standards and rules to confine discretionary power. For example, in the case of selective enforcement at Integrated High, the policy might reflect the principle of equal treatment like this:

"Each student, regardless of race, sex, or age, will be treated equitably by the discipline system of Integrated High. No distinctions between students on these or other irrelevant grounds shall be made unless there are good and substantial reasons for so doing, in which case the bases of the decision will be written into the policy to modify and illustrate it."

A third procedure emanating from the framework of discretionary justice is the use of individual or hypothetical cases to develop rules. For example, consider the hypothetical case of a adolescent girl who comes to school braless and wearing a see-through blouse. Mr. Foster and Mrs. Stanbury could develop a rule governing this action in terms like these:

"Students may dress as they choose providing such dress complies with the requirements of public health and personal safety and does not cause a substantial disruption of educational activities."

It seems likely that going braless in a transparent blouse would cause such disruption; hence such practice would be proscribed.

Systematic concern with structuring discretionary power rests on the acceptance of the principle of openness. The initial requirement should be the collation of the school's discipline policy into one document made available to all members of the school community – students, teachers, para-professional and other staff, parents, and administrators. Such a document, revised annually, would inform all affected parties about the discipline policy of the school, and would include open statements of plans, policy, and rules together with findings, reasons, and precedents. Statements of plans, policy, and rules are self-explanatory but the findings, reasons, and precedents need elaboration through an example:

Case X:
Facts: In 1971, a student involved in a fight pulled a knife on a fellow student, cutting him slightly on the nose. The wound was not serious.
Findings: Eye witnesses corroborated the details of the incident and the first student admitted using the knife. He was suspended from school for 20 school days.
Reasons: The maximum suspension was invoked in this case for three reasons:
1. The possession of offensive weapons is prohibited under the Criminal Code.

135

2. The knife wound, while not itself serious, was potentially very serious and might have resulted in severe injury or death and might also have sparked racial conflict.

3. The school discipline policy calls for the maximum suspension in cases like this.

Precedent: The case, findings, and reasons stated here serve as a precedent for future cases of this type. Cases having essentially similar characteristics will be handled similarly.

Included in the discipline policy, such examples would begin the process of structuring the discretionary power of school disciplinarians.

Finally, the chief method of checking the exercise of discretionary power is to make clear to all affected parties, but *particularly* to students, what avenues of appeal are open to them in the case of a felt grievance.

## Note

Revised version of a paper, "The Exercise of Administrative Discretion in Secondary School Discipline," given at the Canadian Educational Research Association Conference, Laval University, Quebec, June 2, 1976.

The material on pages 121-123 in the present article appears in similar form in Manley-Casimir (1974), and is used here with the permission of *School Review* and the University of Chicago Press.

## References

Becker, H. S. The teacher in the authority system of the public school. In A. Etzioni (Ed.), *Complex organizations*. New York: Holt, Rinehart & Winston, 1965. Pp.243-251.

Black, M. *Models and metaphors*. Ithaca: Cornell University Press, 1962.

Davis, K. C. *Discretionary justice*. Baton Rouge: Louisiana State University Press, 1969.

Friedrich, C. J. Authority, reason, and discretion. In C. J. Friedrich (Ed.), *Authority*. Cambridge: Harvard University Press, 1958. Pp.28-48.

Gulick, L. Politics, administration, and the "New Deal." *Annals of the American Academy of Political and Social Science*, 1933, **169**, 55-66.

Keith-Lucas, A. *Decisions about people in need*. Chapel Hill: University of North Carolina Press, 1957.

Manley-Casimir, M. E. Student discipline as discretionary justice. *Administrator's Notebook*, 1971, **20**(2).

Manley-Casimir, M. E. School governance as discretionary justice. *School Review*, 1974, **82**, 347-362.

Manley-Casimir, M. E. The exercise of administrative discretion in secondary school discipline. Unpublished doctoral dissertation, University of Chicago, 1976.

Manley-Casimir, M. E. Rights in school. In D. Erickson (Ed.), *The urban principalship*. Columbus: University Council on Educational Administration. Forthcoming.

Rawls, J. Justice as fairness. In P. Laslett & W. G. Runciman (Eds.), *Philosophy, politics and society*. Oxford: Blackwell, 1969. Pp.132-157.

Schwab, J. J. The practical: A language for curriculum. *School Review*, 1969, **68**, 1-23.

# Schooling and Ethnic Rights

Vincent R. D'Oyley/OISE

The educational history of Canada's native peoples has rarely been attended to as a source of information on the rights of immigrants and migrants in Canadian schools and in other spheres of the public sector. Yet when we overcome the "official disrespect" accorded to the oral traditions of these groups, we are afforded a dramatic focus for examining the interplay between schooling and culture and between educational rights and group conflicts.

The education of native peoples used to be related to their culture and their social organizations. Their language and skills were rooted in the settling, hunting, and fishing activities of the tribe. Guided by the religious convictions of their elders, the young were taught a reverence for nature, and thus a survival-oriented attitude to nature was interwoven with a deep religiosity. In native society, there was no rigid division of labour, and the youth were prepared for a wide variety of leadership roles. When one purposive activity ended (e.g., buffalo hunting), they had to be ready to engage in others. Intrinsic to native society, and thus to native education, was the socialization of the young into the radically democratic practice of leadership rotation. The conquering Europeans, however, were soon to introduce a cultural hegemony that negated the principles and practices of the native system.

Myths of European superiority provided a taken-for-granted context in which to assert the special rights of the French and British settlers. Native peoples and other non-white minority groups were thus reduced to the status of lower-class citizens and, with the introduction of schooling, this status was reinforced. As a singular official culture emerged, schooling took on the function of socializing the young into the values and organizations of the dominant group.

By the mid-19th century, territorial governments were vigorously outlining the literacy and other educational standards deemed essential for citizenship. In this context, the conformist capacities of immigrants of different racial and cultural groups were assessed.

Some large (and usually poor) immigrant groups were characterized as being "in need of education." In 1848, Ryerson made the following reference to the Irish: "They are notoriously as destitute of intelligence and industry as they are of means of subsistence. . . . The physical disease and death which have accompanied their influx among us may be the precursors of the worse pestilence of social insubordination and disorder" (pp.299-300). He concluded it was in the national interest to "bring the faculties of education within the reach of these . . . unfortunate people that they may grow up in the industry and intelligence of the country and not in the . . . mendacity and vices of their forefathers."

In response to such proddings, school societies, often religiously based, attempted to "civilize" the poor through mass educational ventures. Needless to say, these programs tended to reinforce the "superior"/"inferior" dichotomy.

In spite of the variety and number of immigrant groups involved, the move to Anglo-Canadian domination of school systems was realized by about 1900.[1] The public attitude to non-Caucasian immigrants was harsh. Thus the *Regina Standard* (as quoted in McLeod, 1975) represented the Chinese as "filthy in their habits and a menace to public health," unwilling to "assimilate with the people of any civilized country." Phillips (1957) and Boyd (1976) described the considerable restrictions in schooling to which blacks were often subjected, with laws construed to provide them with separate facilities.

Where immigrant communities were unwilling to establish schools or were uncooperative in maintaining them, officials organized schools for them and supervised their development. Except in Quebec and a few parts of the mid-west, English was generally legislated as the medium of instruction. In the years immediately preceding the 1914-1918 war, officials quarrelled with Ukrainians in the Regina training schools about teachers speaking Ruthenian in the classroom and the use of Ruthenian texts. That confrontation was but part of the conflict over the right to language and culture within the schools, a conflict that continues today.

This past century, governments have stressed compulsory student attendance with successive regulations to lengthen the school year. Such regulations have sought to ensure that all students, regardless of ethnicity, place of birth, or of location within Canada, achieve a minimum educational level. Yet because texts, teacher preparation, instruction, and trusteeship are subject to central control, ethnic minority groups still encounter massive cultural and political obstacles in achieving an education that does not systematically negate their particular backgrounds. Let us look now at the contemporary situation.

**The Demography of Multiculturalism**
In recent years, the enrolment of children from the West Indies, Portugal, Africa, and South America in the schools of Ontario and Quebec has shown a marked increase. In Ontario there has also been an influx of Chinese and East Indian children. The urban schools of the two most westerly provinces have seen a corresponding increase in the enrolment of children from Africa and South America, as well as from China and other Asian countries (see Table 1). This recent and, for some locations, sudden influx of children from unfamiliar racial and cultural sources has elicited a radical challenge to the equity of Canadian schooling and an inadequate organizational response.

The immigration bill being considered in Parliament during the fall of 1977 is likely to recommend that immigration to Canada be reduced, but that newcomers be accepted without regard to race, religion, sex, or age. Additionally, there is some pressure for agreement between federal and provincial governments to move immigrants away from the large urban centres and into locales where planners expect that their presence can be most effectively absorbed. If this plan is attempted, then other school systems must begin to cope with a diversity of immigrant students. The focal point in their efforts will continue to be that of language teaching.

Language of instruction is a crucial factor in understanding lower academic achievement among some immigrants. Educators and representatives of minority groups are divided on the right of children to attend schools where their

138

Table 1/Selected Main Sources of Immigrant Students in Quebec, Ontario, Alberta, and British Columbia (as a Percentage of the Province's Immigration)

| Source | Quebec | Ontario | Alberta | British Columbia |
|---|---|---|---|---|
| West Indies | 15.21 | 13.61 | 5.55 | |
| Portugal | 12.28 | 17.27 | 8.52 | 7.16 |
| Greece | 9.38 | 5.21 | | |
| France | 8.96 | | | |
| Italy | 8.25 | 8.34 | | |
| Middle East | 6.22 | | | |
| Africa (NES) | 5.94 | 8.29 | 13.45 | 21.61 |
| South America | 5.89 | 7.60 | | 3.48 |
| India et al. | | 6.17 | 7.11 | 14.37 |
| China | | 6.11 | 15.72 | 17.46 |
| Asia (NES) | | | 7.11 | 6.16 |
| Europe (NES) | | | 6.10 | |
| Philippines | | | | 3.53 |
| Other (NES) | | | | 5.70 |

Source: Department of Manpower and Immigration 1972 immigration statistics.

mother tongue plays a pivotal role, especially when the objectives, organization, and implementation of such schooling are different from the traditional practices in the minority culture. Some educators emphasize the administrative impossibility of providing instruction in all languages where a school system has pupils from as many as 50 language backgrounds. Others are making an effort to rethink curricula in terms of the multilingual classroom. Their efforts are supported by findings that indicate the great extent to which non-English-speaking students' fluency in English, and general school performance, is enhanced by the sense of emotional well-being that ensues from the affirmation of their own culture and linguistic background. In this regard, Grande's (1975) review of innovations in English language instruction led him to the conclusion that, for new Canadians, a bilingual program of mother tongue and English would be the most feasible, effective, and inexpensive strategy of teaching.

Yet despite the projected feasibility of a multilingual program, the dominant culture's linguistic preferences remain firmly entrenched in the schools. For example, in speaking on behalf of the rights of the Italian-Canadian child and family, Costa and Di Santo (1972) abhorred some of the realities existing in Canadian schools: "The immigrant's language and culture are . . . quite bluntly called 'handicaps,' and success in the schools is equated with their rejection by the young [students]" (p.250). Costa and Di Santo regard uniformity of instruction in English for non-English-speaking students as a denial of a "fundamental democratic right of which we have deprived immigrants for too long." They plead for diversity in instruction via different languages, for "allowing as much as possible for the teaching of immigrant children in their mother tongue, at least for a period of transition. That diversity is the essential element of creativity and inventiveness." How schools respond to such pleading, however, depends mostly on the cultural awareness of teachers, administrators, parents, and students.

## School Responses

Canadian schools are responding in a variety of ways to the current pressures from different ethnic groups for particularized programs. For example, by 1968, 77 elementary and 18 secondary schools in the city of Toronto were regularly providing special English language instruction to 4 214 new Canadian students (excluding kindergarten).

Three main organizational patterns were then in vogue. The Main Street elementary school, with 15 teachers working full time, sought to introduce 119 pupils to the Canadian way of life through the commitment to learn English. In the second organizational pattern, regional reception centres and portable classrooms at selected schools followed the Main Street technique; as their English improved, the "reception" pupils gradually became integrated into life at the regular school. In the third pattern ("withdrawal classes"), the students were withdrawn for some hours from their regular program and given over to the special English teacher. The students came from a wide range of mother-tongue backgrounds: Italian (1 497), Portuguese (875), Greek (666), Chinese (502), Polish (157), Yugoslavian (157). Other language groups numbered fewer than 50 each. Approximately 400 pupils were at each of the age levels from 8 to 16 years.

Data for the Toronto school board in 1975 show significant changes in the constitution of the non-Canadian student population. It increased since 1970 from 25% to 30% of the school population, representing an even greater variety of countries and mother tongues. Non-English-speaking students in this group increased from 41% to 46%. Other language shifts in enrollees are being experienced in Winnipeg, Montreal, and Vancouver. Responding to this large immigrant presence, some school boards are developing language arts curricula similar to those in use in the Toronto area.

In Quebec, Bill 22 (and subsequently the Parti Québecois' Bill 1) has dominated the language issue (Dube, 1975). These bills, probably motivated by the fall in number of French-speaking immigrants to Canada, were expected to enlarge the utilization of French in commercial and legal transactions as well as in schooling. Many groups of parents responded angrily to the legislation. Thus, when Bill 22 was proposed, official representatives of the parents of 44 000 students attending the Montreal Catholic School Commission's English language schools rejected the legislation as vague, undemocratic, unrealistic, and excessive with regard to discretionary powers afforded to non-elected public officials. The subsequent regulatory Orders-in-Council promoted the prominence of French and openly sought the decrease of transfers from the French to the English sector, and of immigrants registering in the English sector. Such objectives highlight some bases surrounding the conflicts embedded in who should define a child's rights to schooling and how those rights ought to be operationalized.[2]

Canadian school systems are ill equipped to meet the needs of immigrant children as long as they remain ignorant of the child's background and way of life. There is now, however, a trend for school systems to establish closer liaison with ethnic communities. This development has occurred mainly in urban boards. Sometimes a school board begins by identifying a teacher with a successful reputation for instructing a particular immigrant or migrant group; that board then redefines the teacher's duties so the teacher may assist other staff members who are assigned to classrooms and programs with a concentration of students from a racial, cultural, or ethnic cluster. Some teachers may also be called upon to explain to groups of parents how the school functions and to summarize for the school the nature of parental aspirations, satisfactions, and uncertainties. But a board may establish other liaison patterns. A few examples follow.

The Board of Education for the City of Toronto has recently established a community relations unit within the student services program: its 24 officers are recruited on the basis of the recommendations and concerns of the immigrant communities. These staff are then responsible to the area superintendent.

In Halifax, Nova Scotia, an ethnic studies department was created in the provincial Department of Education to examine the special learning problems of recent immigrants and to stimulate and improve learning and awareness among Canadian-born minority groups (native persons and blacks) who have had a long tradition of socioeconomic marginality and of failure at school.

In Winnipeg, both urban migration of native Indians from rural areas and the new immigration of groups have been met by training teachers who "know" and understand these groups so that more efficient instruction in basic skills can be provided as well as counselling in overcoming the obstacles of relocation, marginality, and economic deprivation. The trainees in the Winnipeg Centre are themselves residents of the Winnipeg region and their backgrounds are similar to those of that city's core-area pupils.

This scheme indeed has its advantages in its promotion of the hiring of teachers who, because of their identification with their pupils, tend to generate less interference with the educative processes.

In general, it is increasingly being realized that more funds and energy ought to be put towards in-service teacher training so as to permit objectives to be informed by significant community realities and expectations.

## Discussion

The attitudes of the first European settlers, and their subsequent rigour in imposing an Anglo-Canadian culture, language, and organization over groups (with French-Canadian culture stabilized in Quebec and parts of New Brunswick) has resulted in centralized regulations about the operations of the society and the schools.

Currently, immigration has provided Canadian society with larger groups of new types of immigrants, including strong urban concentrations of non-white minorities with whom considerable numbers of the majority race have had no previous personal contact. Often the minorities themselves have had conflicting relationships with one another. For there are among us some who hold destructive stereotypic views about the capabilities of some of the other groups. It is within such a dynamic situation, beckoning for redevelopment in values and understanding, that (1) the Canadian school is now expected to function, (2) the ideals and objectives of education are being re-argued, and (3) the workings of the careful standards embedded in the rights of schooling are being watched. The studies of multiculturalism work groups indicate that where formal school systems atrophy and lose resilience with respect to new clients, vibrant innovations must be forged and ingeniously managed. Only by such purposive actions may schooling appropriate and just for each individual be attained and maintained in Canadian schools.

A few new strategems should be added to those on which Canadian school regulations are founded. The introduction of any ethnic cluster of immigrants to an area requires preparation of the receivers, with articulation between the different levels of bureaucracy — federal, provincial, municipal — of strategies for the achievement of schooling rights. Where education professionals have a history of failure in motivating a linguistic or cultural group, or where the general

141

public is ignorant of particular ethnic or racial presence, federal-provincial ad hoc arrangements should be introduced to promote public acceptance of that group and to facilitate equality of educational opportunity. Such arrangements should involve teacher retraining and the adoption of special curricula aimed at fostering minimum literacy and quantification skills.

Survival of the native peoples continues to require special care. They have lost their ancestral homes and are rapidly migrating from rural areas to the laisser-faire conditions of urban life. In these circumstances, educational innovations instituted by all levels of government can often be of help. But more significant perhaps are their own efforts to redress their rights to economic, political, and cultural autonomy over their territories, and thereby acquire strength and dignity as cultural groups.

The actualization of schooling rights depends, however, largely on teachers with a sensitivity to race relations and to ethnic cultures. Ideally, teachers in this regard should "know" their own culture and that of their audience such that they are willing to treat others as equal. By this approach, teachers and counsellors may begin to develop more subtle knowledge of the barriers to intercultural communication (Da Costa, 1976). For surely, multi-ethnic student populations deserve to be serviced by personnel who are multi-ethnic, who appreciate the significance of multi-ethnicity in the operations and transactions of the school, and who affirm the multilingual and multicultural viability of the community of which the school is part.

The right to schooling is a right to be stated and pursued on behalf of each individual. For one child, that right is served by a minor curricular improvement. For another, only a massive cultural awareness teacher in-service program or a parent education thrust suffices. For another, one residing in Canada's northwest, it may be that only a macro-structural innovation, such as the creation of a Dene nation, provides the cultural and economic climate for appropriate schooling. And for yet another, from a Greek family, say, living in Quebec, the family may feel that there is no opportunity for social and educational justice. The child's claim to self-realization must somehow be balanced with the efforts of francophone neighbours to avoid cultural and linguistic assimilation with a predominantly anglophone North America.

The lack of codification of children's rights does not aid the goal of equal educational opportunity. Complications stemming from this neglect include the fact that (1) ethnic minorities continue to feel the heavy hand of the vertical mosaic through programs promoting the domination of the more powerful language and cultural groups and the retreat of minority culture; (2) low streaming resulting from low performance in specific languages continues to relegate persons from minority groups to low job and economic opportunities.[3] So serious are some of these neglects that they deserve special interventions.

As a national objective, the right to efficient and just schooling must be pursued. The search for strategems and innovations should occupy the most creative minds in the country.

## Notes

[1] In 1875 the Mackenzie government extended its legal rights and principles of government over the Northwest Territories. In 1877 French and English were the working languages but in 1892 English became the only official language and separate schools became a privilege, not a right.

[2] Le Comité central des parents. Bill 22. Point of view expressed by the Central

Parents-Committee of the M.C.S.C. on the contents of Chapter V concerning the language of instruction. June 1974.

[3] This concern in one racial group is discussed in some papers in D'Oyley (1976).

## References

Arpin, C. Bilingualism: A dirty word in the West. *Toronto Star*, Oct.9, 1976, p.B1.

Blake, P. A Dene's views on the pipeline. *Bulletin CAS*, 1976, **17**(1), 24-26.

Boyd, F. S., Jr. *McKerrow: A brief history of blacks in Nova Scotia (1783-1895)*. Halifax: Afro-Nova Scotia Enterprises, 1976.

Costa, E., & Di Santo, O. The Italian-Canadian child, his family, and the Canadian school system. In N. Byrne & J. Quarter (Eds.), *Must schools fail*. Toronto: McClelland & Stewart, 1972.

Crossette, B. Integration problems now vex European schools. *The New York Times*, Nov.14, 1976, p.11.

Da Costa, G. Counselling the black child. In V. D'Oyley (Ed.), *Black students in urban Canada*. Toronto: Ministry of Culture and Recreation, Ontario, 1976.

Deosaran, R. A., & Wright, E. N. *The 1975 Every Student Survey*. Toronto: Toronto Board of Education, 1976.

Dube, C.-H. *Loi sur la langue officielle/Official Language Act. Sanctionée le 31 juillet 1974*. Montreal, Apr. 1975.

Eisenberg, J., & Troper, H. *Native survival*. Toronto: Ontario Institute for Studies in Education, 1973.

*Final report of the Work Group on Multicultural Programs*. Toronto: Toronto Board of Education, 1976.

Foster, M. K. *From the earth to beyond the sky: An ethnographic approach to four Longhouse Iroquois speech events*. Canadian Ethnology Service Paper #20. Ottawa: National Museums of Canada, 1974.

Grande, T. Bilingual education must become a reality. *Canadian Mosaico*, Apr. 1975.

Hawkins, F. *Canada and immigration: Public policy and public concern*. Montreal and Kingston: McGill-Queen's University Press, 1972.

McLeod, K. A. Education and the assimilation of the New Canadians in the North-West Territories and Saskatchewan, 1885-1934. Unpublished doctoral dissertation, University of Toronto, 1975.

Ministère de l'Education, Gouvernement du Québec. *Dossier: 10-04-22. Le projet de loi 22 (Loi sur la langue officielle)*. Vol.3. Aug.5, 1974.

Minority Report. Position of the Anglophone Members of the Central Parents-Committee of the M.C.S.C. regarding Bill 22.

Phillips, C. E. *The development of education in Canada*. Toronto: Gage, 1957.

Rioux, M. *Relations between religion and government among the Longhouse Iroquois of Grand River, Ontario*. Ottawa: Queen's Printer, 1952.

Ryerson, A. E. The importance of education to a manufacturing, and a free people. *Journal of Education for Upper Canada*, 1848, 1.

Sitaram, K. S., & Cogdell, T. R. *Foundations of intercultural communication*. Columbus, Ohio: Merrill (Bell & Howell), 1976.

Verma, G. K., & Bagley, C. *Race and education across cultures*. London: Heinemann Educational Books, 1975.

Wright, E. N. *Students' background and its relationship to class and programme in school: The Every Student Survey.* Toronto: Toronto Board of Education, Dec. 1970.

Wright, E. N. *Programme placement related to selected countries of birth and selected languages: Further Every Student Survey analyses.* Toronto: Toronto Boad of Education, Oct. 1971.

Wright, E. N., & McLeod, D. B. *Parents' occupations, students' mother tongue and immigrant status: Further analyses of the Every Student Survey data.* Toronto: Toronto Board of Education, Dec. 1971.

# Children's Intellectual Rights

Robert MacKay/University of Toronto

This paper considers the question of children's intellectual rights in two ways: first, how the question of rights in general arises, and, second, the rights implied in two educational contexts – testing and classroom lessons.

If all people were homogeneous and equal, presumably the question of the rights of some particular group would never arise. The locus of the question therefore is an heterogeneous, unequal world. The claim of some to have certain rights has, as its reciprocal, the recognition of those rights by some other group. The question of rights exists in the dichotomy of "we" and "they." When the claim to rights is granted, there is a recognition[1] by "we" that "they" equals "we."

The Canadian Bill of Rights refers to the rights of individuals, humans, free men, and free institutions, but neither children nor intellectual rights are mentioned. Closest is the right to freedom of speech but, as I suggest later, this seems inapplicable in schools. The U.N. Declaration of Human Rights is both more clear and extensive but again children's intellectual rights are not covered. Most closely related to the topic is Article 26, the Right to Education. Not only is there a right to education but for school-age children it is to be compulsory. The U.N. Declaration indicates the rights of children with respect to education as follows: "Parents have a prior right to choose the kind of education that shall be *given* to their children" (United Nations, 1968, p.22, my emphasis). In education, then, *someone else* decides what is to be *given* to the child. What is important is the relationship implied in this *giving*. It involves a notion of the ownership of knowledge such that what teachers say is authorized to be what students should absorb. That is, the students have education imposed on them, and it is this that circumscribes their rights.

The raising of children's rights as an issue suggests some recognition that children may be more "we" than "they." This division was not always so: as Ariès (1965) shows, children's separateness from adults is a relatively recent phenomenon. The division has come in part from the increasingly long attendance of children in schools and the attendant separateness of activities, interests, and friends.

Margaret Mead (1942-43) is instructive in noting an important shift in education, a shift from learning to teaching. An emphasis on teaching, she argues, is a shift to proselytization, which assumes a body of knowledge to which each one must be obedient and responsive. A central feature of proselytization is that the proselytizers assume control of the knowledge and the flow of converts. Conceptualized in this way, the relationship of teacher to knowledge is that of possessor. This situation is demonstrated in a student response to an interview.

"Mackay: So I would like to ask you a few things about school in general. Why doesn't the teacher want you to talk in class?
Student: Because he's learned, . . . because he went to school and he knows what he is doing, and he is teaching us because we don't know."

Sharrock (1974) is also instructive in his formulation of the relationship between a corpus of knowledge, a collectivity, and activities. He begins by exploring expressions such as Cheyenne law and Zande medicine and asks if these are simple descriptions or whether they point to relationships between people with respect to a corpus of knowledge. He argues (p.49) that the naming of a corpus of knowledge implies that such knowledge belongs to, or is owned by, a particular collectivity.

"The treatment of corpus names as recognizing a relationship of ownership between collectivity and corpus provides us, then, with a method of interpreting the activities of persons in the society, both those who are collectivity members and those that are not. It provides us with a method of assessing the bona fides of actions and thus of managing the distinction between appearances and realities that is fundamental both to the conduct of everyday life and the accomplishment of sociological work." (p.52)

What is central to the discussion here is the recognition that ownership implies rights in and over things (p.50). To own presupposes control, being master; it implies the possession of a thing (here the facts) that can be sold, lent, or given away. It suggests limited and defined rules of access and acquisition. It suggests order and law.

The concept of the ownership of knowledge is appropriate within the schools where teachers, having been delegated with temporary control of knowledge, are considered managers. However, unlike other forms of control, schools never give up title or object. Schools give only certification that a student has gained possession of (learned) a percentage of the knowledge. Certification can also be withheld. Although it is not common to hear the phrase "teachers' knowledge," I think it clear that such a formulation is appropriate, insofar as the curriculum represents knowledge that is owned and access to teachers' knowledge is through classroom learning. Through lessons and tests, through the giving of correct and incorrect answers, intellectual skills are seen to emerge and thereby to establish the student's status as that of learner.

The notion of intellectual that predominates in schools is largely understood as IQ. Narrow as this interpretation may be, it supports the efficient management of intellectual matters because it is based on empirical criteria. The tension for teachers is between their position as managers of facts and their position in the classroom in which knowledge and knowing defy the criteria of efficient management. Yet this tension is unrecognizable insofar as the community of educators is *mindless* about its own activities. The notion of *mindfulness* provides an analytic way of seeing how the adults, discussed in the following analysis, remain *mindless* to the *unity* (community) that is made possible precisely by the difference they daily recognize between themselves and children – i.e., between we and they. It is in the web or interpenetration of social relations that rights are constituted. A change of rights in any particular community would have as a feature the renewed reflexivity of mindlessness and mindfulness.

Given that intellectual rights are constituted in schools, the question becomes

146

how schools recognize intellectual processes. I examine two ways in which this is done – by testing and by giving lessons.

## Tests

Tests and grades treat intellectual activities as knowable[2] through the methods of science (MacKay, 1974a). There is an assumption in both tests and grades that ignorance (not everyone gets 100%) is distributed in and among individuals. (For some examples of distributions, see Martell, 1974.) A justification then for the schools' claims about students' intellectual abilities is provided by this concept of distributed ignorance, even though the predominant version is that of distributed intelligence. I stress the negative definition of intelligence and knowledge in order to indicate that ignorance creates a relationship of dependency on teachers. There is always more to give or get – not everything is learned. This dependency is based on the teacher's ownership of knowledge. Intellectual rights are circumscribed and defined by the relationship – teacher knowledge/ student.

When the scientific assessment of intellectual abilities is examined, however, several phenomena are brought to light. Roth (1974), in a study of intelligence tests, found that they failed to account for a great deal of intellectual activity. For example, he discovered in the Peabody test that children from all backgrounds displayed greater reasoning abilities than the test gave them credit for.

"The conception of children's intelligence in terms of measurably limited capacity is not justified by our intelligence test data. Instead of being a measure of the children's intrinsic capacity, the test cut-off point on the Peabody imposes arbitrary limits on our knowledge of the children's abilities. This is true of the lowest-scoring black child and the highest-scoring white child, as well as all the children in between. This means that both the geneticists and the environmentalists are wrong in treating the IQ tests as measures of children's intellectual capacities. Furthermore, if IQ tests are incompatible with the teaching processes, then it would be unfounded to attribute relative success in school of black and white children to measured mental ability, even if test scores and school achievement are highly correlated." (p.216)

In my work on standardized reading tests (MacKay, 1974a), I found students to be using the very reasoning and comprehension abilities that the test was designed to measure, regardless of whether the answer was the one designated correct by the test constructor.

These studies, together with others reported in *Language Use and School Performance* (Cicourel et al., 1974), suggest that the scientific techniques used to evaluate children's intellectual abilities and performance in schools not only do not guarantee the recognition of intellectual processes but also render these processes *unavailable* (mindless). They reveal some but they hide others. In other words, some of the abilities of children are being ignored for the sake of efficiency and methodic certainty. Or the intellectual rights of children are being confirmed to the extent that their performance matches a scientific ideal.

## The Orchestration of Teaching

The Ontario Ministry of Education's (1975) policy for elementary education pointed out the centrality of curriculum in schools. "It follows that the curriculum will provide opportunities for each child (to the limit of his or her potential)" (p.4). Curriculum can, in this sense, be seen to be a vehicle to detect ability. Further, the policy recognizes that responsibility for implementation rests with the schools or, at a day-to-day level, with the teachers (p.3). In short, the teachers' function is managerial.

**Teaching and Learning in the Classroom**

I turn now to an analysis of part of a transcript of a classroom lesson on fractions. It is being given to a group of children in grades 5 and 6.

There are several assumptions that I am working from. The first is that it is through the talk that the organization of the class and learning is accomplished. The second is that the teacher's mode of talk, which I characterize as "telling," violates[3] the child's intellectual abilities and cultural embeddedness.[3] The process of "telling," because it assumes children to be passive receptors, detaches the children from their rightful position as active knowers and renders them obedient to an objective set of methods for evaluating their abilities and performance.

"(Noise made by students moving around.)
1. Teacher: Come on Ca., what are you doing? (Continued movement.) All right! Now for the next two weeks, maybe three, I want to begin a new topic in math. All you will work together. No groups, no grade 5s, no grade 6s. Very important topic and I want you to be at school every day. Don't stay home for a cold ( ). S. try to get here by 9:15 or 9:20. All right, some of you had this topic last year in room A; some of you had it in another room; some of you did a lot of it last year in my room. Fractions.
2. Several students: Oh no!"

The teacher begins the lesson by organizing the room. Having gained quiet and attention through his mere presence and through his opening remark to Ca., he justifies the content of the lesson. He announces that it is a new topic and that both grade 5s and 6s will do the work together. These first few statements have determined what the work is to be and altered the usual course of events. Usually the grade 5 and 6 students do their math separately. He establishes his separation from the students – i.e., he points to differences between them and establishes his authority by prescribing special behaviour necessary for their work (e.g., being at school every day).

The last two sentences could be viewed as "mere talk" but they are not. They establish the warrant for how the lesson will proceed. The teacher's assertion about their having studied fractions before provides the grounds for the series of questions at end of 3 below: "Just give me an example of *a* fraction."

The topic of fractions elicits a response from several students (Oh no!) that indicates they do not share the teacher's interest in what is to follow. The teacher does not respond, thereby establishing himself as one who may ignore conversational convention and reaffirming his position vis-à-vis the students. The teacher has established in this first statement: his right to teach, his right to organize the physical environment, the prescribed rules of orientation to the lesson (which, in turn, form the basis for later statements), the conditions of when to come to school, and the fact that some of the students already "know" what is to be talked about.

"3. T: For some of you this will be a review: some of you may have forgotten

148

how to do them even. (For some) it will be brand new. Whatever it is to you, it is an important topic. What is a fraction? (Pause.) What is a definition of a fraction? (Pause.) Any ideas? What does the word fraction mean to you – besides an ugly number? Can you give me an example of a fraction? That you can do. $S_1$. (Pause.) Just give me an example of *a* fraction."

This, in effect, is an unbroken continuation of 1, with the first two sentences repeating the relevance of the lesson. Having established a group who are now *responsible* for knowing about fractions, the teacher can ask what fractions are. After several reformulations of the question, he is explicit about their ability ("That you can do"), and names one ($S_1$) from the group of responsible students. In so doing, he claims his right to control the speaker and to determine who is knowledgeable.

"4. $S_1$: Does a fraction have an inch?
5. T: A what? An example of it? A number?
6. $S_2$: (Whispers – probably to $S_1$.) Four.
7. $S_1$: Four.
8. T: Four? Is that a fraction? (Pause.) What is four? What is four itself? Tell me $S_3$.
9. $S_3$: A whole number.
10. T: A whole number. Now I am asking you to give an example of a fraction. Just to close you in a bit more, if four is a whole number . . . really, the opposite of a whole number is a fraction. (Repeat.) First of all an example of a fraction again. $S_4$?
11. $S_4$: What a fraction is? An example?"

In doing this analysis, the focus is on the teacher – to show how he (and the students) are mindless to their interpenetration. He creates, and is mindless to,[4] student docility. With respect to correct and incorrect answers, he ignores them. Much of the work is his but what is focussed on is the *students'* performance.

Statements 4 to 11 initiate the procedure for arriving at a correct answer. Having established the justification for the question, the teacher responds to an incorrect answer (4) by repeating the question. The incorrect answers culminate in the naming of fractions as whole numbers (9 and 10). This incorrect answer becomes part of the production course for arriving at a correct answer. From the point of view of this paper, it is important to note that so far all the lesson has been teacher-orchestrated. The teacher formulates "clues" (explicitly, 10) to direct the understanding to its intended goal – i.e., he organizes the learning as a differentiation between those who know (himself) and those who do not know but will come to know (the students). Coming to know as the outcome of socially organized learning depends on a flow of questions and answers, incidental talk, asides, queries, irony, etc.

"12. T: $S_5$? (Pause.)
13. T: No? $S_6$?
14. T: Oh come on, think!
15. $S_6$: A number?
16. T: I want an example of a fraction.
17. $S_6$: –

18. T: I know it's Monday. This is terrible. $S_7$?
19. $S_7$: Two.
20. T: Two? Is two a fraction? What is two? $S_7$?
21. $S_7$: A whole number.
22. T: It's a whole number. Two. There are two whole things. I want an example of a fraction. $S_8$?"

There are several things going on in this segment. One is the right to persist in asking questions beyond what, as adults, we would accept. Two is the teacher's right to call for knowledge based on his assertion that some of the students have been taught it before. Questions may be ignored (11, 12) in the interests of getting to the correct answer. Answers come to have their status in the teacher's repetition of the answer. Wrong answers are repeated in the form of a question. Statements 16 and 22 reaffirm the teacher's managerial responsibility towards the students, who are not recognized as participants in what, at a deeper level, is a "shared" enterprise. The teacher's usage of "I" reasserts his authority for seeking (and finally getting) the answer.

"23. $S_8$: Three.
24. T: What's three? Here are three brushes, are they wholes? Huh?
25. $S_8$: Yes.
26. T: Yes. They are whole things. Three is a whole number. Still looking for a fraction. I'm not going to ask you if you've got your hand up. I want someone who doesn't have a clue.
27. $S_9$: One?
28. T: One?
29. Many students: (Laughter.)
30. T: Still working on the same thing. What is this? This one brush. Is it whole or is it a fraction? Think of that much of a brush. That is my example of a fraction. That much of a brush. This is a fraction. Got it now, $S_4$?
31. $S_4$: One-half.
32. T: Very good."

A correct answer is arrived at through recognition of the incorrect ones. This becomes evident in 29, where several students' recognition of $S_9$'s wrong answer marks an orientation to the teacher's concern. I include the teacher's production of the answer only to show the reader that the lesson did move on.

"40. T: Right one-fourth. Another fraction, $S_7$?
41. $S_7$: One-sixth.
42. T: Again.
43. $S_7$: One-sixth.
44. T: Can't quite hear the end of that.
45. $S_7$: One-sixth.
46. T: One-sixth.
47. $S_7$: One-sixth.
48. T: Spell it.
49. $S_7$: Uh. S-i-x-t-h.
50. T: Good."

Here the teacher steps outside of the frame of reference, a lesson in fractions,

150

to deal with spelling and pronunciation. All aspects of the student's learning can be treated without regard to time and place. Before I deal with the significance of this, here are two more excerpts.

"59.  T:  Three-fourths. Another way of saying three-fourths, $S_{10}$? Now I asked you to pay attention to this lesson and you're not doing it.
  60.  $S_{10}$:  Three-quarters.
        T:  Three-quarters. All right. . . .
  61.  T:  I think we know how to identify, or at least name, fractions. They're quite easy. One-half, one-quarter, one-sixth, one-eighth. Repeat these please, $S_{11}$.
  62.  $S_{11}$:  One-half, one-quarter, one-sixth, one-eighth."

In 59, the teacher asserts his authority by reminding the student ($S_{10}$) of rules of conduct. In 61 *he* announces that what was necessary to be known is, in fact, known. *He* speaks *for* the students. $S_{11}$'s repetition of the fractions in 62 establishes proof of the students' knowing. The use of "we" in segment 61 recasts the room — temporarily there is unity between teacher and students.

During the lesson the teacher asserts what I will gloss over as pedagogic rights. These rights (to determine correct answers, behaviours, talking sequence, etc.) are tied to a conception of knowledge that I have characterized as owned. These rights are asserted over not only listening and learning but also the conditions of work. What follows is the last sequence of the lesson.

"157.  T:  Right, pretty simple isn't it?
  158.  $S_4$:  Yep.
  159.  T:  Now there's some work I'm going to do, just simple practice. Grade 5s, in your blue book, page 108 number 1 and number 2. (Writes pages and numbers on the board.) Grade 6s, page 25, 1, 2 and 3. Stop the talking and begin that now. I'm going to come around if you have any questions. Too much chatter. If you have any questions ask either myself or Mr. MacKay, whoever's closer or freer. Don't ask your neighbour please. (Pause.) Grade 6s, I'm sorry, skip number 1 that's a . . . 2, 3, and 4 I want you to do. Number 1 is a number line which I don't agree with. (Pause.) [Teacher leaves room for 2 min.] Neatly please and don't jam your work altogether. You are jamming it too much S."

In the co-production agreement (157-158), the lesson comes to be *seen* as simple and then work is assigned. I want to point to two things here with respect to pedagogical rights — to have students work on their own and to monitor all the activities of the students (e.g., 40-50).

I am arguing that the very speech of teacher and students calls forth and organizes the lesson. The teacher's and students' talk creates the classroom and its rights, indicating that responsibility for the exercise of rights is a moment-to-moment activity. The lesson is shaped within and through the contingencies of interaction, seen but unnoticed. This is important to note because an ideal version of teaching cannot explain how emergent features are part of the lesson. And an ideal version of teaching cannot deal with the orchestration of learning. The lesson then is a co-creation of teacher and students. I have tried to focus on the relationship of knowledge to participants. The teacher's owning of the knowledge produces the possibility for control of students' activities. Here is the locus of students' rights, which seem to be the reciprocal of teachers' rights.

The features and relationships that I have pointed to above in part constitute teaching. This does not imply that teachers do not have different styles but that each style incorporates these features (i.e., ownership, elicitation, etc.) as an integral part of teaching.

The activities of teaching are assumed to lead to learning on the part of the student. In that the teacher's activities promote the emergence of learning, so these same activities define the intellectual rights of students. Students must comply with the rules of good teaching, although these rules may sometimes contravene the interests, frames of reference, abilities, etc., of some of the students. The reciprocal of this is that teachers have the right to see their activities as being in the interest of the student vis-à-vis the learning of a fixed curriculum.

### The Interpretation of Activity

I turn now to a somewhat different conceptualization of these activities to place in relief some of the already presented features. The division between teaching and learning is maintained on the basis of interpenetrating and reciprocal relationships. This reciprocity grants legitimacy to teachers' claims to the ownership of knowledge. In other words, students do affect the way such ownership is achieved. As part of the emergent character of the lesson, there can be seen a tension in this mutual legitimizing of the teachers' enforced claim to ownership. "18. T: I know it's Monday. This is terrible. $S_7$?"

What I see here is that failure to produce correct answers undermines the pedagogical authority of the teacher. Interpenetration is integral to this particular relationship. Tension is also hinted at in the following part of the lesson.

"136. (Class laughs because of something the teacher writes on board.)
137. T. My mind was one step ahead.
138. S: You never make a mistake, sir. (Class laughs.)
139. T: (Inaudible.) Three-quarters plus two-quarters equals five-quarters."

The tension between owner and learner is exposed by the laughter. The danger of the laughter is that it may separate I/they and unite they (the students) against I (the teacher).

The ownership of knowledge is reflexively tied to the concerted activities of both parties. Such interpenetration is unnoticed by the participants except as practical matters (e.g., dealing with the laughter above). This version of teaching rests on the fact that, in the classroom, teachers and students do not recognize that they are collaborators. They are *mindless* before the fragmentation they construct (we/they).

To be more graphic about this interpenetration, imagine a strike in which students, instead of picketing or not attending classes, failed to learn *anything*, claiming that they could not understand what their teachers were getting at. What this would do, besides stopping school based on this form of teaching, would be to bring into the open the practice that gives certain persons the right to determine intellectual abilities *for* others. Education for others has lead to schooling where students are beings-for-others (Vandenburg, 1971). Vandenburg has used this distinction as the basis for arguing that the relationship between teacher and student is commanding.

### Summary and Implications

In this paper I have studied conversation to investigate children's intellectual

152

rights. I stress that it is through analysis of the talk that the social organization of learning and intellectual rights became apparent. What is important here is the creative nature of talk and the responsibility of speakers for their talk (i.e., it is their talk that creates the particular environment here, one of ownership and management).

I began by suggesting that the context for a discussion of rights is an unequal community based on a we/they distinction. I turned to testing and teaching to show how we/they is maintained in classrooms and suggested what rights this implies for children in classroom situations. Teachers who manage their students by managing knowledge are mindless of the unity (we/they) that allows for the differences – teacher as manager, student as learner. I show that the teacher gives knowledge to the students but, through the process of giving, negates the students' rights to be active knowers. Active knowing is subservient to objective method and authority. The teacher's demonstrated rights to ignore the conversational conventions have their reciprocal in the student's lack of rights. The student's rights are those of a docile consumer. Mindful of the unity of teacher and students, I introduced ways in which testing and teaching a lesson ignore children's abilities. This restores the reflexivity[5] of mindfulness-mindlessness, which is an analytic way of perceiving the essentially open and reflexive nature of social life on which equality is ultimately based. Children's rights are to be unequal intellectually. In showing how this inequality stems from careful management of the social organization of learning (teaching), I have pointed to an underlying equality that, in turn, could be a step towards the recognition of children's intellectual rights.

## Notes

This paper is based on some of the data from a study (Children's Culture and Children's Competencies) that was supported by a Canada Council Research Grant.

[1] Although I do not have in mind recognition as only a legal practice the explicitness of the importance of recognition is pointed to in Part I of the Canadian Bill of Rights. "It is hereby recognized and declared that in Canada . . ." (Tarnopolsky, 1966, p.229).

[2] A related example of an act of scientific recognition is available in Kingsley Davis' (1947) article on isolated children. One way Davis is able to show that Isabelle was more social and therefore more worthwhile than Anna was to focus on oral language ability. Oral language ability was given as most important by the social scientific theories he was operating in. Thus he is able to ignore important human attributes about Anna, such as her ability to communicate with a system of gestures.

[3] By cultural embeddedness, I mean the way in which children exist in their own fully constituted culture. A culture is not recognized by curriculum.

[4] This is not a condemnation, for in a state of activity one is necessarily mindless to it. This is analogous to the notions of visible and invisible developed in Merleau-Ponty (1968).

[5] Further evidence to support the integrity of children's intellectual abilities can be found in work on children's culture (e.g., MacKay, 1974b; Silvers, 1976; Speier, 1973).

## References

Ariès, P. Centuries of childhood. New York: Random House, 1965.

Cicourel, A., et al. Language use and school performance. New York: Academic Press, 1974.

Davis, K. Final note on a case of extreme isolation. *American Journal of Sociology*, 1947, **52**, 432-437.

MacKay, R. Standardized tests: Objective/objectified measures of "competence." In A. Cicourel et al., *Language use and school performance*. New York: Academic Press, 1974. (a)

MacKay, R. Conceptions of children and models of socialization. In R. Turner (Ed.), *Ethnomethodology*. Middlesex: Penguin Books, 1974. (b)

Martell, G. *The politics of the Canadian public school*. Toronto: James Lewis and Samuel, 1974.

Mead, M. Our educational emphasis in primitive perspective. *American Journal of Sociology*, 1942-43, **48**, 633-639.

Merleau-Ponty, M. *The visible and the invisible*. Evanston, Ill.: Northwestern University Press, 1968.

Ontario Ministry of Education. Circular P1J1. *The formative years*. Toronto: The Ministry, 1975.

Roth, D. Intelligence testing as a social activity. In A. Cicourel et al., *Language use and school performance*. New York: Academic Press, 1974.

Sharrock, W. W. On owning knowledge. In R. Turner (Ed.), *Ethnomethodology*. Middlesex: Penguin Books, 1974.

Silvers, J. Appearances: A videographic study of children's culture. 1976.

Speier, M. *How to observe face-to-face communication*. Pacific Palisades, Calif.: Goodyear Publishing, 1973.

Tarnopolsky, W. *The Canadian Bill of Rights*. Toronto: Carswell, 1966.

United Nations. The Universal Declaration of Human Rights, 1948. In, *Human rights*. London: Heinemann, 1968. Pp.17-23.

Vandenburg, D. *Being and education*. Englewood Cliffs, N.J.: Prentice-Hall, 1971.

# Family Grouping: A Structural Innovation in Elementary Schools

Ron Buston/Ontario Public School Men Teachers' Federation

Critics of conventional schooling frequently focus on educators' assumption that chronological age is the most effective way of separating children into various classrooms. These critics suggest that the concept of lock-step grading runs counter to the actual diversity and complexity of developmental patterns of childhood. As a result, conventional schools seriously compromise the individual integrity of children by anticipating and arbitrarily influencing the rate at which they grow up. Family grouping is a structural innovation in elementary schools which attempts to limit the amount of control exerted on childhood development and thereby to respect better the rights of young students.

This innovation involves a classroom of children whose chronological age and assessed intellectual growth reflect a differentiation of several years and thus considerable variety in the children's emotional, physical, and psychological functioning. The children remain together with the same teacher for a specified period of time, generally two to four years.

Family grouping aims to promote children's potential for self-determination and to minimize the traumas of enforced entry into school. Although concern rests particularly with the child who does not want to go to school, the innovation of family grouping also addresses itself to the enthusiastic child. This structure reflects belief that educational institutions should care for the positive development of all children, and should maintain rather than crush their natural enthusiasm.

The theoretical model of family grouping is the successful family, and it is from this social structure that we can define the principles of family grouping in schools.

In this paper I provide a rationale for family grouping, together with a description of a prototypical classroom situation and the type of teacher needed to guide it. I then note several implications of family grouping and outline some criticisms. It should be clearly stated at the outset that I am a practical supporter of family grouping and that I have worked as an associate teacher in such a program with children five to seven years old.

For the purposes of this paper I assume that the school staff, the parents, and the local administrators have consented to the concept of family grouping. Resistance is so varied and unpredictable that the concept clearly requires excellent public relations and a relatively autonomous, enthusiastic staff for its implementation. In addition, knowledge of neighborhood needs and attitudes is necessary and evidence from pilot projects makes full implementation easier.

The family, its individual members, and the social structure in which they operate are in a constant state of flux. It follows that the uniqueness of people and the variety of their social situations require that the school be adaptive to their needs and aspirations. Some examples are the constant change in neighborhoods, career requirements, and personal values of any community. Unless the school staff are aware of these community changes and have the sensitivity and skills to respond appropriately, the school and the community may operate in opposing or, at least, non-congruent social spheres. Keddie's (1971) work has shown that teachers' personal and social preconceptions rather than carefully developed understanding and rational evaluation often govern how students are treated in classrooms.

"Ability is an organizing and unexamined concept for teachers whose categorization of pupils on the grounds of ability derives largely from social class judgments of pupils' social, moral and intellectual behavior. These judgments are frequently confounded with what are held to be rational values of a general nature." (p.155)

The traditional grading system that now dominates schools has allowed this hegemony of unreflected and class-derived values to remain because of the teacher's limited one-year commitment to a particular group of children. Family grouping, however, can enhance the school's responsiveness to its community by strengthening the classroom group's cohesion and by allowing individual development of relevant standards over a greater span of time.

If a school and community exhibit a variety of needs, concerns, and values, then it must certainly follow that individuals within these groups will demonstrate even greater variety. As Goodlad and Anderson (1959) found, the "standardized" achievement levels and behavior of children in a variety of tasks and learning activities showed a range of four years in a traditional grade 1 classroom. These findings, which conform to observations of grossly irregular growth patterns, undermine preconceptions of standardized knowledge acquisition and concept development. Family grouping does not pretend to offer a more efficient delineation of intellectual progress, but it does allow the involved parties to be and work together for a longer period of time, free of the constraints of time-tabled growth and pre-planned curricula. By openly incorporating children of a number of ages it allows "fast" and "slow" children to proceed at their own pace and level.

Moreover, teachers in traditional schools do not have sufficient time to individualize programs for specific children. Family grouping gives teachers more time to observe and interact, thus allowing them to assess and accept more effectively their changing role in a changing relationship. As a result, significant program modification to reflect a changed circumstance may take place at any time.

Family grouping contains a number of structural devices that may enhance, besides affecting, teacher–pupil relations, and mutually enrich child–child interaction. While traditional lock-step grading tends to deny the kind of broad social functioning that is commonplace in the adult world and to restrict child–child interaction, family grouping rejects the assumption that children must be protected from themselves and from each other. Teachers are not seen as omniscient vis-à-vis children, and children are encouraged to learn as much from each other as they can from teacher-instigated activities. Obviously this kind of learning is difficult to plan and impossible to assess, but supporters of family grouping recognize its vital importance.

Family grouping also attempts to avoid the trauma that sometimes results when children first go to school. In a traditional school, the young child is expected to cope with a series of changes that would jolt even the most stable of adults. The appearance of new figures of authority, the need to learn a new system of behavior, and the initial lack of support from friends or familiar faces tend to dislocate the child psychologically. By contrast, family grouping attempts to ensure that change is engendered gradually and naturally in a manner congruent with the child's own social thinking and psychological adaptability. Family grouping attempts to minimize the differences between family and school. The family-grouped classroom extends the features of an ideal family into the school by supporting and accommodating individual members. In some situations it may also compensate for the lack of these features in the child's home.

## Our Experience: Entering School

Rather than having all pupils enter a class on the same day, family grouping requires staggered entry based on the child's age and on the child's enthusiasm for the new experience. This is a lengthy and deliberate process preceded by frequent casual visits of parent and child to the school. Children's relationship with their parents is not threatened by any manifestation of teacher power. The presence of older siblings and neighborhood friends suggests a familiar and less threatening social reality to the child. With staggered entry, the teacher can devote more time and energy to the single new entrant and help reinforce a sense of individuality. Other children are also given time to assimilate the single new entrants. In our experience the new arrivals tend to compete for the affections of established children. Acceptance of the new member is generally automatic, just as it is in the successful family at home. In both of these situations, the teacher and the parent strive to create a climate of acceptance before the new member arrives. Ideally, the arrival of the new student, like that of the new baby, is met with anticipation and celebration.

The initial impact of the new arrival is followed by a carefully controlled adjustment and observation period. The teacher assigns the responsibility of "caring" for the new child to one or more of the older class members. No external controls are made evident to the new child unless through a student intermediary. The new student develops an impression of the class as an organic, self-controlling body. The peer group is encouraged to guide the new entrant, on the rationale that children are more tolerant of each other's demands than they are of an adult's. When the teacher and parent are satisfied that the adjustment is successful and that the child has learned to play with others and accept the routines and restraints of the classroom, then the new student can help deal with still newer recruits. As in the family, children move from total dependency on others to a position where others can be dependent on them.

## The Learning Program

The pattern of introduction, gradual assimilation, and independent performance that emerges from the classroom entrance routine is the pedagogical basis of family grouping. As children grow, they are exposed to the course of study, first, through watching older children perform, second, by experiencing their own curiosity and teacher encouragement to perform, and, finally, by working through the particular concept in a more formal group or independent learning structure that is suited to their personality and learning style.

The theoretical basis of our program borrows from the work of Piaget,

157

Bettelheim, and Bruner. It is a growth-oriented program with emphasis on sensory development, explorations of the real world, and verbalization of discoveries and feelings. The Piagetian influence is manifest in a flexible approach to concept development and the conclusion that pressure to succeed, no matter how nobly phrased, causes a loss of equilibrium in the young mind. It may be traditional practice to spend six weeks teaching a five-year-old to add 2 + 5, but we have opted to spend that six weeks in manipulation and grouping of real objects in real situations. We can teach a five-and-a-half-year-old the sum with relative ease when the child is more mature and has experienced a more valuable set of number activities.

This does not mean that the younger child is protected from challenge of the unknown. The average day is built around open-ended situations in both the physical and social spheres. There is much need for observation, assessment, and judgment in real activities. Unlike "school work," these real activities are not pressuring and there is no concept of failure. If one is unsuccessful, one merely tries another activity.

The idea of play in the family-grouped class is given an excellent practical application in Marzollo and Lloyd's (1972) *Learning Through Play*. The authors have devised numerous activities to reinforce sensory development; language development; understanding relationships; sorting, classifying; counting, measuring; problem-solving; exploring; creativity; self-esteem; physical growth. Their ideas are ideally suited to the family-grouped class because the activities can be adapted to various intellectual levels and can be taught by the older children to the younger ones.

The structure of the heterogeneous classroom is much more conducive to integrated learning. The spoken language tends to be more mature because of the presence of the older children, while the younger children are able to pattern their speech after their elders and to become more adept at verbalizing. In the integrated large-group meetings, each child is able to listen at the level of the class yet speak at a personal level. Topics of general interest can be easily adapted to various levels and media without sacrificing interest and enthusiasm. For example, in a nutrition group at our school, the older children purchased and prepared food that was served to the younger ones, who were asked to comment on taste, texture, and color. Each group was able to adapt the subject matter to its own level.

There should be few curriculum dislocations in the family-grouped class if the child sees each learning situation as part of a familiar and reassuring pattern. The desire to learn grows from an atmosphere of positive reinforcement in which one experiences self-worth as an individual and the personal status of being a responsible leader. The intelligent non-achiever soon learns that there are no gains for prolonged inactivity; the genuinely handicapped child can experience success and self-worth by working with students at a similar level yet assuming a modified leadership status within that group. The staunch individualists can remain as such if they wish and can define their own accountability strictly in terms of the teacher's or their own demands. They can opt in or out whenever they wish. The teacher must support the children's decisions and let them function according to their own design. These forms of social play provide an experimental and experiential vehicle that can contribute to mental health by releasing tensions and expanding children's repertoire of behaviors. Bettelheim (1972) suggested that play is children's attempt to make order out of chaos. Children act out their fears in order to overcome them and thereby assert strength over the environment. This strength encourages the children to move on to greater challenges. The teacher cannot realistically guide this process but must stand back and provide only that subtle and quiet leadership needed for physical protection and continued exploration.

Thus, while children in the family-grouped classroom are active instigators of their own learning, teachers protect, observe, and provide basic learning materials. The classroom, like the ideal home, stimulates and reinforces the skills and values deemed important by each child. Independence is looked upon favorably and any attempt children make to devise a personal curriculum and learning structure is encouraged and rewarded.

Significantly, the most frequent complaint we receive from our students is that they want to do formal, rote activities. These complaints are of course answered and result in better quality work habits and performance levels than could have been achieved through compulsory drill. Thus through responding to the interests of the children, the traditionally imposed academic standards are met without sacrificing the intent and structure of family grouping. It is this fact that has most surprised the critics in our community.

The teacher in the family-grouped school may appear at first to be a passive element. This is, however, an inaccurate judgment, which ensues from the shift to a children-centred classroom. The structure of the classroom group is adjusted to allow children to do many of the tasks performed by the teacher in the traditional teacher-centred classroom. Routines and classroom organization are reaffirmed each September by the continuing group of children. Responsibilities such as clean-up, distribution of materials, and correction of work are shared by the teacher and the older children.

As a result of sharing routine duties, the teacher's activities are more focussed on responding to personal requests for learning materials, assistance, and attention. Teachers act as coordinators, integrating such activities as music and physical education. They must be particularly sensitive to the possibilities for developing formal literacy and abstract concepts when these emerge spontaneously from play and activity sessions and the child's own desire to learn. At our school, for example, a teacher-instigated demonstration of hot and cold grew into three frantic weeks of freezing and boiling everything from rocks to red paint and iron magnets. Almost every child wanted to do an experiment and contribute a page to our science book. Several art techniques were learned from observation of 10- and 11-year-olds and resulted in a rare variety of visual expression combining learned and copied techniques. A discarded bingo game and a rubber giraffe provided weeks of explorations into numbers and animal habits. Even though the curriculum was child-centred, by the end of our first year we had managed to learn nearly all of the so-called basic skills required for each child's age grouping. This was done in a spirit of relaxed fun and high personal initiative.

The importance of success as a motivating device cannot be understated. Children often repeat a task several times when they know that success is guaranteed. Their feelings of success, their curiosity, and their exposure to older children combine to motivate them further. One of the most crucial roles of the teacher is to provide opportunity for frequent success, particularly if a child seems unsure or withdrawn.

**Assessing Pupil Progress**
The study of structural innovation in elementary schools has shown that the common element in successful change is greater teacher concern with the whole child. Perceiving a child's growth as an integral psychological and

philosophical progression rather than an externally imposed and unidimensional pattern has contributed greatly to the actualization of this ideal of teaching the whole child. It is an ideal implicit in family grouping, where the curriculum is no longer restricted to courses of study but becomes the sum of all the child's school experiences.

Our redefined curriculum demands that parents and teachers question the validity of traditional academic knowledge and teaching techniques. Young (1971) suggested that literacy, individual work, abstract knowledge and its structuring and compartmentalizing, and the unrelatedness of academic curricula to real experience must be seriously challenged if there is to be any positive change in our social structures. The inability of low-income and minority groups to change their relative positions through education provides evidence to support Young's contention. A school that places singular value on literacy (which is, after all, only one facet of human personality) measures all its students as high or low in terms of this arbitrary standard. When this causes one to overlook other personal and intellectual skills such as practicality, leadership, creativity, and adaptability, then the school becomes an agent of social repression.

Our "reporting to parents" was focussed on a subjective, anecdotal procedure containing only positive comments and suggestions. This type of report gave a good morale boost to all concerned, particularly parents, who much preferred a positive, growth-oriented report card. At the primary school level, we found that a good report card had a positive effect on the parent–child relationship and increased the child's enthusiasm and cooperativeness.

The heterogeneous class and the concept of teaching the whole child accentuate personal differences in a definite manner, without passing absolute judgments. The child's personality defines a learning style, which, in turn, creates a personal standard of achievement. This philosophy is extended to the report card. Teachers who are determined to write good reports on each child become subtly aware of the relativity of their judgments and the social definitions of intelligence that have conditioned their thinking.

Visiting teachers would often politely refer to our children as noisy, precocious, or hyperactive. Our "family" was loud, active, argumentative, and loving. Some days were an emotional and physical strain but the overall results of the program made this worth while. We did not fear this kind of pressure because it was always temporary, unlike the pressure of meeting curriculum demands and skill requirements in the lock-step graded programs.

## The Mechanics of Implementation

Family grouping is no more expensive to operate than a traditional classroom. The school staff have to spend some time in both formal and informal reallocation of supplies and equipment. The time and money saved through minor alterations to equipment and scheduling can be used for individual planning, excursions, and educational "luxuries." The pooling of audiovisual equipment at our school left us with enough money to buy food, pottery clay, toys, and games. The sharing of supervision duties during film and drama presentations left several teachers free to provide individual counselling, talk with parents, or prepare new learning materials.

There must also be congenial sharing among teachers of resources and responsibilities. Willingness to cooperate was a significant factor in the success of the family-grouping experiment. Without fervent commitment on the part of staff, most experiments are doomed. Our approach was positive and constructive with a spirit of open criticism and questioning. If an idea could not be

160

justified in a manner acceptable to all, it was tabled for a later meeting.

This attitude was shared with the children, who, in turn, made their own suggestions about how to alter the classroom and its equipment. Their requests for a woodworking table, more drama, and more soccer games were met when they agreed to some of the compromises that teachers suggested. These compromises were necessitated by timetabling and space restrictions. The process of compromise was an active element in student–teacher relations. Ideas, problems, mistakes, and compliments were openly aired in an ambience of mutual respect and with a sense of humor. We found that doing so increased awareness of and sensitivity to others, drew the individuals closer together, and made further group action easier. Incidents of vandalism, theft, and open aggression became less and less frequent.

The presence of visitors (approximately 10 per week) had no adverse effects on the activities of the group. Some of the curious children would introduce themselves to the strangers, but the majority would ignore them and continue with whatever they were doing.

We rearranged our furniture often and we frequently moved a class into a different room. There is a certain dullness about school rooms, and changing one's location offers a refreshing learning environment. By working in parallel teams of two teachers and 55 students we also lessened the impact of staff turnover and still maintained continuity in the class families.

## Conclusion

Faults in family grouping derive from its position as a social device that runs contrary to several larger social patterns. The pressure of the internalized or socially defined status of knowledge actively counteracts the non-evaluative philosophy of family grouping. Children and parents still use grade names, still compare each other, and are not quick to accept intellectual growth in any form other than in reference to absolute standards.

Family grouping as a device for universal non-evaluative growth is still building its own vocabulary. New concepts and strategies need to be much more widely dispersed and explained before we can expect to lessen the impact of absolute "standards" that dominate most current educational practice. Furthermore, family grouping still supports the notion of status based on age. The direction and strength of primary group power structure are imposed upon the very young. If they are fortunate, they may be able to moderate and humanize these structures that control them, but in most cases they learn to wait until they have grown up before they can rule themselves. Perhaps a highly individualized learning program and a supportive, sympathetic teacher may prove sufficient to counteract this problem.

Despite these weaknesses, family grouping provides continuity between the home and the school with a minimum of psychological and emotional shock. The attention to individual personality is increased, with an equal emphasis placed on interpersonal skills. The extended time period allows teacher and student to interact and to grow together with greater awareness of each other. It is a simple, economical structure to create in any school, provided that staff, parents, and administration share the same positive expectations regarding the program. Classroom teachers have to reassess their role in relation to their clients and their teaching methodology. They have to accept children as the instigators of most of their own learning and encourage them to build their own curriculum in accord with individual personality and learning style. If this can be achieved, family grouping offers both a practical and a humane alternative to the lock-step schooling that now predominates.

## References

Barker-Lunn, J. *Streaming in the primary school*. Sussex, England: King, Thorne and Stace, 1970.

Berson, M. P. *Opening, mixing, matching*. Association for Childhood Education International, 1974.

Bettelheim, B. Play and education. *School Review*, 1972, **81**, 1-13.

Bruner, J. *Toward a theory of instruction*. Cambridge, Mass.: Belknap, 1966.

Dreitzel, H. P. Childhood and socialization. In, *Recent sociology*. No. 5. New York: Macmillan, 1973.

Goodlad, J., & Anderson, R. *The nongraded elementary school*. New York: Harcourt Brace, 1959.

Keddie, N. Classroom knowledge. In M. F. D. Young (Ed.), *Knowledge and control*. New York: Collier and Macmillan, 1971.

Marzollo, J., & Lloyd, J. *Learning through play*. New York: Harper & Row, 1972.

Minuchin, P., & Biber, B. *The psychological impact of school experience*. New York: Basic Books, 1969.

Ridgway, L., & Lawton, I. *Family grouping in the primary school*. London: Ward Lock, 1965.

Skinner, B. F. *The technology of teaching*. Appleton-Century-Crofts, 1968.

Tewksbury, J. L. *Nongrading in the elementary school*. Columbus, O.: Merrill, 1967.

*The nongraded school: An annotated bibliography*. Toronto: Ontario Institute for Studies in Education, 1974.

Wilson, P. S. Plowden children. *Hard Cheese*, May 1973. Liverpool: Liverpool Free Press.

Young, M. F. D. (Ed.) *Knowledge and control*. New York: Collier and Macmillan, 1971.

# School Change and the Implications for Students' Rights

Glenn Eastabrook/Queen's University

"It is extremely difficult as the history of recorded thought and action show to frame correctly the questions or problems of human freedom and control. The correct or proper framing of the questions is almost surely precedent to a proper, correct, or adequate set of answers." (Seeley, 1974)

While I do not presume to think that I can provide a complete framework, I have attempted to pull together some ideas that hopefully will lead to at least a clearer focusing of the questions because of the conviction that we can no longer avoid addressing the challenge. The paper begins with an outline of recent events leading up to the concern over students' rights. A summary of our theoretical assumptions concerning school change[1] is then given. Some of our recent work[2] in two Ontario secondary schools is then presented, where we, in collaboration with student and teacher representatives, attempted to develop a process (and the necessary skills required to facilitate the process) for bringing about changes desired (from their mutual perspectives). I conclude by identifying a number of moral and ethical implications regarding the consideration of students' rights in the process of planned change.

## The Concern with Students' Rights

Ontario did not generally experience the radical demands for students' rights that were so widespread in U.S. schools during the late 1960s and early 1970s (e.g., contrast Libarle and Seligson, 1970, with Levin, 1972, and Quarter, 1972). Although student bills of rights were debated in a number of schools, the issue of rights evolved differently in the United States and Ontario. In contrast to the American experience, policy and action in Ontario were determined at the school board or senior administrative level rather than solely at the student level (e.g., Board of Education, 1973).[3] Another major difference was a concern on the part of central education officials that students should be involved in making decisions about their own schooling (e.g., Ontario Department of Education, 1968; Ontario Ministry of Education, 1975b, 1973/74–1976/77). Similarly, our own studies of parent, teacher, and student perceptions of the student role indicated, in general, widespread support for student involvement (Fullan & Eastabrook, 1972). Yet, despite this support, there appears to have been little actual involvement. A closer examination of the supportive forces suggests several reasons for this paradox. First, although the Ontario Ministry of Education has advocated more student involvement and, indeed, the creation of student councils or forms of student government, there has been little discussion with students or with many teachers as to *how* students might come to play a more active role. Second, there has been hardly any consideration of the implications of student autonomy in terms of course selection. (In 1972, the Ministry secondary school organization and curriculum guidelines, H.S.1, stated that, in effect, no prerequisites existed for secondary school students and no specific subjects were mandatory.[4])

In our review of the literature, we found that there has not been an investigation of the conditions under which there can be a transition from the student role as follower to the student role as initiator. Instead, the focus has been on the reaction of those in the schools to specific events and their consequences. For example, when they observed that students were selecting easy non-academic subjects, or selecting university-oriented subjects without adequate preparation or ability (King, 1972; Laxer, Traub, & Wayne, 1974), the educators (and their critics) decided that students were behaving irresponsibly. When some students began publicly to express their opinions, certain school officials adopted policies "forbidding the publication of defamatory material, such as personal attacks on individuals."[5] While such an attitude may seem just, equitable, and reasonable to those in authority, to the former followers – the newly "liberated" – the new rights seem but myths when defined by a statement to the effect that "now we are all equal but because some do not know operationally what this means, some of us will retain the right to name the game to be played, when and where it is to be played, and to make and revise the rules." It seems to us that one has to address the process of changing and the question of "rights" in that process and not restrict rights considerations to outcomes.

The past two decades have witnessed an awesome expenditure of resources, both human and material, in efforts directed at improving educational environments. It is ironic that then, as now, there has been no consensus as to what the specific objectives should be for these expenditures. Indeed, there has been no consensus as to what the general purpose of the educational experience should be. It is a revealing commentary on our society that only rarely have those most directly affected by the outcomes of the educational process taken part in discussions and in making decisions about this process. In short, in the whole process of schooling, it seems that those most directly involved and affected, in general, find themselves in the role of the bystander.

From our previous studies (Fullan & Eastabrook, 1972), we had found that (1) there were a number of aspects of the schooling process that students (and teachers and parents) wished changed; (2) students at all levels were interested in playing a more active part in the schooling process (i.e., they wanted their points of view to be taken into account, feeling that their ideas and opinions should lead to changes); (3) most parents and teachers supported the concept of student involvement in decision-making; (4) there was little student involvement (indeed little communication between students and teachers and among the students themselves).

**Theory and Methodology**
Two questions emerged from these findings. (1) When there is a desire and when there is support for change, why do things remain the same? (2) Given this desire and support, how can change take place?

A number of researchers have addressed the first question (e.g., see the literature surveys of Fullan, 1972, and Fullan and Pomfret, 1977, and the analysis by Sarason, 1971); their conclusion is that those who are most affected by

164

the schooling process (student and teachers) are not directly part of decision-making procedures. As to the second question, social scientists are still not much beyond the position described by Bennis (1969): "it is a curious fact about present theories that they are strangely silent on matters of directing and implementing change. . . . They are theories of change and not of changing" (p.64). Nevertheless, there are a growing number of potential theoretical contributions from organizational studies (Argyris, 1970; Cox, Erlich, Rothman & Tropman, 1970); interpersonal interaction and communication studies (Likert, 1967; Schmuck & Miles, 1971; Schmuck & Runckel, 1972); and those studies having an actor or user emphasis[6] (Freire, 1970).

Drawing on these studies and using a framework of action research, we began to address the second question. Action research aims to "contribute both to the practical concerns of people in an immediate problematic situation and to the goals of social science by joint collaboration within a mutually acceptable ethical framework" (Rapaport, 1970, p.499).

We have described our theory of change in an earlier paper (Fullan et al., 1977). Briefly, the six major assumptions underlying the theory are:
1. The group members are dissatisfied with aspects of their situation.
2. They are willing to become involved in the process of changing this situation.
3. To do so, they will need to understand their current situation and the problems of all involved in it.
4. They will need opportunities and resources to support the development of their understanding.
5. With this understanding, members can decide courses of action for change.
6. Change can occur only through mutual effort.

On the basis of these assumptions, we began to develop an ethical framework based on three key principles:
1. The guiding principle is that all constituent groups are to be directly involved in all research stages.
2. The constituent groups have control over access to data.
3. Data (including individuals' observations) are not to be used in any judgmental fashion.

These general principles can be specified further in terms of ethical and methodological principles.

Ethical principles:
1. The principal (and current school decision-makers) are to endorse the project.
2. Individuals (in this case students and teachers) are to make decisions regarding participation/non-participation as such.
3. Participating individuals are to be seen as having independent and autonomous rights (e.g., of observation, expression) in all phases of the study.
4. Open, non-judgmental discussions of the data gathering process, the data, and the implications of the data are to be encouraged.
5. The individuals whom the data describe are to have independent and autonomous control over the use and dissemination of them; the principal, and other school decision-makers, are to have control as to whether school data may be made available to people outside the school.

Methodological principles:
1. Time requirements are to be discussed in advance; a substantial proportion

of school time should be designated for the project.

2. Participating individuals shall have a say in determining the questions to be investigated.

3. Individuals' perceptions are valid data.

4. Individuals are to have the opportunity to discuss openly the data/findings within small groups as well as across the groups.

5. Problem-solving skills are necessary to arrive at (a) collective understanding of the meaning of the action, (b) collective approval of approximate solutions and action steps.

6. Only a small amount of data is to be explored at one time (the individual determines the priorities).

7. Participants are to be involved directly in an ongoing evaluation of the project and of its impact. The researcher role will be a part of this evaluation.

We assumed that through the discussion of these principles with each school's major constituent groups (administrators, teachers, and students), the members of these groups would be able to decide whether or not they wished to be involved in the study.

### Student Rights and Change in Two Schools

Our discussion of students' rights is based on research in two schools. One school is a composite secondary (grades 9 to 13), architecturally traditional, with a student body of about 1500, and situated in a relatively new surburban area of a small city. At the time of its construction, the school was intended for a then rapidly growing middle-class suburb. At present, the area includes the whole social spectrum from low-cost family units to middle-class single-family houses. The principal has been with the school since its opening. The staff is relatively young, with an average age of 35. Within the school system, the school has a reputation for being progressive, having a number of innovative features in its program.

The second school was constructed two years ago. Although the building is in a new upper-income-level suburb, the school draws its students from lower-income-level, suburban feeder schools. From its inception, the school has been hailed as a new experience in secondary education. The physical plant incorporates an open-space design and has as its focal point a learning center. Staff for the most part are young (under 30). The student body numbered 260 the first year (grades 9-10) and 500 the second year (grades 9-11). While it is reported to be "common knowledge" that both schools serve a middle-class clientele, observation of their students does not support this position – rather, the students come from a wide range of socially different home backgrounds, with different motivational, achievement, and consumption levels.

### The Larger School

Our work with the larger school centered on problems of communication, primarily in the classroom; a secondary concern was communication between students and administration. During the first year our work was within one department, history. All teachers in the department and 12 of their classes (at least one with each teacher) took part. Four of the teachers and their classes served as a core group. In the second year the project was extended to the English, geography, and science departments and in all 22 teachers and 32 of their classes took part.

Each year our work can be viewed conceptually as progressing through stages: (1) establishing a relationship between researchers and "clients"; (2) identifying areas of common concern and specific research questions; (3) gathering data; (4) feeding back data; (5) attempting to change the situation; (6) evaluating the process. Operationally each phase builds on the previous ones. The first three establish a readiness for change. The last three relate more directly to changing and assessing that change.

We found there are two aspects to establishing a relationship. The first is to develop collaborative support wherein students, teachers, and researchers build norms of mutual trust and openness. Our assumption was that through class discussions of ethical principles this type of support would emerge. The second is to develop the norm of contributing, i.e., to reach a point where each member becomes willing to discuss issues and personal concerns in the classroom. There is a need for the researcher to demonstrate an understanding of both student and teacher points of view, yet not to favor one at the expense of the other. We found as well that it is critical for each member of the class to feel that the project is worthwhile and that all ideas will be taken into account. At this early stage the teacher, or the person in the authoritative role, plays a key part. For example, teachers who invited us into the classroom demonstrated a personal openness to accepting students' ideas as worthwhile and a recognition that their own teaching methods could be improved.

Once individuals agreed to take part in the project the objective was to identify areas of concern, to begin to specify research questions. Two tasks arise at this stage: (1) to provide as many individuals as possible with an opportunity to participate, and (2) to develop a vehicle that can capture all members' ideas and thoughts. Because in the early stages there tend to be barriers that prevent individual participation, we have found it useful to distribute some form of written work, e.g., a short survey to identify student concerns, and to follow this with discussions. Whatever the work used, we believe it should be one to which students can contribute original ideas, as opposed to checking off "yes" or "no" to predetermined stimuli. The students' concerns are recorded and discussed, and any students who wish to extend the discussion meet during noon-hours or other "free" time. The outcome of the discussions is a questionnaire or other mechanism for gathering data.

In general, the data gathering phase is primarily of an organizational or technical nature; the concepts of openness and trust have already been discussed. Up to this point there tends to be relatively little individual risk for students (and teachers) about advancing personal, and perhaps controversial, ideas. However, when students are asked to indicate their true feelings on the questionnaire (or whatever device is used), confidentiality becomes critical. We, as researchers, have always assumed responsibility for gathering data and for its analysis preparatory to distribution or feedback. Since we gather information from all students, a large amount of data is generated. To meet commitments and relevance criteria, data must be fed back quickly. In this feedback phase there is a risk of overwhelming students and teachers with too much information. As well, feedback time eats into regular learning time: the two activities are seen as competing.

In the "changing" phase we find that students are somewhat resistant to identifying and discussing sensitive issues when teachers are present. One basic problem seems to be that students and teachers find it very difficult to transcend the conventional student–teacher roles, even in informal meetings. Thus, our role has been that of facilitator and recorder, attempting to assist teachers and students in clarifying and elaborating each area identified. We have found that the data gathering mechanism(s) should be very brief, focusing on few issues. A sense of futility tends to develop if too many issues are raised without adequate classroom time for debate. By examining a limited number of topics, the difficulty of conventional role-playing can be better addressed.

A second problem is lack of skill in problem-solving. At the time of feedback, we review the principles of constructive use of information: avoiding judgments, searching for and considering alternatives. We emphasize that the basic purpose of these data is to understand people's perceptions of classroom problems and needed changes. Our argument is that the data themselves do not provide solutions but are points of departure; the solutions come through discussion.

A third problem is that basic skills for participation in a collective or group setting are lacking, e.g., interpersonal communication and basic problem-solving in a group context. Students were just not used to talking about sensitive issues either among themselves or with their teachers. This problem was exacerbated by lack of time and the largeness of many classes. A further frustration arose when people began to understand what the issue was but were unable to come up with an acceptable solution. The frustration often resulted in a concern that the researchers were not providing adequate direction.

In our second year we attempted to address the problem of lack of skills by identifying a number of exercises having to do with one-way and two-way communication games and problem-solving exercises. However, we found again that while the students seemed to understand the dynamics underlying the communication games, they were unable to make the transfer to their regular classroom situation. One reason why students did not participate in class discussions was, as a number of students said, because "I might be wrong and other students will laugh at me." Therefore, to facilitate exchange in discussing results, we offered a set of simple guidelines for group discussion and broke each class into small sections. Nevertheless, at this stage the results were disappointing. While students did not lack ideas about specific changes or improvements in their classroom, they seemed incapable of arriving at solutions or developing strategies that might lead to solution. Frequently the changes that they suggested were relatively consistent with conventional or traditional learning/ teaching practices. The following are specific suggestions made by the students with regard to learning:
1. "I would have more discussions in class, and in groups; students should have more of an opportunity to teach the other students a topic they have researched."
2. "If I could change this class I would make it more active. Instead of talking about prisons, or inner-city school problems, we should go to these places and see for ourselves."
3. "Bring more people in from the community."
4. "More use of current news situations in problems, e.g., energy crises."
5. "The evaluation of the student should be on participation, small projects and discussion. I am strongly against the teacher feeding us this course without the student having any say as to its content."

In the second year in one class it was decided that small groups should be formed to discuss curriculum content and methods of instruction and evaluation. The students were to spend three class periods in successive days without the presence of a teacher. At the end of this time their concerns were to be discussed with the teacher. As a result of these discussions to do with the selection of books, independent study, and evaluation methods, specific changes were suggested and attempted. However, after a two-month trial the changes were not judged to be successful by either the students or the teacher. The basic difficulty seems to have been that, as mentioned before, it is a most difficult task to transcend the traditional teacher/student roles that have become ingrained through previous years of schooling and that continue to be reinforced by factors outside the classroom. One teacher, reflecting upon the experiences of his second year, remarked, "After all the basic discussion and reorganization of the class had been set up – courses and so on – I feel that students slipped back into their more traditional roles; they were passive, they wanted me to do the teaching and to give the answers, and their responsibility was to take notes."

Students of both years generally felt that the project had been worthwhile. For example, after the first year over 80% of them suggested that the project be extended to other classes and to other schools. During that first year they felt that they understood better the dynamics of the classroom. However, most of them agreed that hardly any significant change had occurred. The major difference in the second year was that students mentioned more often that they found their class teacher more "approachable."[7] One student expressed the phenomenon: "The importance of the project was finding out that the teacher could talk about and be talked to about class problems." A common complaint was: "The project made us realize the problems. However the solutions were never found." Overall, teachers felt that they had a better understanding of the students' position and that on a one-to-one basis in particular the student–teacher relationship definitely improved. The major difficulties were seen as time related.

### The Smaller School

Our involvement with the smaller school extended over a six-month period, from January to June. Two members of the project's research team had participated in earlier studies at this school (Eastabrook, Fullan, & Clifford, 1974, 1975). Our basic task, as agreed upon by a school staff–student committee, was to monitor the processes whereby students became involved in school-wide decision-making. The formal mechanism for this was a school committee, called the Student Staff Relations Committee (SSRC). The group comprised a small number of students and three staff members. Collectively they represented a model of decision-making that was unique and exciting in function, and rich in possibilities for educational change.

The school itself had a flat (as opposed to a hierarchical) organizational decision-making structure. There were no vice-principals or department heads. Decision-making was undertaken by five school committees: curriculum, budget, aims and objectives, community relations, and student–staff relations. Each made recommendations to the staff and these recommendations became policy. The elimination of department heads and the creation of these committees provided the groundwork for a multiconstituency-based decision-making process. Central to this concept was the development of responsible student attitudes and leadership capabilities. The philosophy was expressed in an early planning document: "Students and staff alike will learn responsibility and leadership through the provision of opportunities to practice them . . . the school climate will be characterized as an open climate which recognizes the inherent nature and dignity of all who work together in a common setting" (from a working paper of Planning Council, March 1973).[8]

The SSRC was the first to have students involved. There was, however, no formal mechanism for student involvement. Membership came through invitations to specific students to attend meetings. This structure provided the opportunity for a small group of students and staff to work together in examining and resolving school issues of mutual concern. Central to this concept was the development of responsible student attitudes and leadership capabilities.

The first problem of the committee, early in the year before we became involved, had been to develop an operational organizational structure and, as well, to establish the legitimacy of the committee in the eyes of the school as a whole. Organizationally, the committee accepted the leadership of one teacher — the one who had invited students to attend. Membership was fluid, varying in terms of the issues that would be discussed at the meeting. Agenda were usually circulated in advance or posted publicly. Eventually a core of members emerged and, in general, there tended to be about 20 to 30 individuals attending each meeting.

A further aspect of the SSRC was its subcommittee structure. This resulted from the concern of the chairperson that there should not be a centralized control. Subcommittees were formed around specific tasks. Again, as was the case with the larger group, membership was voluntary, and a chairperson was cooperatively chosen to focus and to coordinate activities. We became involved when the chairperson of the SSRC asked us if we were willing to attend several meetings to work with the group.

In retrospect, we can see the influence of the teachers, or the staff, in identifying the issues. The foremost issue was that of smoking. Others were vandalism, drug use, student autonomy, evaluation, and involvement. In our initial meeting with the SSRC, the students had relatively little to say and reacted primarily to staff comments or specific invitation to provide input to an idea already started by staff or to a point already made by a staff member. Interestingly enough, when we asked for volunteers for the subcommittee to be responsible for the designing of the questionnaire, only students volunteered. Perhaps because of being the only staff member who attended the first subcommittee meeting, the chairperson of the SSRC assumed the leadership of the smaller group as well.

The designing of the questionnaire took approximately three months. There were several reasons for this delay. One was that the researchers had identified the students' dependency upon them and upon the chairperson, who was the only staff member on the subcommittee. Our concern was that the students increasingly should come to take primary responsibility for the developing of the questionnaire and that we not dominate the questionnaire design. To help the students appreciate or understand the dynamics of the situation, from time to time we reviewed with them our concern. Our role became that of helping students identify specific "do-able" tasks and then supporting them, often teacher fashion, to complete the tasks or, after evaluation, to decide that the task was inappropriate and to select a more appropriate activity. More specifically, our support came in the form of specifying deadlines, rephrasing questions for purposes of clarity or elaboration, helping to identify specific individuals who would be responsible for specific tasks, and through questioning helping the students search for alternative activities. One difficulty in the long questionnaire gestation period was that the members of the parent committee tended to lose touch with the questionnaire designing task. There was an even greater problem with school members who were not a part of the SSRC. The second difficulty was that the members of the subcommittee assumed ownership of the questionnaire and staff

170

members in particular did not feel a part of the whole activity. At the time the questionnaire was administered, the end of the second semester was approaching and other time commitments interfered. As a result the data were not used as extensively as they might well have been. The most comprehensive use of the data was made by the individual classroom teachers, perhaps because students had answered in the context of a specific class for a number of questionnaire items. A second reason may have been that the classroom already had the organization required to at least receive such data – at the school-wide level there was no similar mechanism.

Although we followed conceptually the six stages, we did not build upon each one separately, as we had in the other school. For example, during the feedback stage, we continued to address aspects of the establishing relationships stage. We found that the dependency relationship of students on teachers continued to resurface – this was particularly true at the data feedback and at other "new" activity stages. We found that when researchers and students interacted, the students came increasingly to be more independent. Yet when the chairperson was present, the students continued to rely upon his direction. This seemed to be reinforced when teachers, too, accepted the chairperson's direction in the larger meetings. Still, the teachers spoke directly to the chairperson or to other staff people, while students invariably raised their hand and addressed the group through the chairperson. As a result, student input tended to be dependent upon the chairperson's acknowledgment, or another teacher's, and student opinion was frequently challenged by a number of outspoken teachers who did not wait to be acknowledged. The students were aware of this structured or bureaucratic and normative dependence. A grade 9 student, during an interview, stated: "I was nervous in the committee because of all the teachers present. All through elementary school we had seen the teachers as 'up there,' with the students below, sort of like a high priest in the front of the classroom."

While some of the ideas and concerns of the students that were reflected in the student or in the questionnaire data did come to the attention of some of the committee during the time of our work with its school, in general the data did not seem to be used effectively. The reasons were perhaps twofold. One was that the questionnaire and the data were seen as being owned by members of the subcommittee. An underlying factor, as we have indicated earlier, was the lack of adequate communication between the subcommittee members and the larger committee. The second reason related to the role definitions, a situation alluded to earlier. Although students and teachers were interacting outside the conventional classroom, the student and teacher roles were carried into the committee meetings. We already identified the student dependency phenomenon. However, from the teacher perspective there was active student involvement: when the chairperson or another teacher asked for a specific answer it was very seldom that they did not get at least one student to respond. Teachers and students tended not to see that the students gave short answers, that the students nearly always were dependent on the teacher stimulus, either in the form of a specific question or, a more indirect form of question, a partial statement. There was seldom a balanced discussion between students and staff. In addition to the lack of active support by teachers for student involvement, students themselves did not support each other. One student's opinion did not necessarily gain support from other students. In fact, other students tended to support staff positions. As well, students seldom addressed comments one to another. Rather, their comments were in the form of reactions made to the chairperson.

171

Throughout our work with both the larger committee and the subcommittee, there was always a time constraint. Because the larger committee meetings were weekly, the agenda tended to be very full, leaving little time for reaction on the part of the members. Only stronger members reacted. In fact, the patterns that emerged in the committees seemed to be identical with those in the classroom: a teacher took responsibility for outlining the activities that were to be done, identifying points of entry for the students (e.g., asking specific questions to which students made specific comments), deciding what should be done about students' comments, deciding when the meeting would be over. Paradoxically, in many cases, both students and teachers felt that there *had* been student participation. We attempted to feed process information to both committees to increase student and teacher awareness of their present role limitations, and to support them in becoming more conscious of a more autonomous role that they might play. We found that students and teachers alike became impatient with this, seemingly concerned that the more important business at hand, namely, making decisions, was being frustrated. When we imposed a discussion about process, our discussion had to compete with the more important items on the agenda. As we worked with the subcommittee, when staff members were absent, we did find ourselves able to talk more about process and roles.

Evaluation occurred along two dimensions. One dimension was the evaluation of consciousness raising, the degree or the extent to which students became more aware of the dynamics of a given situation (e.g., the understanding of interpersonal relationships, the effect of societally defined roles on the nature of interaction). The members of the subcommittee did indicate a heightened awareness of the complexity of interpersonal relationships, of interpersonal exchanges both within their own student group and between students and teachers. Gradually, in the subcommittee, the communication flow became more open and relaxed, and centered around a specific task. Students shared their ideas with each other, although they still frequently looked to the researchers for assurance. Often, however, the individual ideas and suggestions competed with each other, and there would be almost staccato exchange where little "listening" occurred. Individual feelings were frequently neglected. The second form of evaluation had to do with the degree to which students' ideas were taken into account for school-wide decision-making. There seemed to be a feeling on the part of many students that, because their ideas had been requested on the questionnaire, the ideas would automatically be taken into account. Staff seemed to feel that the opportunity had been created and the students had taken advantage of the opportunity and that they did state opinions not only on the questionnaire but in meetings as well. However, looking at this latter dimension objectively, we do not find the student ideas and concerns directly being used; the whole exercise culminated in a presentation of the questionnaire results and their implications by the subcommittee student members during two meetings. The students on the subcommittee, rather than verbally express their frustration over their inability to work through viable alternatives given time constraints, reverted to the traditional ways and means of administrative procedures. One student visited the principal. A second put notices up on the bulletin board. The chairperson was "given" control of the activities, and the questionnaire and its data became "lost."[9] The only part of the data that was used visibly was that relating to the smoking issue.

Nonetheless, the students interviewed indicated an optimism about the effect of their work, although they saw there was no direct follow-up on the committee's work. They felt that the chairperson and the principal who were present at most of the key meetings would follow through to bring about a solution based on information that had been gathered. A few students did indicate that the students should carry the work through the feedback stage. One student felt that the student contribution would be considered but that the teachers and principal still would take whatever aspects of the information they wished to use, and would use it as they saw fit, and that there was no guarantee that the changes important to students would in fact be made.

## Discussion

At this point let us review the events that occurred in the two schools. At each school, the traditional authority figures advocated increased student involvement. In both, a formal mechanism was developed whereby students' ideas and concerns might be raised. As well, the ideas and impetus for this formal mechanism were provided by the schools' existing authorities (principals and teachers) in the form of an invitation to the students to participate. It may have been that the students who attended initially did so because they saw no alternative but to comply with the authorities' request. It was interesting that although the students sometimes wrote comments of an uncomplimentary nature on the questionnaires, not one refused to complete a questionnaire or to engage in an interview. Not one verbalized a refusal to participate in the classroom activities. One explanation seems to lie in the existing school structure – given the social definition of the student role, students could not choose alternatives (indeed, were often unaware of the existence of alternatives) and adopted a role of compliance.

It seems then that, in the change process, we must consider student rights from two perspectives: process implications and outcome implications. That is, we must consider students' rights in terms of their being a part of the change process and their being a part (a major part) of the outcomes of the change attempt.

Let us now consider change from two analytical levels: micro or school level and macro or societal level. If we restrict ourselves to the micro (within the classroom or school), we suggest that, in approaching change, the first step is to break existing patterns or at least to arrest them (so that, I would add, the individuals in the immediate situation become aware of what they are doing and why they are doing it). In general, research reports agree that one of the major reasons for lack of success in implementing change has been that the immediate users of the particular innovation are not directly involved in deciding about its adoption and subsequent use (e.g., Fullan, 1972; Fullan & Pomfret, 1977). Yet, it seems to me that the condition of user involvement per se is not sufficient; that there must also be a high degree of homogeneity on the part of the users in terms of both their existing power/authority relationships and ideologies. Otherwise we have found that participation on the part of the inferior members tends to be in a token or gratuitous form. Our observation has been that those in authoritative positions, having provided the opportunity for students to participate and having seen the students use the opportunity as far as presenting themselves and responding to an agenda, are persuaded that students are participating. They do not see that the students' participation is of a passive or dependent nature. Similarly, those without authority (the students) seem to see the opportunity as being sufficient and do not perceive that they still retain their student role – follower of teacher, dependent upon teacher.

173

It is only after the awareness of the societal definitions (Freire's conscientization) develops that they begin to see they are still following and are still dependent. We found that when some students began to transcend the traditional student role, they soon encountered a number of issues that they could not address (e.g., set or "unchangeable" curriculum content, methods of evaluation, and learning modes). We also found that some students began to see the issues in a broader context – so broad that they could not offer suggestions for potential change. This latter group seemed to feel that even though they did not enjoy the present situation they could not change such a complex set of conditions. They reverted more strongly than ever to the student role, stating that it was not their responsibility or even their right to reject current conditions or to entertain new ideas. They became again followers.

Sarason (1972) addressed this problem in his analysis of change failure. One of his conclusions was that individuals who are involved in change, particularly those in key positions, become "trapped" by tradition or convention. When pressure (e.g., of time or of resource scarcity) is experienced, they lose the capacity to consider a range of alternative possibilities and to keep in mind the long-range objectives of the alternative(s). The consequence is that the long-range objectives are lost and former practices are again instituted. His explanation offers insight into our limited success at both schools.

We must address, as well, the matter of change at a broader level than the classroom, the macro level. In the past, educational change did not greatly affect the schooling process. Indeed, until recently, students and teachers led a rather staid existence for, despite great expenditures of effort, time, and money, little alteration in the schooling process came about (e.g., Fullan, 1972). The whole process was quite predictable – one started as a student at about five or six years of age and listened to what the teachers said. One tried to emulate them and to follow their direction and, dependent upon the degree of one's emulating/following capacity, one would experience "academic" success. As noted above, the theories of change had significance for observers but were of little practical use in bringing about change. Currently, however, with an increasing number of educational researchers employing action research approaches and with the research focusing more specifically on techniques of change, the fact of change at the micro level, and at the classroom level in particular, no longer remains problematic. And because of this new condition at the micro level, there are a number of implications that are felt at the macro level. For example, if a new product emerges from the school, will it be "acceptable" as an employee, or as a member of the local community?

Let us now return to the point made by Seeley (1974). The first part of the framing of the question requires addressing the purpose of education. We must ask, "What is the purpose of education?", and this purpose must be addressed on two levels, the societal and the individual. Related to this question is a second, "What are the implications for the student should he/she choose to pursue a direction that is inconsistent or contrary to societally held values?" Then, if the decision should be made to change, the question becomes, "What are the initial givens (those factors that exist right now) in terms of societal expectations of schooling outcomes and definitions of learning activities?"

The basic rights of students, I submit, are:

1.  To know at a given point in time what societal expectations are about schools and schooling.
2.  Subsequently, to have the right to be a part of the decision-making processes

174

that determine which course of action is to be pursued when a change is proposed. In other words, students should have the right to be involved at the action stage, not just at the reaction stage, and to be involved in the consideration of educational processes and their implications.

After all, as one young student stated, "It's our future, isn't it?"

### Notes

Many individuals have contributed to this paper. To each of you, students, teachers, principals, fellow researchers (in particular, John Biss, Julia Clifford, Michael Fullan, Jenny Gehlbach, Donna Lounsbury, Wayne Miles, and Isobel Roncarni), thank you. I hope I have not distorted excessively your realities. I wish also to thank Carolyn Hider for her patient and understanding typing and retyping. The constructive changes made by Gord West and the *Interchange* "anonymous readers" have been greatly appreciated.

[1] A detailed account is found in Fullan, Eastabrook, and Biss (1977).

[2] The author was a part of an OISE research team that included Michael Fullan, John Biss, Susan Light, Julia Clifford, Donna Lounsbury, and Wayne Miles.

[3] In the Toronto experience the activities of senior administrators at the board and school levels tended to be reactionary, i.e., it seems they reacted in anticipation of a student demand for power. For an account of the American experience, see Hendrick and Jones (1972) and in particular ch.8, where from the contributing individuals' perspectives the educators' concerns should be to control and to contain student dissent.

[4] The specific reference is found in Ontario Ministry of Education (1973/74, p.6). It is interesting that, while here and in subsequent issues of the curricular, prerequisites are not explicitly forbidden, one Ontario school board was requested in 1976 by the Ministry to recall and to modify its secondary school handbook for graduating elementary school students because it implied that the high school programs were built on a prerequisite system.

[5] Recommendation 6A from the report of the work group on the proposed student bill of rights, Board of Education for the City of Toronto, p.27.

[6] In looking at the studies of change from just the users' perspective, I note the tendency to employ Quixote-like strategies for change – to tilt at what is immediately visible and to act before the situation is understood. In the end one finds that the situation still persists because a symptom or an unrelated happening was the focus of attack. As well, these Quixote strategies do not take into account the implications of the attack and, if initially successful, they lead to confrontation, not resolution. I must hasten to add that it is not the user emphasis that concerns me – rather, it is the narrowness of the focus and its subsequent limitation.

[7] Because of the rather close relationship that developed between the people at the school and the members of the research team, no quantitative data were gathered at the end of the second year. Instead, personal reactions were noted and while not as "tidy" (we cannot say, e.g., $x\%$ of the students agreed) this form of evaluation is much more useful in that the student reactions are qualified (e.g., conditions for success/lack of success are provided).

[8] It is important to keep in mind that the school did not have a bureaucratic hierarchy – administratively there was no vice-principal, department head structure and decisions were made through a committee structure. In other words, both in terms of other stated philosophy and the administrative decision-making structures, there was a support for all school constituent participation, including that of students.

[9] One should not be left with the impression that the chairperson was insensitive to the student position. On many occasions he demonstrated his empathy with the

175

students and his understanding of their concerns. Yet these attributes may well have, in the long run, restricted student participation – because the chairperson was far more articulate than they, teachers accepted more readily what he said and since their positions were usually presented anyway, why should they risk making blunders in the meetings? The chairperson could speak for them.

## References

Alexander, W. E., & Farrell, J. P. *Student participation in decision-making*. Toronto: Ontario Institute for Studies in Education, 1975.

Argyris, C. *Intervention theory and method: A behavioural science view*. Don Mills, Ont.: Addison-Wesley, 1970.

Bennis, W. Theory and method in applying behavioural science to planned organizational change. In W. Bennis, K. Bennis, & R. Chin, *The planning of change*. (2d ed.) Toronto: Holt, Rinehart & Winston, 1969.

Board of Education for the City of Toronto. Report from the Work Group on the Proposed Students' Bill of Rights. Toronto, May 1973.

Cox, F. M., Erlich, J. L., Rothman, J., & Tropman, J. E. *Strategies of community organization*. Itasca: Peacock, 1970.

Eastabrook, G., Fullan, M., & Clifford, J. *Bayridge Secondary School: A case study of the planning and implementation of education change*. Vol.1: Planning, 1974; Vol.2: Implementation, 1975. Toronto: Ontario Institute for Studies in Education for the Ministry of Education, Ontario.

Eastabrook, G., Fullan, M., Lounsbury, D., & Miles, W. *Students in school wide decision making: A case study*. Toronto: Ontario Institute for Studies in Education. Forthcoming.

Freire, P. *Pedagogy of the oppressed*. New York: Herder & Herder, 1970.

Fullan, M. Overview of the innovative process and the user. *Interchange*, 1972, **3**(2/3), 1-46.

Fullan, M., & Eastabrook, G. *School change project: An interim report*. Toronto: Department of Sociology, Ontario Institute for Studies in Education, 1972.

Fullan, M., Eastabrook, G., & Biss, J. Action research in the school: Involving students and teachers in classroom change. In R. A. Carlton, L. S. Colley, & N. J. MacKinnon (Eds.), *Education, change and society: A sociology of Canadian education*. Toronto: Gage, 1977. Pp.508-522.

Fullan, M., Eastabrook, G., Biss, J., & Gehlbach, J. *Guidebooks to change*. Toronto: Ontario Institute for Studies in Education. Forthcoming.

Fullan, M., & Pomfret, A. Review of research on instructional and curriculum innovation. *Review of Educational Research*, 1977, **47**(1).

Hendrick, I. G., & Jones, R. L. *Student dissent in the schools*. Boston: Houghton Mifflin, 1972.

King, A. *Innovative secondary schools*. Toronto: Ontario Institute for Studies in Education, 1972.

Laxer, G., Traub, R. E., & Wayne, K. *Student social and achievement patterns as related to secondary school organizational structures*. Toronto: Ontario Institute for Studies in Education, 1974.

Levin, M. *Rights of youth*. Don Mills, Ont.: General Publishing, 1972.

Libarle, M., & Seligson, E. (Eds.) *The high school revolutionaries*. New York: Vintage Books, 1970.

Likert, R. *The human organization*. Toronto: McGraw-Hill, 1967.

Ontario Department of Education. *Living and learning.* Report of the Provincial Committee on the Aims and Objectives of Education in the Schools of Ontario. Toronto: The Department, 1968.

Ontario Ministry of Education. *Education in the primary and junior division.* Toronto: The Ministry, 1975. (a)

Ontario Ministry of Education. *The formative years.* Curricula P1J1. Toronto: The Ministry, 1975. (b)

Ontario Ministry of Education. *Secondary school organization and diploma requirements.* Circular H.S.1. Toronto: The Ministry, 1973/74–1976/77.

Parsons, T. The school class as a social system: Some of the functions of American society. *Harvard Educational Review*, 1959, **29**(4), 297-318.

Quarter, J. *The student movement of the sixties.* Toronto: Ontario Institute for Studies in Education, 1972.

Rapaport, R. Three dilemmas in action research. *Human Relations*, 1970, **23**, 499-513.

Sarason, A. *The culture of the school and the problem of change.* Boston: Allyn & Bacon, 1971.

Sarason, A. *The creation of settings and the future society.* San Francisco: Jossey-Bass, 1972.

Schmuck, R., & Miles, M. B. (Eds.) *Organizational development in schools.* Palo Alto: National Press Books, 1971.

Schmuck, R., & Runkle, P. *Handbook of organizational development in schools.* Palo Alto: National Press Books, 1972.

Seeley, J. R. Administered persons: The engineering of souls. *Interchange*, 1974, **5**(3), 1-13.